Eucharist: Symbol of Transformation

William R. Crockett

Eucharist:

Symbol of Transformation

Pueblo Publishing Company

New York

Cover art: Helen Siegl

Design: Frank Kacmarcik

Printed in the United States of America

ISBN: 0-916134-98-9

To Jean

Contents

Preface

At the center of the life of the Christian community is a meal where bread and wine are taken, blessed, broken, and shared in remembrance of the death and resurrection of Jesus and in anticipation of the banquet in the coming reign of God. This simple action has given rise to a long and varied history of eucharistic traditions.

This book is, first of all, a "roots" book. It is intended to introduce Catholic and Protestant, mainline and evangelical Christians to their eucharistic heritage. It is also an ecumenical book. The publication of *Baptism, Eucharist and Ministry* by the Faith and Order Commission of the World Council of Churches represents a milestone in the history of the ecumenical movement. Whereas the book is not written as a commentary on this document, it helps to provide the background for the growing ecumenical consensus on the eucharist.

Ecumenical agreement on the eucharist, however, is not an end in itself. It invites us to reflect on the meaning of our eucharistic celebrations in a world where many go hungry every day. Taking hints from the tradition and taking account of modern symbol theory, the last part of the book develops fresh lines of theological interpretation and explores the relationship between eucharist and justice.

This book could not have been written without the rich experience of ecumenism that has come from contact with colleagues, students, and friends from a variety of Christian traditions. My thanks are due to a number of friends and colleagues, especially Edward Kilmartin, Geoffrey Wainwright, David Holeton, Paul Gibson, and other members of the *Societas Liturgica* who have stimulated my thinking on the eucharist over the years. My thanks are especially due to Stephen Sykes and James F. White, both of whom encouraged me from the beginning and were gracious enough to read the entire manuscript.

My thanks are due also to my colleagues and students at the Vancouver School of Theology who have contributed to the book in many ways. My colleague Lloyd Gaston, in particular, has helped me with the exegesis of the New Testament texts relating to the eucharist. I cannot adequately express my gratitude to the Vancouver School of Theology and particularly to its MacMillan Committee for the sabbatical leave and financial support that they have provided. I am grateful also to Esther North for reading the final proofs.

This book could not have been written without the support of my wife Jean, to whom this book is dedicated, and my daughters Carolyn, Catherine, and Linda, who have lived with "the book" for far too long.

CHAPTER ONE

The Eucharist in the New Testament

INTRODUCTION

The roots of the Christian eucharist lie in the tradition of Jewish meal fellowship and, in particular, in the meals that Jesus shared with his disciples and others.[1] The continuation of this meal fellowship in the earliest Christian communities, together with reflection on its meaning, gave rise to the earliest Christian eucharistic traditions.

A meal in Jewish tradition has a much richer meaning than it has in our modern western culture.[2] Every common meal as well as the meals held on festivals and other special occasions reflect Israelite faith. They are eaten in the context of thanksgiving for Yahweh's gifts given in creation and in Israel's history. This context of thanksgiving is expressed in the table blessings, or *berakoth*, that are prescribed for every meal and that are expanded on festivals to express thanksgiving for the particular events that are being commemorated.[3] Moreover, table fellowship for the Jew is a sign of peace and community. It is for this reason that a scandal was created when Jesus ate with sinners and outcasts. This was immediately seen as a sign of fellowship with them. Against the background of Jesus' message, table fellowship with him constituted the offer of a share in the blessings of the future reign of God.[4]

In all Jewish meals, there is a special blessing recited at the breaking of bread by the head of the household or the host at the beginning of the meal. At festive meals, a special blessing is also recited over the wine cup at the conclusion of the meal. In the New Testament accounts of the Last Supper, when Jesus took the bread, broke it, and "gave thanks" (said the blessing) over it, and "after supper" took the cup and "gave thanks" over it, he was repeating the customs and reciting the table blessings familiar to every Jew and which the disciples would have known from their earliest childhood.

The New Testament contains a number of meal traditions. Apart from the Last Supper itself, there are several references to meals in the gospel traditions: meals eaten with publicans and sinners, the feeding stories, and meals connected with the resurrection. Meals are also an important element in the parables and sayings of Jesus.[5] There are references to a bread breaking tradition in Acts,[6] and Revelation 3:20 reflects an early Christian meal tradition. Norman Perrin thinks that meal fellowship played a more important role in the ministry of Jesus than the present redaction of the gospels indicates. According to Perrin, Jesus' practice of eating with tax collectors and sinners so offended his fellow Jews that this was toned down in the gospel tradition. Outside the New Testament, there are references to early Christian meal traditions in the *Didache*[7] and in the apocryphal New Testament writings.[8] This evidence for various meal traditions in the New Testament and in early Christian literature is significant because it makes it clear that the question of eucharistic origins is more complex than it is often thought to be. It also makes it clear that the history of the interpretation of the eucharist in the early Church cannot be seen exclusively in relation to the Last Supper.

In taking account of the meal traditions in the New Testament, we shall adopt a tradition history approach. This means taking into account three stages of historical development in the formation of the New Testament writings. The earliest stage is Jesus' earthly ministry and the traditions concerning his death and resurrection. The second stage is the stage of oral tradition within the earliest Christian communities. The third stage is that of the present New Testament documents. This is the "redaction" stage of the gospel tradition. The material from the first two stages is taken up by the evangelists and edited from their own theological perspective.[9] These three stages are most clearly evident in the formation of the gospel tradition, but they are evident in varying degrees in the composition of the rest of the New Testament as well. To adopt a tradition history approach to the eucharist in the New Testament is to acknowledge that there is a development in the history of eucharistic traditions. It is commonly recognized that there are different Christologies in the New Testament and that these Christologies have different histories.[10] We also recognize development in both the form and the understanding of the Church and the ministry in the New Testament. We shall find that the eucharistic traditions in the New Testament have a similar history.

We must beware of reading back into the New Testament texts the questions, formulations, and theological perspectives characteristic of later periods. While the New Testament can cast light on our questions concerning the eucharist, it can do so only as we try to allow the perspectives present in the texts themselves to address us in their own historical context. This means that in approaching the eucharistic texts, we need to view them from within their own historical setting and from within the theological perspectives that are present in that setting and not from within the framework of the later history of ideas. In this chapter, we shall attempt to unravel some of the most important strands of eucharistic tradition in the New Testament and to draw out the theological perspectives that they contain.

THE LAST SUPPER TRADITION

We have indicated that the history of the interpretation of the eucharist in the early Church cannot be seen exclusively in relation to the Last Supper tradition, but needs to be seen in relation to the wider context of the variety of meal traditions reflected in the New Testament writings. The same point can be made with respect to the Last Supper tradition itself. There are a number of strands that need to be separated out if we are to understand its history. We can even speak of a number of Last Supper traditions that have been combined in different ways.

There is, first of all, a Last Supper tradition that preserves an eschatological interpretation of the supper. This is contained in the eschatological saying in Mark 14:25 and in Matthew 26:29, which follows the words of institution. Luke has the same saying in a double form, but preceding the words of institution (Lk 22:15–18). This double form of the eschatological saying is con-

3

nected by Luke with the thought of the passover. There is also a reminiscence of the eschatological perspective in Paul's commentary on the words of institution in 1 Corinthians 11:26.

There are three Last Supper traditions that connect the Supper with the death of Jesus. The first of these is the tradition of the eucharistic words of Jesus over the bread and cup, which link them with his approaching death. The tradition of the eucharistic words is found in the Last Supper accounts in all the synoptic gospels and in Paul (Mk 14:22–24, Mt 26:26–28, 1 Cor 11:23–25, and Lk 22:19–20 ["long text"]), but not in John. There is a pre-Pauline formula that gives an early Christian interpretation of the eucharistic words in 1 Corinthians 10:16. A second Last Supper tradition connects the eucharist with the death of Jesus by interpreting it as a "memorial" (*anamnesis*) of his death. This tradition is present in Luke 22:19 in connection with the bread saying, and in 1 Corinthians 11:24–25 in connection with both the bread and the cup sayings. It is absent from the Marcan and Matthean accounts of the Last Supper and from the Johannine account. A third Last Supper tradition links the eucharist with the death of Jesus by interpreting it as a Christian passover celebration. The synoptic gospels place the account of the Last Supper in a passover context and identify it as a passover meal. In John's gospel, the Last Supper is placed in the context of passover time, but it is held on the evening before the feast of the Passover. Paul may know the tradition of the interpretation of the eucharist as a Christian passover celebration (1 Cor 5:7–8), but if he does, he does not connect it with the Last Supper tradition. Finally, there is a Last Supper tradition that connects the eucharist with the theme of the covenant. This covenant motif is found in Jesus' eucharistic saying over the cup (Mk 14:24, Mt 26:28, 1 Cor 11:25, and Lk 22:20 ["long text"]).

We must try to draw out the theological perspectives present in these separate strands of tradition. Our primary aim will be to illuminate the background and meaning of these theological perspectives. We shall also attempt to see what the evidence suggests with regard to the history of these traditions and the reasons for the ways they are combined in the present texts.

4

The central theme of the message of Jesus is the proclamation of the future reign of God.[11] This theme has its roots in early Israelite tradition, but is present in a heightened form in postexilic Judaism and in late Jewish apocalyptic. It is particularly against this later background that Jesus' message of the kingdom of God is to be understood. One central thread in this tradition of eschatological expectation is the portrayal of the future reign of God under the image of an eschatological meal. According to this tradition, at the end time, God will provide a great feast or banquet, and those who share in the blessings of eschatological salvation will sit down at table and eat and drink in the presence of God. The most striking text in the Old Testament for this form of Jewish eschatological hope is found in the apocalyptic passage in Isaiah 25.

"On this mountain the Lord of hosts will make for all peoples a feast of fat things, a feast of wine on the lees, of fat things full of marrow, of wine on the lees well refined. And he will destroy on this mountain the covering that is cast over all peoples, the veil that is spread over all nations. He will swallow up death for ever, and the Lord God will wipe away tears from all faces, and the reproach of his people he will take away from all the earth; for the Lord has spoken."[12]

Another example is to be found in Ethiopian Enoch:

"And the righteous and elect shall be saved on that day, And they shall never thereafter see the face of the sinners and unrighteous. And the Lord of Spirits will abide over them, And with that Son of Man shall they eat. And lie down and rise up for ever and ever."[13]

The Qumran community practiced meals that were given an eschatological interpretation. F. M. Cross, Jr., cites the Qumran document IQSa[14] as evidence that meals were held in which the community anticipated liturgically the banquet of the kingdom.[15] These meals were also given a messianic interpretation. The Qumran passage begins:

"This is the order of the session of the 'men of Name who are invited to the Feast' for the communal council when God sends the Messiah to be with them."

The document goes on to give details regarding the seating and the procedures to be followed with regard to bread and wine at a meal at which the priest (the Aaronic Messiah?) and the Messiah of Israel are the most prominent figures. The account concludes with the following rubric:

"And they shall act according to this prescription whenever the meal is arranged, when as many as ten solemnly meet together."

Cross believes that this final rubric indicates that the arrangements prescribed in the document are those of the common meal of the community and that the presence of the priest and the Messiah of Israel indicates that the meal is interpreted as an anticipation of the messianic banquet at the end time in which the priestly head and the lay head of the community represent the Messiahs of Aaron and Israel. This text, therefore, provides evidence for the presence in late Judaism not only of the idea of the kingdom of God under the form of an eschatological meal, but also of the idea of a common community meal as a present anticipation of this eschatological meal.

It is against this background that we can understand the role that meal fellowship and meal teaching played in the public ministry of Jesus. Table fellowship with Jesus during the public ministry was a visible sign of the dawning of the future reign of God. It was an acted parable. It was both the offer in the present of the possibility of a new kind of relationship with God and with one's neighbor, and an anticipation of the fellowship to be expected in the future in the consummated kingdom of God. The fact that Jesus was depicted in the popular imagination as a "glutton and a drunkard" testifies to the central role that this table fellowship played during the ministry of Jesus. The fact that such table fellowship was extended even to "tax collectors and sinners" scandalized his fellow Jews. Whereas John the Baptist was viewed as an ascetic, "the Son of man" was seen to come "eating and drinking."

6

"For John came neither eating nor drinking, and they say, 'He has a demon'; the Son of man came eating and drinking, and they say, 'Behold, a glutton and a drunkard, a friend of tax collectors and sinners!' "[16]

The same theme is found in Mark 2:15–19a. Here a wedding motif is introduced:

"And as he sat at table in his house, many tax collectors and sinners were sitting with Jesus and his disciples; for there were many who followed him. And the scribes of the Pharisees, when they saw that he was eating with sinners and tax collectors, said to his disciples, 'Why does he eat with tax collectors and sinners?' And when Jesus heard it, he said to them, 'Those who are well have no need of a physician, but those who are sick; I came not to call the righteous, but sinners.' Now John's disciples and the Pharisees were fasting; and people came and said to him, 'Why do John's disciples and the disciples of the Pharisees fast, but your disciples do not fast?' And Jesus said to them, 'Can the wedding guests fast while the bridegroom is with them?' "

The kingdom of God is likened to a great supper in Luke 14:15–24. In Matthew's version of the same parable, the Supper is portrayed as a wedding feast. The most explicit saying of Jesus likening the future kingdom of God to a feast, apart from the eschatological saying in the Last Supper tradition, is the following saying in Matthew and Luke.

"I tell you, many will come from east and west and sit at table with Abraham, Isaac, and Jacob in the kingdom of heaven."[17]

"And men will come from east and west, and from north and south, and sit at table in the kingdom of God."[18]

The portrayal of the kingdom of God under the form of a meal is, therefore, a central feature both of the activity and of the sayings and parables of Jesus.

It is against this background that we can understand the eschatological saying in Mark 14:25 (Mt 26:29 parallel):

"Truly, I say to you, I shall not drink again of the fruit of the vine until that day when I drink it new in the kingdom of God."

The eschatological perspective in the Last Supper tradition takes up the theme of the future reign of God under the image of an eschatological meal, which we have found in Jewish literature and in the teaching and practice of Jesus, and views the eucharist as an anticipation in the present of this future eschatological meal. The eschatological saying in Mark 14:25 is taken up and reworked into a double saying with a passover motif in Luke 22:15–18.

"And he said to them, 'I have earnestly desired to eat this passover with you before I suffer; for I tell you I shall not eat it until it is fulfilled in the kingdom of God.' And he took a cup, and when he had given thanks he said, 'Take this, and divide it among yourselves; for I tell you that from now on I shall not drink of the fruit of the vine until the kingdom of God comes.' "

Luke also includes several other sayings on the theme of table fellowship that are marked by this eschatological perspective, and that include a "serving" theme.

"For which is the greater, one who sits at table, or one who serves? Is it not the one who sits at table? But I am among you as one who serves. 'You are those who have continued with me in my trials; as my Father appointed a kingdom for me, so do I appoint for you that you may eat and drink at my table in my kingdom and sit on thrones judging the twelve tribes of Israel.' "[19]

John's gospel has these same motifs in a Last Supper context. In Chapter 13, the "serving" theme is made explicit in Jesus' washing of the disciples' feet. The Farewell Discourse (Chaps. 14–17) that follows also has a strong eschatological orientation, although in John, this now appears in an atmosphere of realized eschatology.[20] John, on the other hand, does not contain the tradition of the eucharistic words over the bread and the cup. The evidence from Luke and John suggests that the eschatological perspective, perhaps combined with the "serving" theme, once stood as an independent tradition that was only later combined with the tradition of the eucharistic words.

The Tradition of the Eucharistic Words

The tradition of the eucharistic words of Jesus over the bread and the cup have, in the history of eucharistic thought, eclipsed all the other strands of early Christian tradition as the focal point from which the whole eucharistic tradition has been interpreted. From the point of view of the history of traditions, this needs to be put in perspective. In the first place, the tradition of the eucharistic words is not a universal feature of the Last Supper tradition in the New Testament. In John's gospel, the eucharistic words are absent altogether from the account of the Last Supper. Moreover, in the synoptic gospels, it is likely that the eschatological sayings that are combined in the present texts with the eucharistic words originally formed an independent tradition that was only subsequently combined with the tradition of the eucharistic words. Secondly, there are significant differences between the different versions of the eucharistic words in the synoptic gospels and in Paul, which indicates that the eucharistic words themselves contain a history of traditions. Thirdly, there are other meal traditions in the New Testament that are independent of both the Last Supper tradition and the tradition of the eucharistic words, although these various traditions show signs of mutual influence. Finally, the eucharistic words are not found in the *Didache*, which contains the earliest examples of eucharistic table prayers that we possess. This does not diminish the importance of the eucharistic words, but enables us to gain some historical perspective on their place in the tradition. When the eucharistic words become the exclusive focal point for the interpretation of the eucharist, some important traditional perspectives are lost sight of that only come into the light when the eucharistic words assume their proper role alongside these other perspectives in the history of traditions.

There are four accounts of the eucharistic words in the New Testament: Mark 14:22–24, Matthew 26:26–28, 1 Corinthians 11:23–25, and Luke 22:19–20 ["long text"]. We can best begin our discussion of these different accounts by placing them alongside each other in columns, and giving them in the order in which the words occur in the Greek text.[21]

1 Cor 11:23–25	Lk 22:19–20	Mk 14:22–24	Mt 26:26–28
The Lord Jesus	And	And as they were eating	As they were eating
on the night when he was delivered up			
			Jesus
took bread	taking bread	taking bread	taking bread
and having given	having given	having said	and having said
thanks	thanks	the blessing	the blessing
broke	broke	broke	broke
(it)	(it) and gave (it)	(it) and gave (it)	(it) and giving (it)
	to them	to them	to the disciples
and said	saying	and said	said
This	This	Take this	Take eat this
is my body	is my body	is my body	is my body
which (is) for you	which for you (shall be) given		
this do in my remembrance	this do in my remembrance		
In the same way	And	And taking	And taking
also the cup	the cup in the same way	(the) cup	(the) cup
after supper	after supper		
		having given thanks he gave (it)	and having given thanks he gave (it)
		to them and they all drank of it	to them
saying	saying	and he said to them	saying
			Drink of it all
This cup	This cup	This	(of you) for this
is the	the	is	is
new covenant	new covenant		
in my blood	in my blood	my blood of the covenant	my blood of the covenant
	which for you (shall be)	which (shall be)	which for many (shall be)

| | poured out | poured out
for many | poured out
to the forgive-
ness of sins |
| this do as often
as you drink
(it) in my
remembrance | | | |

If we examine Mark and Matthew first, we will observe that they are the closest to each other in form. Matthew is simply a slightly expanded and stylistically reworked version of Mark, which reflects a shift from a narrative to a more stylized liturgical form. The only significant theological difference between them is the addition in Matthew of the phrase "for the forgiveness of sins." These two accounts, therefore, represent a single tradition.

If we turn to Luke next, we must observe that there is a problem concerning the text. The Lucan text exists in two forms, the so-called "short text," which ends with the words "this is my body" (v. 19a) and which lacks verses 19b and 20, and the so-called "long text," which contains these latter verses. Of the more than 5,000 Greek manuscripts of the New Testament that we possess, only one of them (Codex D) contains the "short" text. This textual reading is contained in a few of the translations. Most, but not all, New Testament scholars today accept the genuineness of the "long" text.[22] We shall proceed on the assumption that the "long" text is original.

If this is the case, then Paul and Luke have four principal features in common that are either absent from or occur in a different form in Mark and Matthew: (a) Paul and Luke speak of Jesus taking the cup "after supper." This means that the words over the bread and the words over the cup were separated by a meal. The thanksgiving over the bread took place before the meal and the thanksgiving over the cup took place at the conclusion of the meal. This was normal Jewish custom. By contrast, in Mark and Matthew, there is no hint at all that the two actions were separated by a meal. (b) The form of the cup saying is different in Paul–Luke and in Mark–Matthew. In Paul–Luke, the cup saying contains the phrase "the new covenant in my blood," whereas Mark and Matthew contain the wording "my blood of the covenant." (c) The "for you" or "for many" phrase is connected with the cup saying in Mark and Matthew. Paul has it in connection with the bread saying only. Luke has it in connection with both the bread and the cup sayings. (d) Paul and Luke contain the command to repeat the Supper (the so-called *anamnesis* formula), "Do this (as often as you drink it) in remembrance of me." This command is absent from both Mark and Matthew.

There are also certain differences between the Pauline and the Lucan accounts. We have already observed that Paul has the "for you"–"for many" phrase in connection with the bread saying only in contrast to Mark and Matthew, who connect it with the cup saying. Luke has it in the same form as Paul, "for you" rather than "for many" (Mark–Matthew), but has it in connection with both the bread and the cup sayings in contrast to Paul. Secondly, the command to repeat the supper occurs after both the bread saying and the cup saying in Paul, but only after the bread saying in Luke. A third difference is that Luke incorporates the additional words "which (shall be) poured out (for you)" in the cup saying. There are, further, certain stylistic differences. Paul's account is closer to normal Greek style, while Luke's account reflects a more Semitic idiom. The similarities between Paul and Luke indicate that they are drawing on the same tradition. The differences between them, however, makes the hypothesis of mutual literary dependence unlikely. It appears, therefore, that Paul and Luke have drawn on the same tradition, but have done so independently.[23] If this analysis is correct, then we have two independent traditions of the eucharistic words in the New Testament, Paul–Luke and Mark–Matthew.

These two traditions contain both earlier and later elements, so that it is difficult to assign to either of them an absolute priority in time. On linguistic grounds Mark appears to be older since it is more Semitic in idiom than Paul.[24] Luke, however, also contains a number of Semitisms.[25] On other than linguistic grounds Paul–Luke appears on the whole to be the earlier tradition.[26] The principal evidence for this is (a) the presence of the phrase "after supper" in the Pauline–Lucan tradition, and (b) the form that the cup saying takes in that tradition. The presence of the phrase "after supper" in the Pauline–Lucan tradition reflects an earlier stage in the development of the eucharist when the actions connected with the bread and the cup were still separated by a common meal. The absence of this phrase in Mark and Matthew indicates a later stage in liturgical tradition when the two actions took place together either at the end or apart from a common meal. This would indicate that Paul and Luke are drawing on an earlier tradition of the eucharistic words than Mark. This tends to be confirmed when we examine the differences between the forms of the cup saying in the two traditions. In Paul–Luke, the cup saying reads: "This is the new covenant in my blood." In Mark–Matthew, it reads: "This is my blood of the covenant." We shall later be concerned to show that these two forms of the cup saying reflect two different Old Testament covenant traditions. At the moment, we are concerned with the question of the respective ages of the two forms of the saying. In the Marcan–Matthean tradition of the eucharistic words, there is a direct parallelism between the form of the bread saying and the form of the cup saying: "This is my body"; "This is my blood. . . ." In Paul–Luke, there is a lack of parallelism: "This is my body"; "This cup (is) the new covenant in my blood." In Mark–Matthew, the words "body" and "blood" are parallel terms. In Paul–Luke, the parallel is between "body" and "covenant," not between "body" and "blood." The likelihood is that the nonparallel version of the cup saying is earlier, since it is more difficult to account for the subsequent appearance of the sayings in a nonparallel form if they were originally parallel sayings. On the contrary, there is a tendency for liturgical texts to develop a more pronounced parallelism through continued usage.[27] If this is correct, then the Marcan–Matthean form of the cup saying represents an assimilation to the form of the bread saying through continued liturgical usage, in which a parallelism was produced between the two sayings that was not present in the earlier form of the tradition. The nonparallel version of the sayings, therefore, represents a stage when the actions in connection with the bread and the cup were still separated by a meal, whereas in Mark and Matthew, we have a reflection of a stage when the bread and the cup actions took place together at the end or apart from a common meal. The lack of parallelism would not be apparent as long as the two actions were separated by a meal, but when the two actions came together, there would arise a tendency for the two sayings connected with them to be assimilated in form. If this analysis is correct, then the bread saying and the cup saying were originally self-contained rather than parallel sayings. This is important for determining their earliest meaning. If they were not originally parallel sayings, then they must be interpreted as self-contained sayings, and our exegesis of them must not proceed from the initial assumption of their parallelism.[28]

The function of the eschatological perspective in the Last Supper tradition was to link the celebration of the eucharist to the offer of a share in the blessings of eschatological salvation. From the eschatological perspective, to share in the eucharistic bread and cup was to share already by anticipation in the future meal of the kingdom of God. The function of the eucharistic words in the Last Supper tradition was to link the celebration of the eucharist to Jesus' redemptive death. From the perspective of the eucharistic words, to share in the bread and the cup means to share in the redemptive power of his death. The bread saying and the cup saying reflect that perspective in different ways. According to the cup saying in its Pauline–Lucan form, those who participate in the eucharist receive a share in the new covenant (the new eschatological order of salvation) that has been established on the basis of Jesus' death. According to the cup saying in its Marcan–Matthean form, those who participate in the eucharist receive a share in his "blood," but this also means a share in his death, because "blood" is a description of the death of Jesus understood as a saving event.[29] According to the bread saying, those who participate in the eucharist receive a share in the body of Christ given in death. A further perspective becomes visible here that was only implicit in both forms of the cup saying. Both the bread and cup sayings view participation in the eucharist as a share in the redemptive power of Jesus' death. The bread saying, however, also speaks of a share in his "body." In Hebrew anthropology, the human person is not viewed as a unity of "body" and "soul" (a Greek conception), but is viewed as an embodied person. The term "body," therefore, refers to the whole person and not to one constituent part of human nature. The bread saying, therefore, signifies that in the eucharist, we have a share not only in the saving power of Jesus' death, but also a share in his person.[30]

The most difficult question that needs to be raised in relation to the eucharistic words is whether in the New Testament itself, they are to be understood in a "realist" or in a "symbolical" sense. Do they mean, "This is my body" or "This signifies my body"? This is the form that the question took in the early medieval eucharistic controversies and at the time of the Reformation, but the question itself presupposes a different framework of understanding than that which is present in the minds of the New Testament writers. Moreover, within the New Testament itself, the tradition of the eucharistic words has passed through three stages of transmission, that of the Palestinian–Jewish church tradition, that of the Hellenistic–Jewish mission, and that of the Gentile mission. What did they mean, therefore, in each of these environments?

This is impossible to say with certainty since the New Testament contains only one authentic commentary on the meaning of the eucharistic words in 1 Corinthians 10:16[31], and we shall argue later that this represents the understanding of them present in the stage of the Hellenistic–Jewish Christian mission, but does not tell us what they meant in either the Palestinian–Jewish environment or in a totally Gentile-Christian environment. 1 Corinthians 10:16 interprets them as a "communion" or "participation" (koinonia) in the blood of Christ and a "communion" or "participation" in the body of Christ. We shall attempt to show later that the term koinonia here is to be understood in an analogous way to the sharing, fellowship, or communion with Yahweh that was associated by Hellenistic Jews with participation in the meals associated with the Jewish sacrificial cultus. What, however, did they mean in the Palestinian–Jewish environment? Three analogies suggest themselves from the Semitic sphere of thought and from the background of the words and actions of Jesus during his public ministry. None of these, however, can be proven from the texts. They may be helpful, however, since they warn us at least against importing our own thought forms back into the New Testament.

J. Jeremias suggests that the eucharistic words can be interpreted in the first instance on the analogy of a parable.[32] If the earliest community meals of the postresurrection Church are a continuation of the common meals that Jesus held with his disciples and others during his ministry, then the analogy that first suggests itself as both one that has its roots in the Palestinian environment and one that has direct links with the teaching and activity of Jesus in connection with meals is that of a parable. On this analogy, the eucharistic meal is an acted parable signifying the offer of eschatological salvation to all those who accept the invitation to table fellowship. The eucharistic words specify that this offer of eschatological salvation includes a share in the redemptive power of Jesus' death as the event by which the new eschatological order of salvation is being established.

A second possible analogy stems from the Jewish view that participation in a common meal mediates a share in the blessing recited over the gifts of food and drink.[33] We have already observed that in Jewish practice, a common meal binds those who share in it in a table fellowship and that this table fellowship is always understood as an expression of Israelite faith. When the head of the household or the host recites the blessing over the bread, breaks it, and hands a piece to each person to eat, the meaning of the action is that those who share in the meal are made recipients of the blessing associated with it. The same is true of the "cup of blessing." Drinking from it mediates a share in the blessing. The eucharistic words, therefore, on this analogy not only symbolize the meaning of the actions connected with the bread and the cup, they also interpret the content of the blessing given in the distribution of the bread and the cup. They signify that those who share in the eucharistic bread and cup receive a share in the redemptive power of Jesus' death by which the beginning of the final salvation is already ushered in.

Using a third semitic analogy, H. Schürmann interprets the giving of the bread and the cup on the analogy of a prophetic sign ôt.[34] A prophetic sign both represents the divine action symbolically and anticipates and realizes it in an initial way. On this view, the bread and the cup, with the accompanying words, not only represent Jesus' saving death symbolically, but the bread and the cup are gifts that offer a share in the salvation that they signify. The accompanying words thus characterize the nature of the gifts given.

If these analogies provide likely clues to the understanding of the eucharistic words in the earliest Palestinian Church, then the eucharist was understood in these communities in what the later Church called both a "realist" and a "symbolical" sense. These strictly Jewish analogies interpret the bread and the cup as not only "symbolizing," "signifying," or "representing" the redemptive significance of Jesus' death, but as offering a share in the "blessing" or "gift" of eschatological salvation brought about by that death and a share in the body of Jesus that was given up to death.

The Covenant and Redemption Motifs
In our discussion of the tradition of the eucharistic words, we spoke of the relation of the eucharist to the covenant theme and of its relation to Jesus' redemptive death. We must now bring out the background and meaning of these ideas more clearly. We shall begin with a discussion of the covenant idea and discuss the redemption motif in relation to it.

Whether or not the covenant motif ever stood alone as an independent theological perspective on the eucharist, it at any rate became linked very early in the Last Supper tradition with the theological interpretation of Jesus' death, so that we have no knowledge of its history as an independent theological perspective.[35] According to this perspective, the eucharist is understood as a meal celebrating the renewal of God's covenant. Meals were one of the features that frequently accompanied the concluding of a covenant in the Old Testament, so that the idea of a covenant meal is very old.[36] The covenant motif occurs in the cup saying in both the Pauline–Lucan and the Marcan–Matthean traditions of the eucharistic words, where it is in each case linked with Jesus' death as the means by which God's renewal of the covenant with the people has been accomplished. It occurs in two different forms in each of these traditions. In Paul–Luke, it takes the form: "the new covenant in my blood," whereas in Mark–Matthew, we have the phrase: "my blood of the covenant." These two forms reflect two different Old Testament covenant traditions, which in turn provide different theological interpretations of Jesus' death.

The Pauline–Lucan form of the saying is an allusion to the new covenant in Jeremiah 31:31–34.

'Behold, the days are coming, says the Lord, when I will make a new covenant with the house of Israel and the house of Judah, not like the covenant which I made with their fathers when I took them by the hand to bring them out of the land of Egypt, my covenant which they broke, though I was their husband, says the Lord. But this is the covenant which I will make with the house of Israel after those days, says the Lord: I will put my law within them, and I will write it upon their hearts; and I will be their God, and they shall be my people. And no longer shall each man teach his neighbor and each his brother, saying, 'Know the Lord,' for they shall all know me, from the least of them to the greatest, says the Lord; for I will forgive their iniquity, and I will remember their sin no more."

The Marcan–Matthean form of the saying is an allusion to the Sinai covenant and its accompanying ceremonies.

"Moses . . . rose early in the morning, and built an altar at the foot of the mountain, and twelve pillars, according to the twelve tribes of Israel. And he sent young men of the people of Israel, who offered burnt offerings and sacrificial peace offerings of oxen to the Lord. And Moses took half the blood and put it in basins, and half of the blood he threw against the altar. Then he took the book of the covenant, and read it in the hearing of the people; and they said, 'All that the Lord has spoken we will do, and we will be obedient.' And Moses took the blood and threw it upon the people, and said, 'Behold the blood of the covenant which the Lord has made with you in accordance with all these words.' Then Moses and Aaron, Nadab and Abihu, and seventy of the elders of Israel went up, and . . . they beheld God, and ate and drank."[37]

These two covenant traditions are in marked contrast to each other. In the account of the Sinai covenant in Exodus, the elements of sacrifice and of sprinkling with blood are both features of the covenant ceremony. Jeremiah, on the other hand, contrasts the new covenant with the Sinai covenant. Here there is no mention of sacrifice or blood. God accomplishes the renewal of the covenant with the people, including the forgiveness of their sins, by means of a direct interior renewal of the heart without external rites. Jeremiah's account of the new covenant belongs to the Old Testament tradition of eschatological prophecy, whereas the account of the Sinai covenant in Exodus belongs to the sphere of the sacrificial cultus.

In the Pauline–Lucan cup saying, the new covenant spoken of in the prophecy of Jeremiah, a future eschatological covenant, has become a present reality through the death (in the blood) of Jesus. Those who share in the cup share in the reality of this new covenant relationship between God and humanity concluded on the basis of Jesus' death. Jesus' death is understood from this standpoint as the means through which the fulfillment of the eschatological prophecy of Jeremiah has taken place. Two ideas are combined here that are not combined in the immediate Old Testament background of the saying, the ideas of the fulfillment of eschatological prophecy and the death of Jesus. God's future reign has become a present reality through the death of God's servant Jesus. Even now, those who share in the eucharistic cup, share in the blessings of the future reign of God. This conception of Jesus' death as bringing about the fulfillment of eschatological prophecy points to Jesus' death as in some sense a "redemptive" death. This is the beginning of a process of theological reflection that is expanded as further Old Testament motifs are drawn upon to specify the particular sense in which it is redemptive. This process is already present in the Lucan addition of the words "which is poured out" to the cup saying. Here Luke alludes to Isaiah 53:12 and specifies the interpretation of Jesus' death as a death on the analogy of the death of the suffering servant of Yahweh.[38]

The Marcan–Matthean version of the cup saying, on the other hand, links the covenant motif to the Sinai tradition rather than to the sphere of eschatological prophecy. The redemptive significance of Jesus' death now comes to be interpreted against the background of the Old Testament tradition of cultic sacrifice.[39] According to this perspective, those who share in the eucharistic cup have a share in the fruits of Jesus' death interpreted on the analogy of a cultic sacrifice. In the present context, the fruit of Jesus' sacrificial death is the renewal of the covenant relationship between God and humanity, which was first established on Sinai, and is now renewed by Jesus' death.

When the earliest Christian communities began to interpret the meaning of Jesus' death as a redemptive event, there were a number of options open to them from the Old Testament background for interpreting its redemptive significance. What we are concerned with here are the particular options that appear in the tradition of the eucharistic words. We have seen that the two versions of the cup saying present two different Old Testament backgrounds for understanding the redemptive significance of Jesus' death. Paul–Luke, by linking Jesus' death to the idea of the new covenant in Jeremiah 31, treats Jesus' death as the fulfillment of eschatological prophecy. Mark–Matthew, on the other hand, by linking the cup saying to the Sinai covenant, presents Jesus' death under the image of a covenant sacrifice. The "for many" phrase in Mark 14:24 and Matthew 26:28 and the phrase "which is poured out" in Mark 14:24, Matthew 26:28, and Luke 22:20 are a direct allusion to Isaiah 53:12b:

". . . he poured out his soul to death, and was numbered with the transgressors; yet he bore the sin of many."[40]

In this case, the Old Testament figure of the suffering servant comes into view as the particular Old Testament motif used to interpret the redemptive character of Jesus' death.

The eucharistic words interpret Jesus' death as a redemptive event, but they provide us with different models for the interpretation of its redemptive significance. When we share in the bread and the cup, we receive a share in the power of Jesus' redemptive death, but the tradition of the eucharistic words does not bind us to one particular way of understanding how it is redemptive "for us."

The Eucharist as Anamnesis

In the Pauline–Lucan Lord's Supper tradition, the *anamnesis* phrase, "Do this . . . in remembrance of me" is combined with the tradition of the eucharistic words. This phrase is absent from the Marcan–Matthean tradition. We can, therefore, treat it as a theological motif independent of the tradition of the eucharistic words,[41] but closely linked with them in the sense that it specifies in a further way the relation between the eucharist and the death of Jesus.

The background and interpretation of the *anamnesis* phrase has been a matter of controversy, depending upon whether the Jewish or the Hellenistic background is regarded as the primary source both for the expression itself and for its meaning. H. Lietzmann held that both the expression and the idea derive from Greek memorial feasts for the dead.[42] J. Jeremias, on the other hand, holds that it derives from the Old Testament and from Judaism, and that it has its origin in Jewish liturgical tradition. Moreover, he goes two steps further. He holds that we have here a formula of remembrance that comes from the passover feast (Ex 12:14) and that the meaning of the passover memorial is that "God remembers" Israel in the passover celebration rather than that "Israel remembers" Yahweh.[43] The meaning of these expressions will be made clear in the course of our discussion.

The difficulty with Jeremias' position is that it rests on three presuppositions, none of which can be proved: (a) that the Last Supper was a passover meal, (b) that the earliest Christian communities regarded the eucharist as a Christian passover celebration, and (c) that the meaning of the passover memorial is that "God remembers" Israel rather than that "Israel remembers" Yahweh. With respect to the first of these presuppositions, according to the accounts of the Last Supper in the synoptic gospels, the Last Supper was a passover meal. According to the account in John, however, the meal was held on the evening before the passover festival began, and, therefore, could not have been a passover meal. Attempts to make these chronologies agree have ended largely in failure. Moreover, whereas the synoptics put the institution narrative in the framework of a passover meal, there is no hint in the institution narrative itself that the meal is a passover meal. There is no reference, for example, to the passover lamb, or to the unleavened bread, or to the bitter herbs, which are invariable elements in the passover meal. It appears, therefore, that the passover framework within which the synoptic accounts are set reflects the theological understanding of the meal on the part of the evangelists rather than the original character of the meal.[44] With regard to the second of Jeremias' presuppositions, the evidence suggests that some but not all of the early Christian eucharistic meals were regarded as Christian passover celebrations.[45] Finally, with respect to the third presupposition, D. Jones and H. Kosmala have shown on the basis of a careful study of the Jewish parallels that Jeremias' interpretation of the phrase *eis anamnesin* in the exclusive sense of "God remembers" rather than "Israel (or the Church) remembers" cannot be sustained.[46] The specific connection of the phrase in Paul–Luke, therefore, with either the passover meal or with Jeremias' interpretation of the meaning of the passover memorial cannot be proved. This does not rule out a connection with the Jewish sphere of thought or with the passover itself, but it rules out the possibility of establishing the passover as the specific origin of the phrase *eis anamnesin* and its meaning in the context of the Pauline–Lucan Last Supper accounts.

G. Bornkamm agrees with Lietzmann that there are clear parallels between the phrase *eis anamnesin* here and similar formulas in the Hellenistic memorial feasts of the dead. He points out further that these meals also contribute the motif of a connection between the phrase and the death of a particular person, which the Old Testament parallels do not. However, the parallel does not extend to the meaning of these meals, which have a widely different significance than that of the eucharist.[47] F. Hahn concluded from all this that while the primary background for the phrase itself must be sought in the Hellenistic background and specifically in the formulas connected with Hellenistic memorial meals, the evidence from both the Hellenistic and the Jewish backgrounds is too uncertain to establish the specific content and meaning that the formula has in Paul–Luke.[48] It appears, therefore, that the question has reached an impasse.

Is this the case? In our judgment, the present impasse is not incapable of resolution, at least up to a point. In the first place, it can be observed that the phrase as it is used in Paul–Luke is a traditional formula that belongs to the pre-Pauline and pre-Lucan Church tradition. The question we then have to ask is whether it belongs to the Palestinian–Jewish Church tradition, to the sphere of the Hellenistic–Jewish Christian mission, or to the stage of the Gentile mission. The fact that plausible parallels can be established from both the Jewish and the Hellenistic backgrounds and that the phrase is found in the Septuagint suggests that the formula came into the tradition during the stage of the Hellenistic–Jewish Christian mission. If it belonged to the Palestinian–Jewish church tradition, then it is hard to explain both the clear Hellenistic parallels and the absence of the formula in Mark–Matthew. It is further generally agreed that the manifest differences between the Hellenistic memorial meals and the Christian eucharist are sufficiently wide to make it impossible to derive the specific meaning of the formula from these meals. The most that can be derived from this source is the terminology of the phrase itself and the motif of a connection between the idea of a memorial and the death of a particular person. The question remains, therefore, where does the idea of "memorial" come from in this instance? There does not appear to be in the Hellenistic background any clear idea of a "memorial" that would fit in this context. We are justified, therefore, in looking to the Jewish sphere as the general background for the content and meaning of the formula. We cannot, however, without further evidence, establish a definite connection either with any one specific meaning that the term "remembrance" had in Israelite tradition, or with any specific Old Testament cultic context.

The Hebrew verb zkr ("remember") has a wider semantic range in Hebrew than it normally has in English. We are accustomed to thinking of memory in primarily psychological terms, as the mental recollection of a past event. While Hebrew includes this psychological meaning, "remembering" in the Old Testament moves beyond the sphere of psychological processes to include the sphere of action.[49] This is particularly true in liturgical or cultic contexts, but this usage is not confined to the cult. The verb *zkr* is used in the Old Testament with "God" as its subject, and also with "Israel" as its subject. The phrase "God remembers" has its origin primarily in the cultic context, and occurs most frequently in the psalms, where the object of God's memory is the covenant people. The essence of God's remembering consists in God's acting toward Israel on the basis of the covenant. The phrase "Israel remembers," in contrast to the phrase "God remembers," does not have its primary origin within the sphere of the cult, but, in its original meaning, has a primarily psychological sense.[50]

In Deuteronomy and Deutero-Isaiah, however, the phrase is extended and takes on a new and highly theological significance. The Deuteronomist is writing in a situation in which Israel no longer has direct access to the redemptive events of the past. It is for this reason that memory now takes on central theological significance. Israel is still constituted by the redemptive events of the past, but memory now provides the link between past and present.[51] Deutero-Isaiah also employs the verb *zkr* in a theological sense that extends far beyond the general psychological meaning. Moreover, in Deutero-Isaiah, the phrase "Israel remembers" takes on a distinctive eschatological meaning.[52] Here the people are in exile, and the problem is to relate the present experience of the people both to the former covenant history and to the future. "Memory" thus takes on both a past and a future sense. The function of remembering God's past deeds is to point to Yahweh's sovereignty over history and to the divine purpose in history. God's sovereignty and historical purpose, however, are not confined to the past, but encompass the beginning and the end of history.

"By linking herself to the past in memory, Israel becomes part of the future, because past and future are one in God's purpose."[53]

Memory, therefore, serves not only to link Israel to the past redemptive action of Yahweh, but also to God's future promise.

The question arises, however, how does memory function in this way? How does it link past, present, and future? In order to explain this theological function of memory in the Old Testament, B. S. Childs employs the concept of "actualization."[54]

According to Childs, when Israel "remembers" the past, the redemptive events of her history are somehow "actualized" in the present. This only applies, however, to Israel's act of remembering. The problem of making a past event contemporaneous is not involved in God's memory, because God is always present. The problem is how a generation that is removed in time from the Exodus generation can experience the redemptive events of the past as efficacious in the present.

Two theories have been advanced by Old Testament scholars to explain how memory provides this link. One theory, represented, for example, by S. Mowinkel, uses the theory of the relationship between myth and cult in the ancient Near East to explain this relationship. According to this theory, what takes place in the cult is the reenactment of the myth that constitutes the identity of the religious community. In this dramatic recapitulation, the content of the myth is renewed and the participants in the cultic rite experience its elemental power. This concept of "actualization" is not indigenous to Israel. It belongs to the wider sphere of the religions of the Near East. According to Mowinkel, however, the content of the dramatic reenactment can be either mythical or historical. What takes place in Israel's cult is the dramatic reenactment of the redemptive events of the past. The act of remembrance, according to this theory, consists in cultic reenactment.[55]

The difficulty with this theory is that it too easily assimilates Israel's understanding of historical redemption to mythical categories. As Childs points out, the fundamental category that determines Israel's understanding of her redemption is that it consists in a series of unrepeatable historical events, not in a timeless myth.[56] This constitutes a fundamental change in perspective from the surrounding cultures and, therefore, a general theory of the relationship between myth and cult based on the history of religions cannot be applied unilaterally to an understanding of Israelite tradition and worship.

This insistence on the historical character of the events of redemption in Israelite tradition has given rise to a countertheory, represented, for example, by M. Noth,[57] which stands at the opposite end of the spectrum from the myth and ritual theory. According to this theory, "remembrance" consists in the recital in the cult of the historical acts of the past that established Israel's existence. These acts share the quality of genuine historical events. They have a once-for-all character and are unrepeatable. "Actualization" does not occur through the dramatic reenactment of the original events, but by means of an act of remembrance, the worshipers experience an identification with these events.

Childs believes that the "recital" theory correctly safeguards the "once-for-all" historical character of the redemptive events in Israel's history as over against the timeless aspect of the myth and ritual theory. Nevertheless, he believes that this second theory, while correctly emphasizing the historical aspect in the process of actualization, has tended to ignore the dynamic quality of historical events. Historical events are unrepeatable, but they are not static. They have a dynamic quality about them that affects later generations.[58] According to this understanding, the Exodus occurred only once, but each later generation can become contemporaneous with the Exodus generation, because succeeding generations stand before Yahweh in an analogous position to the Exodus generation. An event from the past initiates a genuine encounter in the present. "Actualization," according to this interpretation, does not happen automatically simply by correctly performing the cultic rite. Neither, on the other hand, is it a purely subjective act of mental recollection on the part of the worshiping community. What is involved is an encounter between Yahweh and the people. According to the Old Testament, redemptive history is not a purely objective happening. It represents a fusion of God's action and Israel's response, which cannot be analyzed into purely objective or subjective factors, but can only be understood in personal and relational categories. What takes place in the act of remembrance is a contemporary encounter between Yahweh and the covenant people in which Israel is called to faithful obedience to Yahweh in the totality of its life in the present. The act of remembrance thus has a profoundly ethical thrust that transcends a purely objective cultic action. It is concerned with faithful response in the present, not simply with the recollection of past events. This call to obedience in the present, however, does not take place apart from the redemptive events of the past, because Israel's present relationship to Yahweh is constituted by those past events. That is why these events must be "remembered" or "actualized." The continuity between present and past, however, does not consist in the repetition of the original events, but in the fact that each generation shares in the same redemptive reality that is mediated both by the original events themselves and by the act of "remembering" them.

So far, we have spoken broadly of the meaning of "remembering" in the Old Testament background, and of the understanding of the act of remembrance as "actualization." We must now try to be more precise and see if we cannot relate the *eis anamnesin* phrase more specifically to its Jewish background. In our discussion of the Old Testament background, we have given primary consideration to the verb *zkr*. *Anamnesis*, however, is a noun and we need to ask what noun from the root *zkr* would be its Hebrew equivalent. In the Septuagint and the other Greek versions of the Old Testament, there are four noun forms from the root *zkr* that are translated by *anamnesis: azkarah, hazkir, zeker,* and *zikkaron.*[59] *Azkarah* refers to the portion of the Old Testament cereal offerings that were burnt by fire as a "pledge" or "memorial" by the offerer. The term is only translated once by *anamnesis* in the Septuagint, the normal Greek rendering being *mnemosunon*, and this one instance appears to be a translator's error. It is, therefore, hazardous to build too much on this term, especially since the translation of the term itself as "memorial" is not certain. The second possible noun equivalent, *hazkir*, is translated by *eis anamnesin* twice in the Septuagint in two Psalm titles. Its meaning in these instances, however, is obscure and provides no real basis for understanding the New Testament use of *anamnesis*. The third noun, *zeker*, describes the uttering of a name, or the name itself, in the context of the act of cultic proclamation. Its primary meaning, therefore, is connected with "naming" rather than with "remembering," although the two are closely related. Moreover, in the Septuagint, *zeker* is almost always translated by *mnemosunon* or *mneme* and never by *anamnesis*. The most obvious Hebrew equivalent for *anamnesis*, therefore, in our context is *zikkaron*.

In the Old Testament, *zikkaron* is used with both a passive and an active meaning.[60] In its passive sense, it refers to something that is itself worthy of remembrance. The passive sense, however, carries no significant theological meaning in the Old Testament. In its active meaning, it is used in the sense of a memorial that calls something else to remembrance, and carries important theological significance. Moreover, in the active sense, it carries cultic connotations with it in almost every instance. It can refer to a cultic object, to a cultic activity such as the blowing of trumpets (Nm 10:10), or to a cultic festival, namely the Passover (Ex 12:14). The only occurrence of *anamnesis* for *zikkaron* in the Septuagint is at Numbers 10:10, where it refers to the cultic act of blowing the silver trumpets. In the Hebrew literature contemporaneous with the New Testament, however, nearly all the references are to the observing of festivals, the sounding of bells, or the blowing of trumpets.[61] Most significant, however, is the repeated use of *zikkaron* in the embolism (liturgical addition) that follows the third pericope of the cup blessing on the day of the new moon and festivals, including the passover.

". . . may the *remembrance* of ourselves and of our fathers and the *remembrance* of Jerusalem, the city, and the *remembrance* of the Messiah, the son of David, your servant, and the *remembrance* of your people, the whole house of Israel, arise and come, come to pass, be seen and accepted and heard, be remembered and be mentioned before you for deliverance, for good, for grace, etc."[62]

If it is against this background that the *eis anamnesin* phrase is understood in the Pauline–Lucan Lord's Supper tradition, then the eucharist is a memorial in a way analogous to the way in which Jewish cultic acts and festivals, including the passover, are memorials, although the passover does not provide the exclusive background for an understanding of the eucharistic memorial. The eucharist is a memorial in the sense that in the liturgical action, the redemptive death of Jesus is "actualized" in such a way that Christians can participate here and now in its redemptive reality.

28

In 1 Corinthians 10:16, Paul gives us the only commentary in the New Testament on the tradition of the eucharistic words.[63]

"The cup of blessing which we bless, is it not a communion (*koinonia*) in the blood of Christ? The bread which we break, is it not a communion (*koinonia*) in the body of Christ?"

In this text, sharing in the eucharistic bread and cup is interpreted as a "communion" or "participation" (*koinonia*) in the blood of Christ and a "communion" or "participation" (*koinonia*) in the body of Christ. What is meant by "communion" in this context?

It is important to observe first of all that Paul is following a traditional interpretation here, so that we are dealing with a pre-Pauline formula. The expressions "the cup of blessing which we bless" and "the bread which we break," which introduce the formula, reflect both Jewish meal practice and the liturgical language of Hellenistic Judaism. We are dealing, therefore, with a formula that, like the *anamnesis* formula, probably belongs to the context of the Hellenistic–Jewish Christian mission. The meaning that the word *koinonia* apparently has in the formula fits perfectly with the normal usage of the word in a Hellenistic–Jewish milieu. On the other hand, such a meaning would be impossible on Jewish soil that had not undergone Hellenistic influence. This is borne out by a study of its history.[64]

The basic idea contained in the word *koinonia* is that of relationship, but this relationship is understood in different ways in the Greek and Hebrew spheres of thought. In Greek religious thought, it implies a direct union with the deity. In the Old Testament, on the other hand, the Hebrew word group *habur-*, which is translated in the Septuagint by the word group *koinon-*, is used to express the relationship between human beings, but is never used to express the relationship of human beings to Yahweh. Although in the Old Testament, the relationship between Yahweh and the covenant people is understood in the most intimate terms as one of dependence, belonging, and trust, the sense of distance that the devout Israelite feels in the presence of God distinguishes Israelite faith from Greek religion in a fundamental way. This applies also to the sense of fellowship experienced in Jewish meals and especially in the meals connected with the sacrificial cultus. Even here the word group *habur-koinon-* is avoided. Occasionally, "fellowships" (*haburoth*) are mentioned in later rabbinic literature and the meals held on occasion by these groups are referred to as *haburah* meals, but the language used here describes the relationship between the participants rather than the relationship between the participants and God.

A shift, however, takes place in the sphere of Hellenistic Judaism. Philo, for example, uses *koinonia* and its cognates to express the religious sharing and fellowship between God and human beings. Here the Old Testament faith is expressed in the idiom of Greek thought. Thus, Philo can speak of a close fellowship between the righteous and God in the cultus, and especially in the sacrificial meals. 1 Corinthians 10:16 speaks of the eucharist as a *koinonia* in the blood of Christ and a *koinonia* in the body of Christ. Such a direct way of speaking would have been impossible in a Jewish sphere that had not been influenced by Greek conceptions. However, since the term is used here in the context of a formula that reflects Jewish rather than Greek meal practices, we conclude that the formula belongs in its pre-Pauline context to the sphere of the Hellenistic–Jewish Christian mission rather than to the stage of the Gentile mission. This means that the idea of the eucharist as a "communion" in the body and blood of Christ does not derive from the Hellenistic mystery cults during the period of the Gentile mission, but has its background in a Jewish milieu, although a Jewish milieu that has undergone Hellenistic influence. The eucharistic words are understood both in the sense of a communion in the body of Christ and in the sense of a communion in his redemptive death ("in the blood of Christ"). The *koinonia* formula, therefore, transmits into a Hellenistic environment the two perspectives that we have already seen to be present in the Palestinian Church tradition. "*Koinonia*" means communion in the death of Jesus understood as a redemptive event. It also means communion in the body (in the person) of Christ.

In verse 17, however, where Paul gives his own interpretation of the traditional formula, he uses it as the starting point for a new direction of thought.[65] "Because there is one loaf," he says, "we who are many are one body, for we all partake of the one loaf." Here communion in the body of Christ through the act of sharing in the one loaf implies being bound together in one body, the Church. The body of Christ, therefore, which in the traditional formula had a Christological meaning is taken up by Paul and given a new creative interpretation. Communion in the body of Christ implies community in the body of Christ.

What is the source of this ecclesial interpretation of the "body" concept in Paul? That is one of the unresolved problems in Pauline studies. Three principal sources have been suggested: (1) Hebrew thought with its conception of human beings as embodied persons and its conception of Israel as a corporate personality, (2) Gnostic Adam-speculation, and (3) The Stoic conception of the cosmos as a living body or organism in which gods and humanity form a unity and where each member is regarded as a limb of the whole.[66] Two examples from Stoic literature will illustrate this conception:

"All that you behold, that which comprises both God and humanity, is one—we are the parts of one great body."[67]

"The principle which obtains in single organisms with regard to the limbs of the body applies also in separate beings to rational things constituted to work in conjunction. But the perception of this will come home to you better, if you often say to yourself, I am a limb of the organized body of rational things."[68]

The Stoic conception appears to be the one that is primarily in the background in 1 Corinthians 12:12–27[69] and may also find some reflection in the present text.

With regard to the second alternative, E. Käsemann thought that "almost the whole of Paul's interpretation of the primitive eucharistic tradition bears the mark of the fact that he has adopted and adapted the gnostic myth of an Archetypal Man, who is also the Redeemer." "Only on this basis," he held, "can we explain historically Paul's distinctive combination of the Sacrament and the

Church as the Body of Christ."[70] This archetypal man is conceived as having a giant body that embraces countless members. If this is the background of Paul's thought here, then Christ is viewed as having a body in which many can be incorporated by entering into communion with him.

There are, however, serious difficulties with this hypothesis. In the first place, Gnosticism itself as a developed system (i.e., as a sect with a definite body of literature and teachings) cannot be definitely traced before the second century. We cannot, therefore, speak of Gnosticism in connection with the background of the New Testament writings as though it were a fully developed system. It is better to speak of a Gnosticizing atmosphere that is certainly present in the New Testament background and that led to the development of Gnosticism itself. In the second place, the assumption that a full-blown myth of the archetypal man was present in the New Testament environment is probably false. The conception of a primal man, which has its roots in both Iranian religion and Jewish thought, did form part of Gnostic speculation, but it was just that—speculation. The traces of this conception that have been collected, however, do not form a unified mythological structure or system of thought. Paul's "body" concept, therefore, may well owe something of its background and form to Gnosticizing reflection of this type, but we cannot speak of dependence on a fully developed Gnostic myth.[71]

Whether Hebrew, Gnostic, or Stoic conceptions form the primary background for Paul's "body" concept, in any case, Paul does not construct his doctrine of the Church on the basis of any of them. His starting point is reflection on verse 16, in which the concept of the body of Christ is used in its Christological sense. The ecclesiological idea of the Church as the body of Christ derives, in this context, from the Christological idea. It is the result of Paul's reflection on the implications of the bread saying and its traditional interpretation for the community of believers. Communion in the body of Christ implies community in the body of Christ. The basis, therefore, of the conception of the body of Christ in verse 17 is not the analogy with Hebrew, Gnostic, or Stoic conceptions, but reflection on the fact that communion in the body of Christ through the partaking of one loaf in the eucharist forms the many into one body. The Hebrew conception of the human being as an embodied person, and the extension of this idea to include the whole community of Israel, would appear to be the ultimate background against which such an idea could arise in Paul's mind, although we should not rule out the importance that Gnostic and Stoic conceptions may have had both in prompting the idea in the first place and giving shape to it once Paul had conceived it.

What are the implications of this communion (= community) in the body of Christ for Paul? In Chapter 11, Paul draws out the implications of his ecclesial interpretation of the eucharist for the social relationships within the body of Christ. The question of eucharistic celebration in this chapter emerges as a practical social problem.[72] Apparently, the Lord's Supper was celebrated in Corinth in the context of a community meal where some members of the community arrived early and ate all the food and drank all the wine, leaving nothing for the poorer members of the community when they arrived.

". . . when you assemble as a church, says Paul, I hear that there are divisions among you. . . . When you meet together, it is not the Lord's Supper that you eat. For in eating, each one goes ahead with his own meal, and one is hungry and another is drunk. What! Do you not have houses to eat and drink in? Or do you despise the church of God and humiliate those who have nothing?"[73]

Paul then goes on to give his account of the institution of the Lord's Supper, after which he comments as follows:

"Whoever, therefore, eats the bread or drinks the cup of the Lord in an unworthy manner will be guilty of profaning the body and blood of the Lord. . . . For any one who eats and drinks without discerning the body eats and drinks judgment upon himself. . . . So then, my brothers and sisters, when you come together to eat, wait for one another—if any one is hungry, let him eat at home—lest you come together to be condemned. . . ."[74]

s passage has been interpreted in a highly indi-
Unworthy reception of the Supper has been re-
sin, and "discerning the body" has been inter-
ically. This interpretation, however, misses the
ₒlects the social context that Paul is addressing
...ᵤ fails to see the connection between Paul's ecclesial interpretation of the body of Christ in 1 Corinthians 10:16–17 and
the "discerning of the body" referred to in 1 Corinthians 11:29.
In Chapter 10, Paul makes it clear that by sharing in the one loaf
and the one cup, those who have assembled are constituted as a
koinonia, a community. Because there is one loaf, all who share
in that one loaf become one body, one community in Christ. In
Chapter 11, Paul draws out the implications of this ecclesial
interpretation of the eucharist for the community's social relationships.

In Paul's view, to have communion in the body of Christ is to
have community in the body of Christ. The Christological and
the ecclesiological themes stand together and cannot be separated from each other. Christian existence is embodied social
existence lived out in community. To participate in the Lord's
Supper means to be transformed in the totality of one's bodily
existence and in the totality of one's social relationships.

". . . those who eat and drink without 'discerning' or
'recognising' (*diakrino*) the body, i.e., the community constituted
by breaking the one bread . . . eat and drink for judgment (*krima*
v. 29). . . ."[75]

The community that assembles to celebrate the Lord's Supper
while the poorer members of the community are deprived of
food stands in theological self-contradiction.

NOTES

1. For the role of table fellowship in the ministry of Jesus, see Norman
Perrin, *Rediscovering the Teaching of Jesus* (New York: Harper & Row,
1967), 102–108.

2. Cf. Joachim Jeremias, *The Eucharistic Words of Jesus* (London: SCM
Press, 1966), 232.

3. For the background of Jewish meal traditions and the Jewish table blessings, see Louis Finkelstein, "The Birkat Ha-Mazon," *Jewish Quarterly Review*, n.s., 19 (1928–1929): 211–262.

4. Perrin, 102–108.

5. Cf. Ernst Lohmeyer, *Lord of the Temple* (London: Oliver & Boyd, 1961), 79ff.; and Oscar Cullmann and F. J. Leenhardt, *Essays on the Lord's Supper* (London: Lutterworth, 1958), 8–16.

6. Cf. Acts 2:42,46; 20:11; 10:41.

7. Chaps. 9, 10, and 14.

8. Cf. Hans Lietzmann, *Mass and Lord's Supper: A Study in the History of the Liturgy* (Leiden: E. J. Brill, 1979), 196–203.

9. For an introduction to redaction criticism, see Norman Perrin, *What is Redaction Criticism?* (Philadelphia: Fortress Press, 1969).

10. Cf., for example, Reginald H. Fuller and Pheme Perkins, *Who is this Christ?* (Philadelphia: Fortress Press, 1983).

11. Cf. Rudolph Bultmann, *Theology of the New Testament*, 2 vols. (New York: Charles Scribner's Sons, 1951), 1:4–11.

12. Is 25:6–8.

13. Ethiopian Enoch 62:13–14.

14. Col. 2, lines 11–22.

15. Frank Moore Cross, Jr., *The Ancient Library of Qumran and Modern Biblical Studies*, rev. ed. (Grand Rapids, MI: Baker Book House, 1980), 85–90. Cf. also K. G. Kuhn, "The Lord's Supper and the Communal Meal of Qumran," in Krister Stendahl (ed.), *The Scrolls and the New Testament* (New York: Harper & Bros., 1957).

16. Mt 11:18–19a.

17. Mt 8:11.

18. Lk 13:29.

19. Lk 22:27–30. Cf. Heinz Schürmann, *Le Récit de la Dernière Cène* (Lyon: X. Mappus, 1966).

20. Raymond E. Brown, *The Gospel According to John*, The Anchor Bible, 2 vols. (New York: Doubleday & Co., 1966–1970), 2:601–603. For the eucharist in John's gospel, see John Reumann, *The Supper of the Lord: The New Testament, Ecumenical Dialogues, and Faith and Order on Eucharist* (Philadelphia: Fortress Press, 1985), 17–21.

21. See Patrick McGoldrick (ed.), *Understanding the Eucharist* (Dublin: Gill & Macmillan, 1969), 28.

22. Jeremias, *Eucharistic Words*, 139–159.

23. *Ibid.*, 186–187.

24. *Ibid.*, 173–186.

25. *Ibid.*

26. Günther Bornkamm, *Early Christian Experience* (London: SCM Press, 1969), 136–137.

27. Eduard Schweizer, *The Lord's Supper According to the New Testament* (Philadelphia: Fortress Press, 1967), 14.

28. *Ibid.*, 15.

29. *Theological Dictionary of the New Testament*, s.v. "haima" (hereafter cited as *TDNT*).

30. Bornkamm, 139.

31. *Ibid.*

32. Joachim Jeremias, *The Parables of Jesus*, rev. ed. (New York: Charles Scribner's Sons, 1963), 227–229.

33. Jeremias, *Eucharistic Words*, 232–237.

34. Heinz Schürmann, "Jesus' Words in the Light of his Actions at the Last Supper," in Pierre Benoit (ed.), *Concilium*, vol. 40 (New York: Paulist Press, 1969). Cf. also H. Wheeler Robinson, "Hebrew Sacrifice and Prophetic Symbolism," *Journal of Theological Studies*, 43 (1942): 131–139.

35. Cf. Ferdinand Hahn, "Die alttestamentlichen Motive in der urchristlichen Abendmahlsüberlieferung," *Evangelische Theologie* 27 (1967): 341. For the covenant concept, see Reumann, 34–41. For the following discussion, see also Helmut Merklein, "Erwägungen zur Uberlieferungsgeschichte der neutestamentlichen Abendmahlstraditionen," *Biblische Zeitschrift*, 21 (1977): 88–101 and 235–244.

36. *TDNT*, s.v. "diatheke."

37. Ex 24:4–11.

38. Schürmann, "Jesus' Words," 129.

39. *Ibid.*, 129–130.

40. Jeremias, *Eucharistic Words*, 226ff.

41. Hahn, 341.

36

42. Lietzmann, 205ff.

43. Jeremias, *Eucharistic Words*, 237–255.

44. Schweizer, 29–32.

45. Bernard Lohse, *Das Passafest der Quartadecimaner* (Gütersloh: Bertelsmann, 1953), 62–89.

46. Douglas Jones, "Anamnesis in the LXX and the Interpretation of 1 Cor. 11:25," *Journal of Theological Studies* 6 (1955): 183–191; H. Kosmala, " 'Das tut zu meinem Gedächtnis,' " *Novum Testamentum*, 4 (1960): 81–94.

47. Bornkamm, 140–141.

48. Hahn, 341–342. Reumann also concludes after reviewing recent scholarship that "the meaning of anamnesis thus remains unsettled in biblical studies" (33).

49. Brevard S. Childs, *Memory and Tradition in Israel* (Naperville, IL: Alec R. Allenson, 1962), 9–30.

50. *Ibid.*, 31–50.

51. *Ibid.*, 50–56.

52. *Ibid.*, 58.

53. *Ibid.*

54. *Ibid.*, 75–85.

55. Sigmund Mowinckel, *The Psalms in Israel's Worship*, 2 vols. (Oxford: Basil Blackwell, 1962), 1:15–22.

56. Childs, 82.

57. Martin Noth, "Die Vergegenwärtigung des Alten Testaments in der Verkündigung," *Evangelische Theologie*, 12 (1952–1953): 6–17.

58. Childs, 82–85.

59. For the discussion that follows, see esp. David Gregg, *Anamnesis in the Eucharist*, Grove Liturgical Studies, no. 5 (Bramcote, Notts.: Grove Books, 1976), 17–23.

60. Childs, 66–70.

61. Gregg, 21.

62. D. Hedegard, *Seder R. Amram Gaon* (Lund, 1951), 152.

63. Bornkamm, 139.

64. For the following discussion, see *TDNT*, s.v. "koinonia."

65. Ernst Käsemann, *Essays on New Testament Themes* (Naperville, IL: Alec R. Allenson, 1964), 110.

66. Ernst Käsemann, *Perspectives on Paul* (Philadelphia: Fortress Press, 1971), 103.

67. Sen. *Ep.* 95.52.

68. M. Aur. Ant. *Medit.* 2.1; 7.13.

69. Hans Conzelmann, *1 Corinthians* (Philadelphia: Fortress Press, 1975), 211–214.

70. Käsemann, *Essays*, 109.

71. Markus Barth, *Ephesians*, The Anchor Bible, 2 vols. (New York, Doubleday & Co., 1974), 1:16.

72. Elisabeth Schüssler Fiorenza, "Tablesharing and the Celebration of the Eucharist," in Mary Collins and David Power (eds.), *Concilium*, vol. 152 (New York: Seabury Press, 1982), 5ff.

73. 1 Cor 11:18, 20–22.

74. 1 Cor 11:27, 29, 33–34.

75. Fiorenza, 10.

CHAPTER TWO

The Eucharist in the Early Church

THE EUCHARISTIC PRAYER

First and Second Centuries
The Eucharistic Prayer is the great Prayer of Thanksgiving said
over the bread and the cup in the eucharistic liturgy. In the East,
it is generally called the anaphora. In the West, it became known
as the canon of the mass or the prayer of consecration. Today, in
the liturgical revisions that are taking place in most of the western Churches, it is commonly called the Eucharistic Prayer. In
the early Church, it was the Eucharistic Prayer that formed the
heart of the liturgy, and the words of institution, when they
came to be inserted in it, formed an integral part of this prayer.
The origin of the Eucharistic Prayer lies in the Jewish table
prayers of blessing and thanksgiving (*berakoth*),[1] and above all in
the thanksgiving said over the cup at the end of the meal, the
birkat ha-mazon.[2] The clearest example in early Christian literature
of this dependence on Jewish models is seen in the table prayers
in the *Didache*.[3]

This is the pattern already reflected in the Last Supper accounts
in the New Testament. At the beginning of the meal, Jesus said
the traditional Jewish blessing over the bread. At the end of the
meal ("after supper"), he said the thanksgiving over the cup.
There is evidence in the New Testament itself that at a very early
period, the eucharist and the common meal were separated from
each other. The meal either took place before the eucharist was
celebrated (apparently the situation in Corinth when Paul was
writing) or it took place apart from the eucharist altogether as an
agape meal. Once the meal was separated from the eucharist, the

berkoth said separately over the bread and the cup were combined into a single prayer of thanksgiving recited over the bread and the cup together. This single prayer was modeled after the thanksgiving over the cup rather than after the bread blessing, and it is this thanksgiving over the cup, the *birkat ha-mazon*, which became the primary inspiration and model for the Eucharistic Prayer.[4]

The text of the *birkat ha-mazon* translated from the *Siddur Rav Saadya* is as follows:

"Blessed are you, Lord our God, King of the universe, for you nourish us and the whole world with goodness, grace, kindness and mercy.

"Blessed are you, Lord, for you nourish the universe.

"We will give thanks to you, Lord our God, because you have given us for our inheritance a desirable land, good and wide, the covenant and the law, life and food."

"On the feasts of Hanukkah *and* Purim, *here follows an embolism.*

"And for all these things we give you thanks and bless your name for ever and beyond.

"Blessed are you, Lord, for the land and for food.

"Have mercy, Lord our God, on us your people Israel, and your city Jerusalem, on your sanctuary and your dwelling place, on Zion, the habitation of your glory, and the great and holy house over which your name is invoked. Restore the kingdom of the house of David to its place in our days, and speedily build Jerusalem.[5]

"(On the day of the new moon and festivals, including the Passover, the embolism *ya'aleh we-yavo* is added.)"

It will be seen from this text that the basic form of the *birkat ha-mazon* is composed of three sections or pericopes with the following structure: blessing–thanksgiving–supplication. The second and third pericopes provide for "embolisms" (additions or expansions) on feast days.

Recent research in the history of the Eucharistic Prayer indicates that the earliest Christian Eucharistic Prayers do not follow this pattern exactly, but rather tend to conflate the first two pericopes and give to the whole revised pericope the note of thanksgiving characteristic of the second section of the Jewish prayer. This revised pericope is then developed in a specifically Christian direction and becomes a thanksgiving for redemption (and also for creation) that is oriented in a Christological direction.[6] This was the first and fundamental way in which the Jewish model was transformed by Christian tradition. This remodeling can already be seen in the prayer of thanksgiving after the meal in the *Didache*, Chapter 10.

"And after you have had your fill, give thanks thus:

"We give thanks to you, holy Father, for your holy Name which you have enshrined in our hearts, and for the knowledge and faith and immortality which you have made known to us through your child Jesus: glory to you for evermore.

"You, almighty Master, created all things for the sake of your Name, and gave food and drink to mankind for their enjoyment, that they might give you thanks; but to us you have granted spiritual food and drink and eternal life through your child Jesus. Above all we give you thanks because you are mighty; glory to you for evermore. Amen.

"Remember, Lord, your Church, to deliver it from all evil and to perfect it in your love; bring it together from the four winds, now sanctified, into your kingdom which you have prepared for it; for yours are the power and the glory for evermore.

"May grace come, and may this world pass away.

"Hosanna to the God of David.

"If any is holy, let him come; if any is not, let him repent. Marana tha. Amen."[7]

The dominant note of thanksgiving can readily be seen in paragraphs one and two of this prayer. The prayer has been touched up in a Christological direction, but the theology is still Jewish–Christian. Paragraph three follows the pattern of supplication characteristic of the third pericope of the Jewish prayer. Two characteristics of this supplication can be noted. The supplication begins with "remember," and the whole pericope is dominated by the eschatological theme of the coming kingdom. Here, too, it is in line with Jewish tradition and with the earliest Christianity.

Third Century

The next stage of remodeling involved the expansion both of the new revised first pericope of the Christian prayer (originally, the first two pericopes of the *birkat ha-mazon*) and of the original third Jewish pericope of supplication, which has now become the second pericope in the Christian prayer. This expansion apparently took place in the following ways. Two different patterns, in fact, seem to have been followed. The predominant pattern, found in the *Apostolic Tradition of Hippolytus*,[8] which contains the oldest western form of the Eucharistic Prayer that has come down to us, and in virtually all of the later developed anaphoras was to expand the first pericope of thanksgiving to include the institution narrative from the Last Supper and an anamnesis. If L. Ligier is right, the inspiration for this pattern was the practice of inserting commemorative embolisms at the conclusion of the second Jewish pericope of thanksgiving on the festivals of Hanukkah and Purim.[9] The second pericope of the Christian prayer was then expanded into an epiclesis and concluded with a doxology. The pattern that emerged is thus the following:

Thanksgiving for (creation) and redemption

Institution narrative and Anamnesis

Epiclesis and Doxology

This is exactly the structure of the anaphora in the *Apostolic Tradition of Hippolytus*.

"And when he has been made bishop, all shall offer the kiss of peace, greeting him because he has been made worthy.

"Then the deacons shall present the offering to him; and he, laying his hands on it with all the presbytery, shall say, giving thanks:

42

"The Lord be with you.

"And all shall say:

"And with your spirit.
Up with your hearts.
We have (them) with the Lord.
Let us give thanks to the Lord.
It is fitting and right.

"And then he shall continue thus:

"We render thanks to you, O God, through your beloved child Jesus Christ, whom in the last times you sent to us as a savior and redeemer and angel of your will; who is your inseparable Word, through whom you made all things, and in whom you were well pleased. You sent him from heaven into a virgin's womb; and conceived in the womb, he was made flesh and was manifested as your Son, being born of the Holy Spirit and the Virgin. Fulfilling your will and gaining for you a holy people, he stretched out his hands when he should suffer, that he might release from suffering those who have believed in you.

"And when he was betrayed to voluntary suffering that he might destroy death, and break the bonds of the devil, and tread down hell, and shine upon the righteous, and fix a term, and manifest the resurrection, he took bread and gave thanks to you, saying, 'Take, eat; this is my body, which shall be broken for you.' Likewise also the cup, saying, 'This is my blood, which is shed for you; when you do this, you make my remembrance.'

"Remembering therefore his death and resurrection, we offer to you the bread and the cup, giving you thanks because you have held us worthy to stand before you and minister to you.

"And we ask that you would send your Holy Spirit upon the offering of your holy Church; that, gathering her into one, you would grant to all who receive the holy things (to receive) for the fullness of the Holy Spirit for the strengthening of faith in truth; that we may praise and glorify you through your child Jesus Christ; through whom be glory and honor to you, to the

Father and the Son, with the Holy Spirit, in your holy Church, both now and to the ages of ages. Amen."[10]

In recent years, attention has come to focus more and more upon an anaphora that in its original form appears to be at least as old if not older than the Eucharistic Prayer of Hippolytus, i.e., the so-called anaphora of the Apostles Addai and Mari.[11] L. Bouyer believes that "everything leads us to believe that this prayer is the most ancient Christian eucharistic composition to which we can have access today."[12] Addai and Mari is of particular interest not only on account of its age, but also because of its intrinsic importance. The Eucharistic Prayer in Hippolytus, despite its antiquity, already shows the stylistic features of a studied literary piece, and was probably a model prayer composed by Hippolytus for the occasion of a bishop's ordination, although in both form and content, it reflects both earlier traditions and the Jewish model that provides its inspiration. Addai and Mari, on the other hand, was and still is the actual prayer of a worshiping community, being used to this day by the East Syrian Church called Chaldean or Malabar, though in a developed form. Moreover, it has a very definite Semitic character, having been composed originally in Syriac and if, as appears most likely, it belongs to the tradition of the ancient Church of Edessa, it is an example of a tradition of the Eucharistic Prayer that was untouched until much later by Hellenistic modifications.

The difficulty, however, is that despite its interest, Addai and Mari bristles with difficulties both of a textual nature and with respect to its content. Up until 1966, the earliest known manuscript of this anaphora was from the sixteenth century. In that year, however, William F. Macomber made the sensational discovery of a tenth–eleventh-century manuscript in the church of Mar Esa ya in Mosul, which pushed the textual evidence back half a millenium.[13] Nevertheless, the text is still very late and has certainly undergone considerable development. The establishment of the earliest form of the text, therefore, is highly problematic. The most interesting internal features of the document, however, are the lack of an institution narrative and the apparent lack of an anamnesis. Two clauses in the text resemble an anamnesis, but they look more like parts of an intercession than like an anamnesis of the type we find in Hippolytus. Furthermore, the epiclesis rather than the institution narrative-anamnesis appears to be the high point of the prayer, so that it exhibits the following structure:

Thanksgiving for creation and redemption

Intercessions

Epiclesis

Doxology

More recently still, attention has been drawn to another anaphora, the so-called Third Anaphora of the Apostle Peter, commonly referred to by the first word in the Syriac, *sharar*, which is also in the East Syrian tradition and which appears to be a twin of Addai and Mari.[14] However, in its present form, it is also late and exhibits some differences from Addai and Mari, notably the presence of an institution narrative and an anamnesis. T. Talley, however, points out that this prayer, despite its present considerably developed form, shows "an acute sensitivity to the formal details of Jewish meal prayers . . . (which) might be a sign of very great antiquity. . . . "[15] Moreover, he points out that the last part of this prayer, which begins in the present text with the clause "We offer before you, Lord, this sacrifice in memory of all righteous and holy fathers etc.," is strongly reminiscent of the festal embolism in the third pericope of the *birkat ha-mazon*, the ninth-century text of which reads as follows:

". . . may the remembrance of ourselves and of our fathers and the remembrance of Jerusalem, the city, and the remembrance of the Messiah, the son of David, your servant, and the remembrance of your people, the whole house of Israel, arise and come, come to pass, be seen and accepted and heard, be remembered and be mentioned before you for deliverance, for good, for grace, etc."[16]

This rather striking parallel between the Jewish embolism and the last part of *sharar* leads me to the following very tentative suggestion. If this section of the prayer is indeed very early, then is it possible that in *sharar*, the anamnesis was originally part of the last pericope of the prayer and took a supplicatory or intercessory form following the Jewish model, and that the institution narrative-anamnesis unit in the present text of the prayer is a later addition to bring it into line with other eastern anaphoras?

If this is the case, this would shed light on the difficulties encountered in Addai and Mari. The absence of an institution narrative and anamnesis would be explained by the fact that the development of the East Syrian anaphora took a different path than that taken by Hippolytus, although both were based on Jewish models. Whereas in Hippolytus, the institution narrative-anamnesis took the form of an embolism added to the thanksgiving pericope of the prayer on the analogy of the festal embolisms of Hanukkah and Purim, the memorial in the East Syrian anaphora developed by way of analogy to the new moon and Passover embolism, was developed within the second rather than the first pericope, and took on the supplicatory character of that embolism. This would explain why the only clauses in the Mar Esa ya text of Addai and Mari that are anamnetic in character are embedded in the intercessory section of the prayer. It would also reinforce the observation of Dom H. Engberding, reechoed by other scholars, that the intercessory material in Addai and Mari is very old.[17] A final indication is to be found in the *Didache*, where it is the supplication that begins with "remember," and there is no explicit anamnesis in the thanksgiving pericope.

If this hypothesis has any substance, it goes a long way toward explaining the evolution of the Eucharistic prayer into its developed forms. Addai and Mari and *sharar* were marked by a different kind of evolution from the *birkat ha-mazon* than that manifested by Hippolytus. The path taken by Hippolytus, however, was that taken by all the eastern anaphoras except the East Syrian. Eventually, the East Syrian tradition itself came under the influence of the dominant pattern and an institution narrative-anamnesis was inserted into the ancient prayers. The evidence in the later manuscripts, which contain an institution narrative-anamnesis, of awkward "joins" in the construction of the prayer at this point tend to confirm this suspicion. Our hypothesis would also reinforce Cutrone's observation that the epiclesis is really the high point of the prayer in Addai and Mari, to which the thanksgiving section of the prayer naturally leads up.[18] This would be, in fact, the true original structure of the prayer, with the original anamnesis forming an integral part of the epicletic supplication. In the present text of *sharar*, in fact, the commemorative intercessions lead directly into the epiclesis and doxology. The insertion of the institution narrative and anamnesis between the thanksgiving section and the concluding intercessions–epiclesis–doxology would thus constitute a break in the original structure of the prayer.

Can we go even further? In a seminal article,[19] Geoffrey Cuming has suggested that the Strasbourg papyrus, formerly thought to be an early fragment of the Eucharistic Prayer in the Liturgy of St. Mark, is in fact a complete Eucharistic Prayer that can be dated as early as the second century and is the earliest Eucharistic Prayer we possess in the Egyptian tradition. It has the complete structure of a Jewish berakah:

Thanksgiving for creation
Supplication (Intercessions)
Doxology

"to bless [you] . . . [night] and day. . . .

"[you who made] heaven [and] all that is in [it, the earth and what is on earth,] seas and rivers and [all that is] in [them]; [you] who made man [according to your] own image and likeness. You made everything through your wisdom, the light [of?] your true Son, our Lord and Savior Jesus Christ; giving thanks through him to you with him and the Holy Spirit, we offer the reasonable sacrifice and this bloodless service, which all the nations offer you, 'from sunrise to sunset,' from south to north, [for] your 'name is great among all the nations, and in every place incense is offered to your holy name and a pure sacrifice.'

"Over this sacrifice and offering we pray and beseech you, remember your holy and only Catholic Church, all your peoples and all your flocks. Provide the peace which is from heaven in all our hearts, and grant us also the peace of this life. The . . . of the land peaceful things towards us, and towards your [holy] name, the prefect of the province, the army, the princes, councils. . . . [*About one-third of a page is lacking here, and what survives is in places too fragmentary to be restored.*]

"[for seedtime and] harvest . . . preserve, for the poor of [your] people, for all of us who call upon [your] name, for all who hope in you. Give rest to the souls of those who have fallen asleep; remember those of whom we make mention today, both those whose names we say [and] whose we do not say . . . [Remember] our orthodox fathers and bishops everywhere; and grant us to have a part and lot with the fair . . . of your holy prophets, apostles, and martyrs. Receive(?) [through] their entreaties [these prayers]; grant them through our Lord; through whom be glory to you to the ages of ages."[20]

There are a number of striking features about this prayer. In the first place, it contains a thanksgiving for creation (incorporating a prayer of offering), but no thanksgiving for redemption. Secondly, the intercessions begin with "remember" in a manner analogous to the new moon and Passover embolism of the *birkat ha-mazon*, the third pericope of the *Didache* prayer, and the intercessions in *sharar*. Thirdly, there is no Sanctus, institution narrative, or epiclesis. If this is a complete prayer, therefore, it may represent a stage in the development of the Eucharistic Prayer that is even earlier than Hippolytus or Addai and Mari.

The thanksgiving for creation in this prayer is based on Psalm 146:6 and retains a purely Jewish character with no Christological reworking. This remains characteristic of the Eucharistic Prayer in Egypt even in its fully developed form in the Liturgy of St. Mark in contrast to Hippolytus and the East Syrian tradition. The prayer of offering, quoting Malachi 1:11, parallels the *Didache*, Justin Martyr, and Irenaeus, all of whom quote the Malachi text and understand the eucharist as a sacrifice of thanksgiving on the analogy of a Jewish gift-sacrifice.[21] *Anamnesis* takes an intercessory form as it does in *sharar*. The absence of an institution narrative also parallels the East Syrian tradition.

Fourth to Sixth Centuries

In the fourth century, a variety of rites came into existence. These rites can be grouped according to liturgical families belonging to different regions, which exhibit certain distinctive characteristics. There are three liturgical families belonging to the eastern end of the Mediterranean, which are commonly referred to as the oriental or eastern rites. These three liturgical families are (a) the West Syrian or Antiochene tradition, (b) the Egyptian or Alexandrian tradition, and (c) the East Syrian tradition. We have already spoken of the anaphoras of Addai and Mari and *sharar*, which belong to the East Syrian tradition. These rites, however, probably stem in their original form from as early as the third century or even earlier.

The West Syrian tradition had its two major centers of influence in Jerusalem and Antioch. An early anaphora of Antiochene type (ca. A.D. 375) is the anaphora in the so-called *Apostolic Constitutions,* Book VIII, which draws on and greatly expands the anaphora in the *Apostolic Tradition of Hippolytus.*[22] The Jerusalem liturgy is exemplified by the Liturgy of St. James (ca. A.D. 400), which is probably a conflation of earlier liturgies of Antioch and Jerusalem.[23] The developed Byzantine liturgies of St. John Chrysostom[24] and St. Basil,[25] still in use today, are liturgies of the West Syrian type. There survives, however, an early recension of the anaphora of St. Basil, known as the anaphora of Basil of Caesarea, which probably stems from Asia Minor in the first half of the fourth century.[26]

The Liturgy of St. Mark, which we have already referred to, is the developed liturgy of the Egyptian Church. If Cuming is right, the Egyptian prayer evolved from the model found in the Strasbourg papyrus in something like the following way. The Sanctus came to replace the original doxology. The Sanctus was then followed by an epiclesis asking God to "fill" the sacrifice with his blessing, linking the epiclesis to the last sentence of the Sanctus, "heaven and earth are full of your glory." The institution narrative and anamnesis were then inserted after the epiclesis and a second epiclesis was added after the anamnesis, probably under the influence of the West Syrian model. The intercessions remained in their original place, following the thanksgiving. We can chart the differences in structure of the anaphoras of Antiochene and Alexandrian type as follows.[27] There was mutual influence, however, between the West Syrian and Egyptian liturgies, so that it should not be thought that these types developed in complete isolation from each other.

Antiochene	Alexandrian
Thanksgiving	Thanksgiving
Sanctus	Intercessions
Thanksgiving	Sanctus
Institution Narrative	Epiclesis I
Anamnesis	Institution Narrative
Epiclesis	Anamnesis
Intercessions	Epiclesis II
Doxology	Doxology

It can be seen from the chart and from an examination of the anaphoras concerned, that the earlier models of the Eucharistic Prayer have been considerably amplified both by the embellishment of the existing structure of the prayer and by certain additions, notably the *Sanctus*, the spread of intercessions, and the appearance of a second epiclesis in anaphoras of the Alexandrian type. We shall see in a later section that the sacrificial element also becomes more prominent. By the middle of the fifth century, the Eucharistic Prayer had generally attained its definitive structure in the East.[28]

In the West, there were at first a number of local and regional liturgies, the Ambrosian rite (Milan), the Mozarabic rite (Spain), the Celtic liturgy (Ireland, etc.), and the Gallican rite (Frankish-Germanic kingdoms) as well as the Roman rite, which was used in Rome itself and the surrounding areas.[29] These regional liturgies were eventually absorbed into the Roman rite, which finally supplanted them. The origins of the Roman canon are veiled in obscurity. It attained a virtually fixed form by the end of the sixth century, but the only certain evidence of its earlier evolution is found in the *De sacramentis* of St. Ambrose, who quotes the central part of the Eucharistic Prayer current in his day and describes the first part of the canon.[30] The parallels are obvious between the evidence of the *De sacramentis* and the later text of the Roman canon, but evidence for the development between Ambrose and the final redaction is scant.

The Roman canon is cast in the form of a series of interconnected short prayers, the structure and unity of which present a number of problems. The theme of sacrifice is more prominent in this Eucharistic Prayer than in any of the eastern anaphoras. The institution narrative-anamnesis is framed by sacrificial prayers, and the sacrificial theme is woven into the series of commemorations and intercessions that appear between the *Sanctus* and the institution narrative. Moreover, between the *Sanctus* and the doxology, the note of praise and thanksgiving is subsumed under the note of supplication.

Does the Roman canon have a structural unity? Ralph A. Keifer has argued that it does and that the unifying theme is that of a sacrifice of praise.[31] The presentation of the sacrifice of praise, however, has been recast in the form of a supplication of the divine majesty, which has biblical roots, but which has been influenced by the Roman form for the supplication of an emperor. If this is correct, then the Roman canon exhibits the fundamental character of the early anaphoras, but like them bears the stamp of its own culture. The structure of the Roman canon is set out in the following chart in relation to the pattern of the Eucharistic Prayer that we have already discerned. The Latin phrases by which the parts of the Roman canon are normally identified are the opening words of each prayer in the series. Keifer's rationale for the prayer down to *Supplices te rogamus* is also supplied.[32]

Structure	Prayer Series	Rationale
Praise and Thanksgiving	Opening dialogue	We praise you
	Variable Preface	
Sanctus	Sanctus	
Commemorations-Intercessions	Te igitur	We offer (for the whole church)

	Memento, Domine	We offer (for particular persons)
	Communicantes	We offer (in union with . . .)
Sacrificial prayers	Hanc igitur	We offer (for special needs)
	Quam oblationem	Accept our offering
Institution narrative	Qui pridie	Because Christ commands it
Anamnesis	Unde et memores	In his memorial, we offer
Sacrificial-epicletic (?) prayers	Supra quae	Accept our offering as you did those of the old covenant
	Supplices te rogamus	Make it pleasing to you and beneficial for us
Commemorations-Intercessions	Memento etiam Nobis·quoque peccatoribus	
Doxology	Per quem haec omnia	

Theology of the Eucharistic Prayer

The function of the Eucharistic Prayer is to render praise and thanksgiving to God over the bread and the cup for creation and redemption. In thanking God, the Church followed the Jewish custom of summing up its faith in what God had done. The prayer is, therefore, primarily a recital of the mighty works of God. It is thanksgiving, *anamnesis*, and proclamation rolled into one. Within the context of this basic function of the Eucharistic Prayer, however, the theology of the prayer develops in two directions. On the one hand, the way in which this praise and thanksgiving is rendered is shaped by the theological genius and cultural milieu of the region in which the prayer is developed. On the other hand, the various additions and expansions that mark the historical development of the prayer become the focus of theological reflection.

Once the Jewish prayer became Christianized, the motive of the thanksgiving became explicitly Christological, the recalling of what God had done in Jesus. Gradually, therefore, the Christological outlook and redemptive vision of the various early Christian communities impressed themselves on the character and shape of the prayer. In the earliest Eucharistic Prayers, this theological vision is expressed primarily within the categories of Jewish Christianity. In the more developed eastern anaphoras, the cosmic vision of redemption as a divine plan of salvation encompassing the whole of creation and the Trinitarian vision of God dominate the structure of the prayer. The goal of this thanksgiving and *anamnesis* of the divine activity, however, is the praise of God's glory on the basis of God's works. Nothing could be closer to the whole spirit of Jewish prayer, but when Jewish prayer becomes the prayer of eastern Christians, it comes to bear the imprint of the eastern theological vision. Likewise, when the sacrifice of praise came to be offered by a Church saturated by the culture of the late Roman empire, its prayer, too, although remaining a prayer in praise of the divine glory, was offered in the style of a supplication addressed to the Roman emperor. In their theology, therefore, the Eucharistic Prayers of the early Church reflect both the theological variety and cultural diversity characteristic of the regions in which they were produced.

The theology of the early Eucharistic Prayers, however, was not only an expression of the theological visions characteristic of the different faith communities that produced them, it was also a function of the development of the structure of the prayer itself. At the beginning, all that was necessary was a simple prayer of thanksgiving-supplication on the Jewish model. Such a prayer is itself an *anamnesis* of the mighty works of God, because the only way a Jew knows how to give thanks to God is by recounting Yahweh's mighty works. Moreover, Jewish prayer always ends in supplication toward God both on the basis of what Yahweh has done and on the basis of the divine promise for the future. There is, therefore, both an anamnetic and an eschatological thrust to all Jewish prayer.

It was natural, however, that these themes, implicit in all Jewish prayer, should become explicit in the Christian prayer, especially when there were at hand Jewish models for such additions and expansions to the primary pericopes. It was in this way, it seems, that the anamnesis and the epiclesis developed within the structure of the prayer. It was natural also that when the institution narrative was inserted into the prayer it should stand in closest connection with the anamnesis, because it provided the specific warrant for the Christian anamnesis in the command to "Do this for a memorial of me." These elements, along with the sacrificial element, became the focus both of liturgical development and theological reflection. In the next two sections, we shall trace the development of the epiclesis and the sacrificial theme. We will then look at the kind of exegesis that was characteristic of early Christian writers and at the kind of philosophical frame through which they perceived reality, because these traditions also had a vital impact on their eucharistic theology.

EPICLESIS

In the eastern Churches, the epiclesis or invocation of the Holy Spirit in the Eucharistic Prayer has had special importance. More recently, the recovery of the tradition of the Eucharistic Prayer in the West has also meant a recovery of the epiclesis. The importance of the epiclesis is acknowledged in the World Council of Churches document *Baptism, Eucharist, and Ministry*, where the Invocation of the Spirit is one of the principal themes discussed in connection with the eucharist. In this section, therefore, we want to trace the evolution of the epiclesis and discuss its theological significance.

The origin of the epiclesis has been a matter of debate among liturgical scholars. The most likely theory is that it developed out of the third supplicatory pericope of the *birkat ha-mazon*, which is a prayer for the restoration of Jerusalem.[33] If this is the case, the epiclesis has an eschatological origin. It is essentially a prayer for the coming of the kingdom. An early piece of evidence for this is the Aramaic acclamation *Maranatha*, "Come Lord Jesus." *Maranatha* occurs in the New Testament in its Aramaic form in 1 Corinthians 16:22 and in Greek translation in Revelation 22:20 in what appear to be liturgical contexts. In the *Didache*, it concludes the epicletic section of the meal prayer in Chapter 10.[34]

More substantial evidence for the eschatological character of the epiclesis is found in the theme of gathering the Church into unity in the kingdom, which occurs in a number of the early epicleses. G. Cuming has pointed out that the phrase "gathering . . . into one" in the epiclesis in Hippolytus finds a parallel in John 11:52, "to gather into one the children of God who are scattered abroad."[35] A. Kavanagh has also called attention to the theme of unity in the high priestly prayer in John 17:20–24:

"may they all be one, even as thou, Father, are one in me and I in thee . . . that they may be one even as we are one, I in them and thou in me, that they may become perfectly one. . . . "[36]

The theme of unity is also found in the *Qibbus galuyoth* petition in the Eighteen Blessings in the synagogue liturgy:

"Sound the great horn for our freedom, and lift up the ensign, to gather our exiles, and proclaim liberty to gather us from the four quarters of the earth to our land. Blessed be thou, JHWH, who gatherest the dispersed of thy people Israel."[37]

There is a parallel to this prayer in the epicletic section of the meal prayers in Chapter 10 of the *Didache*:

"Remember, Lord, your Church, to deliver it from all evil and to perfect it in your love; bring it together from the four winds . . . into your kingdom. . . . "[38]

The Jewish prayer refers to the gathering together of the *diaspora* of Israel. In the *Didache*, this is transposed into a prayer for the eschatological gathering of the Church into the kingdom.

We have already referred to the presence of this theme in Hippolytus. The unity theme is also found in two early examples of the Egyptian liturgy and in the form of a direct reminiscence of the *Didache*. In the *Euchologion* of Sarapion, it occurs in the institution narrative rather than in the epiclesis,[39] but in the *Deir Balyzeh* papyrus, it occurs in the first epiclesis:

"Fill us also with the glory from (you), and vouchsafe to send down your Holy Spirit upon these creatures (and) make the bread the body of our (Lord and) Savior Jesus Christ, and the cup the blood . . . of our Lord and . . . (And) as this bread was scattered on (the mountains) and hills and fields, and was mixed together and became one body . . . so this wine which came from the vine of David and the water from the spotless lamb also mixed together became one mystery, so gather the catholic Church. . . . "[40]

The theme of unity is also found in the anaphoras of Alexandrian and Byzantine Basil:

" . . . Make us all worthy to partake of your holy things for sanctification of soul and body, that we may become one body and one spirit, and may have a portion with all the saints who have been pleasing to you from eternity.[41]

" . . . Unite with one another all of us who partake of the one bread and the cup into fellowship with the one Holy Spirit; . . . that we may find mercy and grace with all the saints who have been well-pleasing to you from of old. . . . "[42]

The eschatological note is struck in the epiclesis in Addai and Mari, but here it is not expressed as a supplication for the gathering of the church into unity, but as a supplication for the benefits of redemption:

"come and rest on . . . this offering . . . and bless and sanctify it, that it may be to us . . . for . . . the great hope of resurrection from the dead, and new life in the kingdom of heaven. . . . "[43]

From this eschatological background in the supplicatory section of the Jewish birkat ha-mazon, the epiclesis developed in a variety of directions and reflects a rich theological history, which we shall illustrate from the liturgical texts.

"In Judaism, this supplicatory section grew quite long on certain festival occasions. It seems that from these prayers for Jerusalem and the consummation of the Messianic hope emerged the supplications in the third part of the early anaphoras. Among the supplications, often at the head of them, were prayers for fruitful communion. Some of these invoked the Logos, some the Spirit; some invoked blessing on the elements, some on the congregation, some on both. But other supplications were present, too. Thus, the growth of the epiclesis of the Spirit can be seen as a developing tendency within a broader scope of supplications."[44]

How did the epiclesis develop from a supplication for the gathering of the Church into the kingdom into an explicit invocation of the Spirit over the gifts and the community? It appears that the epiclesis of the Spirit has its origins in a Spirit-Christology, which only later developed into an explicit epiclesis of the Spirit in the specifically Trinitarian sense.[45] In early Christian literature prior to the fourth century, "Holy Spirit" can refer to the spirit of the risen Christ rather than to the third person of the Trinity. There is evidence that the terms *Logos* (Word) and *Pneuma* (Spirit) were often interchangeable in the Christian literature of the period prior to the fourth-century Trinitarian debates. In the New Testament, Paul does not distinguish sharply between the spirit of Christ and the "Holy Spirit." In 2 Corinthians 3:17, for example, Paul says that

" . . . The Lord is the Spirit, and where the Spirit of the Lord is, there is freedom."

G. Dix lists a number of patristic texts where the Logos is equated with the Spirit. Justin, he says,

"takes it for granted that the words *pneuma hagion*, 'Holy Spirit,' mean the *Logos*, and he applies *this* theology to the Eucharist."[46]

He then quotes other patristic writers, including Hippolytus, to show that this is not an isolated instance. Hippolytus, for example, can write:

"For he was Word, he was spirit, he was power. . . . For what was begotten of the Father but the spirit, that is to say, the Word."[47]

The epicleses in the *Apostolic Tradition of Hippolytus* and in Addai and Mari are the earliest clear examples of the epiclesis that we possess. Both are explicit epicleses of the Spirit, but if the origin of the invocation of the Spirit in a Spirit-Christology is correct, then it is not certain that this is a definite reference to the third person of the Trinity. Both the epiclesis in Hippolytus and the epiclesis in Addai and Mari ask that the Holy Spirit "come" (Addai and Mari) or be "sent" (Hippolytus) on "this offering of your servants" (Addai and Mari) or "the offering of your holy Church" (Hippolytus). This reference to the community's offering should probably not be interpreted exclusively in relation to the elements, but it probably refers more widely to the whole eucharistic action as an act of offering on the analogy of a communion-sacrifice. This would explain the close connection between the petition over the gifts and the petition for the communicants in both these epicleses.[48]

"And we ask that you would send your Holy Spirit upon the offering of your holy Church; that, gathering her into one, you would grant to all who receive the holy things (to receive) for the fullness of the Holy Spirit for the strengthening of faith in truth."[49]

" . . . May your Holy Spirit, Lord, come and rest on this offering of your servants, and bless and sanctify it, that it may be to us, Lord, for remission of debts, forgiveness of sins, and the great hope of resurrection from the dead, and new life in the kingdom of heaven, with all who have been pleasing in your sight."[50]

The elements are not here envisaged as objects separated from the eucharistic action, but in the language of the epiclesis in the *Testamentum Domini* as reconstructed by Botte, as "drink and . . . holy food" for the nourishment of those who receive them.[51] In the early Church, "offering," "consecration," and "communion" were not regarded as three isolated moments in the liturgical celebration, but as three aspects of a dynamic liturgical action.

"More is involved in 'consecration' than the transformation of bread and wine into the sacramental body and blood of Christ. Considered liturgically, in terms of the whole eucharistic prayer, 'consecration' is a processive offering to the Father of the whole assembly—Christ's body which is the church . . . the offering-sacrifice of the body of Christ which is the church *makes* the sacramental body of Christ—under the forms of food for Christian nourishment. . . ."[52]

An interesting example of an early epiclesis is that found in the anaphora of Basil of Caesarea (commonly referred to as "Alexandrian" Basil).[53] This is one of the earliest surviving anaphoras, dating probably from the first half of the fourth century in Cappadocia. From there, it may have been brought to Egypt by St. Basil about A.D. 357. This anaphora, however, is Antiochene rather than Alexandrian in character, so that it is more clearly linked to the West Syrian rather than to the Egyptian tradition of the epiclesis. It was later amplified, probably by St. Basil himself, into the developed anaphora that bears his name. The early character of the epiclesis in this anaphora is in part attested to by its use of verbs. The verbs found in the early epicleses often furnish important clues to the developing theology of the epiclesis.[54] The verb *hagiazo* (sanctify) still reflects a predominantly Jewish understanding of the consecration of the gifts, which remains within the perspective of the Jewish *berakah*. The verb *anadeiknumi* (show forth), however, reflects a shift from the eschatological perspective toward an "epiphany" theology, where the Spirit is invoked on the gifts in order that they may manifest the presence of Christ.[55] As in Addai and Mari and Hippolytus, the Spirit is invoked on both the community and the gifts, and the theology of the epiclesis exhibits an intimate connection between the sanctification of the gifts and the sanctification of the community. We have already commented on the unity theme and the eschatological orientation of this epiclesis, which provide further evidence of its early character.

In the latter half of the fourth century, three factors affected the development of the Eucharistic Prayer as a whole and the epiclesis in particular. (1) The Jewish *berakah* prayer form was transformed into a Hellenistic literary composition with the piling up of phrases and subordinate clauses for rhetorical effect on the model of the Hellenistic schools. The essential elements of the *berakah* remain, but it is now vastly expanded and unified. The anaphoras of St. Mark and St. James and the Byzantine anaphoras of St. John Chrysostom and St. Basil all reflect this development. (2) The fourth-century Trinitarian controversies also had an influence on the development of the Eucharistic Prayer in two respects. The overall structure of the prayer now takes a definite Trinitarian form, and the language of the epiclesis reflects Trinitarian orthodoxy. (3) The petition over the gifts in the epiclesis becomes an explicit petition for the consecration of the elements.[56]

In the Egyptian tradition, all these factors are apparent in the developed liturgy of St. Mark. The anaphora has an evident Trinitarian structure and there is a long clause in the second epiclesis that reflects the fully developed doctrine of the Holy Spirit that emerged from the fourth-century Trinitarian debates.[57] A number of verbs are used to describe the activity of the Holy Spirit in relation to the gifts: *gignomai* (become), *hagiazo* (sanctify), *teleiow* (perfect or consecrate), and *poiew* (make), all of which reflect different theological nuances. The verb *hagiazo* still reflects a predominantly Jewish understanding of the consecration of the gifts that remains within the perspective of the *berakah*. *Teleiow*, used in apposition to it, lies close to this perspective, but translates it into a Hellenistic key. With the use of the verbs *gignomai* and, especially, *poiew*, we have a model of the divine activity in relation to the elements that bears a closer analogy to the natural processes of change and production and has a more philosophical ring.

Although these verbs are not used here in a technical theological sense, they give us a clue to the developing theology of the epiclesis. The language of "becoming" and "making" carries us into a different theological sphere than that reflected in the language of "sanctification" and "manifestation." This reflects both a move toward a more explicitly consecratory epiclesis and the use of more naturalistic and philosophical models for interpreting the eucharistic mystery. It is interesting to note, however, particularly in a highly developed epiclesis like that of St. Mark, how this emphasis on the consecration of the gifts is still linked inseparably with the invocation of the Holy Spirit on the community. The epiclesis begins with the phrase "Look on us," which immediately orients it toward the community. Moreover, the bread and wine are not described as objects, but as food and drink (loaves and cups), which reflects early tradition. The gifts are also specifically linked with the act of communion in the phrase "that they may become to all of us who partake of them. . . . "

In the West Syrian tradition, the anaphora in the Jerusalem liturgy of St. James exhibits the characteristics of the later fourth-century anaphoras already noted. The epiclesis in the liturgy of St. James stands in the tradition of Alexandrian Basil, particularly with its emphasis on the close connection between the petition over the gifts and the community.[58] The phrase "upon us and upon these . . . gifts" repeats the opening phrase of the epiclesis in Basil of Caesarea, which now becomes characteristic of epicleses of the Antiochene type. The epiclesis of St. James, however, differs from that of Basil in two respects. The language of epiphany is replaced by the language of "making" or "production" in the petition over the gifts, and in the petition for the communicants, the dominant note struck is no longer the eschatological gathering of the community, but the present establishment of the community as a bulwark of unity against heresy. This reflects a period of intense theological controversy.

Although a highly developed literary composition, the Byzantine liturgy of St. Basil remains remarkably close to Jewish models, and reflects early tradition. The language used to speak of the Spirit's activity in relation to the gifts is the language of "blessing," "sanctification," and "epiphany," all of which are characteristic of early tradition.[59] The eucharistic elements are spoken of as "antitypes" (*antitupa*) of the body and blood of Christ, reflecting the understanding of the relationship between symbol and reality characteristic of the patristic period. We have already seen how the petition for the communicants retains the traditional theme of eschatological unity.

The developed epiclesis in the Byzantine Liturgy of St. John Chrysostom is also an epiclesis of the Antiochene type.[60] It has the characteristically close connection between the petition over the gifts and over the community. The petition for the communicants also reflects the eschatological emphasis. The most striking feature of this epiclesis, however, is found in the petition over the gifts, where not only is the language of "epiphany" replaced by the language of "making," but two phrases are inserted asking that the Holy Spirit "change" (*metaballo*) the elements into the body and blood of Christ. This use of conversionist language first appears in the Catechetical homilies of Cyril of Jerusalem in his commentary on the epiclesis and is reflected also in the writings of other fourth-century Greek fathers.[61] When mediated to the West through Ambrose, the language of "change," "conversion," or "transformation" in connection with the elements became the basis for the western medieval doctrine of transubstantiation.

The language of production and change that appears in these later examples of the epiclesis appears on the surface to represent a fundamental shift from Jewish and biblical models to naturalistic or philosophical models. It is not always perceived, however, that Biblical models are also available for the interpretation of this language in the models of creation—new creation and resurrection—eschatological transformation. When viewed from this perspective, the roots of this kind of language in earlier tradition can be perceived. From this perspective, especially when the relation between the gifts and the community is firmly maintained, the language of "making" and "change" suggests that the transformation of the gifts and the community are already by way of sacramental sign the anticipation of the transformation of all things that the New Testament speaks of in the language of resurrection and new creation. As early as Justin Martyr, we find the use of the verb *metaballo* in a eucharistic context, although here it is used in relation to the community rather than in relation to the elements:

"For we do not receive these things as common bread or common drink; but just as our Savior Jesus Christ, being incarnate through the word of God, took flesh and blood for our salvation, so too we have been taught that the food over which thanks have been given by a word of prayer which is from him, (the food) from which our flesh and blood are fed by transformation (*metaballo*), is both the flesh and blood of that incarnate Jesus."[62]

The link between this eschatological transformation and the Holy Spirit is already present in the theology of Paul in Romans 8. If this interpretation is correct, then the language of the later epicleses in the eastern liturgies still reflect their eschatological roots.

SACRIFICE

In the New Testament, the eucharist is nowhere explicitly called a sacrifice, although Paul strongly hints at a sacrificial interpretation when he compares the eucharist to Jewish and pagan communion-sacrifices,[63] and the accounts of the institution of the eucharist are couched in language that has sacrificial overtones.[64] On the other hand, beginning with the *Didache*, the earliest Christian literature outside the New Testament uses sacrificial language to describe the eucharist, and this usage becomes common in the liturgical texts and theological literature of the patristic period.[65]

The modern Christian labors under a twofold disadvantage in approaching this literature. On the one hand, sacrifice, at least as the ancient world understood it, is an almost foreign language to us. The living reality of the ancient sacrificial cultus is not part of our culture. On the other hand, we are the heirs of the Reformation controversies over the sacrifice of the mass, and it is hard for us to read the ancient texts without importing that history back into the literature.

In contrast to modern culture, sacrifice was a universal feature of religion in the ancient world. G. Dalman indicates that in Jewish practice, "Every meal, especially when bread was used, was looked upon as sacrificial. . . ."[66] Ancient sacrifice, however, cannot be brought under a single definition or concept, since it was performed with a variety of different rites and these rites express a variety of motivations. In our attempt to understand the background against which the early Christians used the language of sacrifice, we shall first provide a brief description of Jewish sacrificial practice. We can describe that practice under three headings: gift-sacrifices, communion-sacrifices, and sin-offerings.[67]

Gift-Sacrifices

In Jewish religion, there were two kinds of gift-sacrifices: holocausts (*'olah*), and vegetable or cereal offerings (*minhah*). The holocaust was an animal sacrifice in which the entire animal was burnt. The normal *minhah* was an offering of fine flour. A special example of the *minhah* is the first-fruits offering, i.e., the offering of a portion of the new crop at harvest time. In the *minhah*, a portion of the offering is burnt on the altar as an *'azkarah* (memorial or pledge). The word *minhah* means "gift," and in preexilic times, the term was used more broadly for both animal and vegetable sacrifices. Its usage was later confined to vegetable and cereal offerings. The holocaust, however, is also a gift-offering; indeed, it was considered the best form of gift-offering because animals and meat were more expensive.

Communion-Sacrifices

In ancient Israel, the communion-sacrifice (*zebah, zebah sh'lamim,* or *sh'lamim*) was the most frequent type of sacrifice. Communion-sacrifices were, like the holocausts, animal sacrifices. The difference, however, was that only part of the animal was burnt, the rest being shared in a sacrificial meal by the priest, the offerer, and the family or guests. The covenant-sacrifice that concluded the giving of the law on Mount Sinai (Ex 24:9–11) was a communion-sacrifice.

The Greek *thusiai* were communion-sacrifices and parallel the Jewish communion-sacrifices in many respects. They were joyful feasts in which a part of the slaughtered animals was burnt on the altar and the rest shared in the sacrificial meal. Paul compared the eucharist to both Jewish and Greek communion-sacrifices in 1 Corinthians 10.

Sin-Offerings

The communion-sacrifice and the holocaust were the principal forms of sacrifice in preexilic Israel. Sin-offerings (*hatta'th* and *'asham*) arose later and reflect an increasing awareness of sin and ritual purity together with a need for atonement. The sin-offerings, like the communion-sacrifices and holocausts, were animal sacrifices, but particular importance was attached to the blood ritual associated with them, blood being understood as a means of atonement.

"For the life of the flesh is in the blood; and I have given it for you upon the altar to make atonement for your lives; for it is the blood that makes atonement, by reason of the life."[68]

In later Judaism, the Day of Atonement became "the day" of atonement for sin, and on this one day of the year, the High Priest entered the Holy of Holies in the temple and sprinkled the blood of the sin-offerings on the mercy-seat itself.

Passover

The Passover is in a category by itself, since it was considered both a memorial and a sacrifice. It was a memorial of the event of the exodus, but because the passover lamb was regarded as a sacrifice, it was considered a sacrificial meal.

The purpose of sacrifice was not spelled out in either the Old Testament or in Greek literature, but has to be inferred from the texts. This means that any modern attempt to interpret the purpose of ancient sacrifice must of necessity take the form of a theory. According to R. de Vaux, Jewish sacrifice was essentially an acted prayer. It was a symbolic action that expressed both the interior dispositions of the offerer and God's response to this prayer.[69] According to this interpretation, the interior disposition is of the utmost importance. In accordance with this understanding, Israelite sacrificial practice received a powerful critique and a progressive interiorization and spiritualization in the prophets, in the psalms, and in the later wisdom literature. In the light of this development, sacrifice ceased to have any significance as an outward observance apart from the inward disposition that accompanied it.

This development illustrates a fundamental feature of Jewish sacrificial practice, namely, its progressive transformation by Yahwist faith. In the surrounding cultures, gift-sacrifices often carried with them the idea of seeking the favor of the gods or striking a bargain with them. This was entirely contrary to Israel's faith. According to Israelite faith, Yahweh is sovereign over all creation. Nothing could be offered to God that had not already been received as a gift. The gift-offering, therefore, was essentially a sacrifice of thanksgiving. Moreover, the gifts offered in sacrifice, whether crops or domestic animals, were offerings of gifts that were needed to support life. They expressed in some way, therefore, the desire of the offerer to offer to God the life that had first been received.

The communion-sacrifices were also sacrifices of praise and thanksgiving, but they also gave particular expression to the covenant relationship with Yahweh as well as expressing joyful fellowship among the worshipers. The communion-sacrifices, therefore, were also called covenant-sacrifices. In the sacrificial meal, the covenant relationship between Yahweh and the people was expressed, but as we have already seen, this excluded the notion of communion as a direct union with deity such as was characteristic of Greek sacrificial meals.[70] The communion-sacrifices were joyful occasions, and at the beginning of Israel's history, the communion-sacrifice was the most frequent kind of sacrifice offered, because it was regarded as the most complete kind of sacrifice, including both the ideas of gift and communion.

We have spoken already of the progressive interiorization and spiritualization that took place in Jewish tradition in regard to sacrificial practice. This development does not represent a repudiation of sacrifice, but an assertion of the worthlessness of sacrifice without the interior disposition of the heart that must accompany the outward act. Sacrifice, therefore, becomes an ethical as well as a cultic category. The preexilic prophets uttered some violent attacks on sacrifice. They contrast the futility of sacrifice with obedience to Yahweh and with the doing of righteousness and justice.[71] The psalms also contain a vigorous condemnation of sacrifice.[72] Yet the psalms also accompanied the processions and sacrificial rites associated with the daily temple worship. As hymns accompanying the sacrificial rites, they gave expression to the meaning implicit in the rites while at the same time providing a corrective to a sacrificial worship that only emphasized outward observance. Eventually, with the destruction of the temple, the outward sacrificial cultus was replaced altogether by the interior disposition, so that prayer, repentance, obedience, and works of mercy came to be regarded as the equivalent of sacrifice.

In early Christianity, this tradition of the spiritualization of sacrifice had a profound effect on the Christian attitude to sacrifice. At the same time, the language of sacrifice provided a vocabulary, and the ancient sacrifices a set of models for describing both the redemptive work of Christ and Christian life and worship, including the eucharist.[73] When the eucharist came to be described as a sacrifice, the analogies that came most readily to mind were the gift-sacrifices and communion-sacrifices. Only later, when the eucharist came to be identified in some way with the sacrifice of Christ on the cross, did it come to be understood on the analogy of a sin-offering. It is this latter development that lies behind the medieval idea of the sacrifice of the mass.

The primary perspective reflected in the early Christian liturgical texts is that of thanksgiving, not sacrifice. This note of thanksgiving is the fundamental characteristic of the tradition of the Eucharistic Prayer with its roots in the Jewish table prayers of blessing. Neither in the *Didache* nor in the account of the early eucharist in Justin Martyr is there any mention made of sacrifice as an element in the Eucharistic Prayer itself. Nevertheless, when both writers come to describe the eucharist, they quite spontaneously describe it as a sacrifice. How are we to account for this? Sacrifice is not something added to the thanksgiving, but a way of describing the meaning of the act of thanksgiving itself. There is an analogy here with the anamnesis. The anamnesis is not something added to the act of thanksgiving. Rather, it is a way of describing how thanksgiving is made, i.e., by making memorial of the mighty deeds of God in creation and redemption. The same holds true for the description of the eucharist as a sacrifice. Thanksgiving is made by offering sacrifice. The eucharistic action as a whole, an action of thanksgiving-memorial, is here being described as a sacrifice of thanksgiving on the model of a gift-sacrifice.[74]

This perspective comes out clearly in the early texts. The meal prayers in the *Didache* 9–10, which are modeled on the traditional Jewish *berakoth*, do not mention the theme of sacrifice. Rather, they are marked by the dominant note of thanksgiving. However, when the author describes what takes place on the Lord's Day, the eucharist is called a sacrifice.

"On every Lord's Day—his special day—come together and break bread and give thanks, first confessing your sins so that your sacrifice may be pure. Anyone at variance with his neighbor must not join you, until they are reconciled, lest your sacrifice be defiled. For it was of this sacrifice that the Lord said, 'Always and everywhere offer me a pure sacrifice; for I am a great king, says the Lord, and my name is marveled at by the nations.' "[75]

We find in this text the first use of Malachi 1:11 as a prophecy of the eucharist. This text is frequently quoted in this sense in early Christian literature. We also see here very clearly the ethical requirement for participation in the sacrificial meal.

In Justin Martyr's *Dialogue with Trypho*, 41, we find a description of the eucharist as an act of thanksgiving in which remembrance is made of the suffering of Christ. The Jewish cereal-offering is used as a type of the bread of the eucharist, and Justin refers to the bread and the cup as "sacrifices which are offered in every place by us," quoting Malachi.

"The offering of fine flour . . . which was handed down to be offered by those who were cleansed from leprosy, was a type of the bread of the eucharist, which our Lord Jesus Christ handed down to us to do for the remembrance of the suffering which he suffered for those who are cleansed in their souls from all wickedness . . . so that we might give thanks to God, both for creating the world with all things that are in it for the sake of humanity, and for freeing us from the evil in which we were born, and for accomplishing a complete destruction of the principalities and powers through him who suffered according to his will. Hence God speaks about the sacrifices which were then offered . . . through Malachi, one of the twelve (prophets):

'My will is not in you, says the Lord, and I will not receive your sacrifices from your hands; for, from the rising of the sun to its setting, my name has been glorified among the nations, and in every place incense is offered to my name and a pure sacrifice, for my name is great among the nations, says the Lord. . . . '

"He is prophesying about the sacrifices which are offered in every place by us, the nations, that is the bread of the eucharist and likewise the cup of the eucharist, saying that we glorify his name. . . . "

Irenaeus also understands the eucharist as a sacrifice of thanksgiving on the analogy of a gift-sacrifice.

"Now we make offering to him, not as though he stood in need of it, but rendering thanks for his gift. . . . "[76]

He also quotes Malachi as a prophetic anticipation of the Church's sacrifice, and observes that the sacrifice can only be pure if it is offered with the right dispositions. Irenaeus places particular emphasis on the analogy between the eucharist and the Jewish offering of first-fruits.

"Again, giving directions to his disciples to offer to God the first-fruits of his own created things . . . he took that created thing, bread, and gave thanks, and said, 'This is my body.' And the cup likewise, which is part of that creation to which we belong, he confessed to be his blood, and taught the new oblation of the new covenant; which the church receiving from the apostles, offers to God throughout the world. . . . "[77]

In the third century, we begin to see the theme of sacrifice appearing in the Eucharistic Prayer itself. In the Eucharistic Prayer in the *Apostolic Tradition of Hippolytus*, we find the sacrificial theme in both the anamnesis and the epiclesis.

"Remembering therefore his death and resurrection, we offer to you the bread and the cup, giving you thanks because you have held us worthy to stand before you and minister to you. And we ask that you would send your Holy Spirit upon the offering of your holy Church; that, gathering her into one, you would grant to all who receive the holy things (to receive) for the fullness of the Holy Spirit for the strengthening of faith in truth."[78]

In the anamnesis, the phrase "giving you thanks" qualifies the meaning of "we offer to you the bread and the cup," so that the model in the background here is that of a sacrifice of thanksgiving. In the epiclesis, the phrase "the offering of your holy

Church" does not refer exclusively to the elements but refers to the eucharistic action as a whole that culminates in the act of communion (partaking of the holy things). This close link between offering and communion exemplified in the epiclesis is characteristic of a communion-sacrifice.

The Eucharistic Prayer in Addai and Mari does not have an anamnesis of the type we find in Hippolytus and the sacrificial theme appears primarily in the epiclesis.

" . . . May your Holy Spirit, Lord, come and rest on this offering of your servants, and bless and sanctify it, that it may be to us, Lord, for remission of debts, forgiveness of sins, and the great hope of resurrection from the dead, and new life in the kingdom of heaven, with all who have been pleasing in your sight."[79]

The structure of the epiclesis in Addai and Mari parallels closely that in Hippolytus and we can observe the same close link between offering and communion characteristic of a communion-sacrifice.

From these beginnings, the sacrificial theme spread fairly rapidly to the other parts of the Eucharistic Prayer. In the Egyptian liturgy, the sacrificial theme first appears in the opening thanksgiving of the Eucharistic Prayer, as in the Strasbourg papyrus, then in the first epiclesis, and later in the anamnesis. From there, in both the Egyptian liturgy and the West Syrian liturgies, it spread to the commemorations and intercessions. In the West, the entire canon, apart from the opening dialogue and preface, became a prayer of offering, and the theme of thanksgiving became overshadowed by the theme of sacrifice. If R. Keifer's analysis is correct, however, the fundamental model underlying the Roman canon is still that of a sacrifice of thanksgiving.[80]

Alongside these developments in the Eucharistic Prayer, early Christian reflection on the eucharist also began to make a connection between the eucharist and the sacrifice of Christ. This is expressed in three different ways in the patristic literature. A first line of reflection connects the eucharist with the sacrifice of the cross by way of the eucharistic memorial. The eucharist is identified with the sacrifice of Christ, because the eucharist celebrates the anamnesis of Christ's death. This line of thinking stands in continuity with the Old Testament understanding of a liturgical memorial and with the anamnesis formula found in the eucharistic words of Jesus in the New Testament. This line of reflection is found, for example, in both Cyprian in the West and John Chrysostom in the East.

"For if Jesus Christ, our Lord and God, is himself the chief priest of God the Father, and has first offered himself a sacrifice to the Father, and has commanded this to be done in commemoration of himself, certainly that priest truly discharges the office of Christ, who imitates that which Christ did; and he then offers a true and full sacrifice in the church to God the father, when he proceeds to offer it according to what he sees Christ himself to have offered. . . . "[81]

"And because we make mention of his passion in all sacrifices (for the Lord's passion is the sacrifice which we offer), we ought to do nothing else than what he did. For Scripture says, 'For as often as you eat this bread and drink this cup, you show forth the Lord's death until he comes.' As often, therefore, as we offer the cup in commemoration of the Lord and of his passion, let us do what it is known the Lord did."[82]

"What then? Do we not offer every day? We offer indeed, but making a memorial of his death. . . . This is done for a memorial of that which was done then. For 'Do this,' he said, 'for my memorial.' We do not offer another sacrifice, as the high priest of old, but we always offer the same, or rather we make the memorial of his sacrifice."[83]

A second line of reflection connects the eucharist with the eternal pleading of Christ's sacrifice in heaven in line with the epistle to the Hebrews. From this perspective, the earthly liturgy is a participation in the heavenly liturgy.

"We must . . . realize that we perform a sacrifice of which we eat. . . . It is indeed evident that it is a sacrifice, but not a new one and one that (the priest) performs as his, but it is a remembrance of that other real sacrifice (of Christ). Because the priest performs things found in heaven through symbols and signs, it is necessary that his sacrifice also should be as their image, and that he should represent a likeness of the service of heaven. . . . Christ our Lord . . . performs . . . (his) priestly service in heaven. . . . He performs a real high priesthood and offers to God no other sacrifice than himself. . . . "[84]

In Augustine, we find a third line of reflection that connects the eucharist with the sacrifice of Christ, not directly, but by way of the ecclesial interpretation of the eucharist found in Paul and the root metaphor of the body of Christ. From this perspective, the eucharist is a sacrifice in the sense that in the eucharist, the church itself is offered in union with Christ its head.

"Such is the sacrifice of Christians. 'We, the many, are one body in Christ.' This is the sacrifice, as the faithful understand, which the church continues to celebrate in the sacrament of the altar, in which it is clear to the church that she herself is offered in the very offering she makes to God."[85]

Augustine also connects the sacrifice with the memorial and re- tains the close connection between offering and communion char- acteristic of the early anaphoras.

"Christians also make the memorial of this sacrifice in the holy offering and partaking of the body and blood of Christ."[86]

In the earliest period, therefore, the term sacrifice was used of the eucharist as a descriptive metaphor for the action of thanksgiving-memorial as a whole. At this stage, the gift-sacrifice and the communion-sacrifice provided the primary models for applying sacrificial language to the eucharist. When the eucharist became more closely linked to the sacrifice of Christ on the cross, this was primarily interpreted through the biblical concep- tion of anamnesis, although it was also linked to the heavenly intercession of Christ. Augustine's distinctive contribution is his ecclesial interpretation of the eucharistic sacrifice. In the course of the Middle Ages, in the popular imagination at least, the eu- charist came to be seen as almost a sin-offering in its own right. It was this that called forth the protest of the reformers, who saw in this development a threat to the atonement that Christ accomplished once for all on the cross.

Apart from the liturgy itself, the two fundamental frameworks within which early Christian writers viewed the eucharist were biblical typology and Platonism. We shall discuss the biblical typology of the Church fathers in this section and their Platonism in the next. Although these two frameworks have quite different backgrounds, they overlap in practice. This is reflected, for example, in the way in which the word "type" itself is used in patristic literature. In some contexts, the word "type" refers to certain Old Testament prefigurations of the eucharist, whereas in other contexts, the bread and wine of the eucharist are referred to as "types" or "figures" of heavenly realities in a Platonic sense. Sometimes, therefore, it is biblical typology that forms the immediate background of a particular eucharistic passage, sometimes Platonism and sometimes a combination of the two. Since biblical typology and Platonism are underlying frameworks rather than carefully worked out theoretical approaches, we should not look for a clear definition of principles or a perfectly consistent application of method in the early theology of the eucharist.[87]

In the patristic period, two principal methods of exegesis were employed in the interpretation of scripture: typology and allegory. As a method of exegesis, typology is intended to demonstrate the unity between the Old and New Testaments by seeking to establish correspondences between events, persons, and realities. This assumes that the Bible contains a history of salvation and that there is a consistency in the pattern of God's redemptive activity in both testaments. The events, persons, and realities of the Old Testament were regarded as "types," "images," or "shadows" that prefigured events, persons, and realities in the New Testament. Typological exegesis, therefore, is the search for correspondences and relationships within the framework of historical revelation.

Allegorical interpretation in contrast to typology is the search for secondary or hidden meanings that are thought to underlie the literal meaning of the text. This secondary or hidden meaning may or may not have a direct connection with historical revelation. There were two traditions of allegorical exegesis in the ancient world, one stemming from the Jewish rabbinic schools and the other from the Hellenistic philosophical schools. The former is more closely related to typology since the hidden meaning of a passage is still related to the framework of historical revelation. An example of this type of allegorical interpretation is found in Paul's exegesis of the story of Sarah and Hagar in Galatians 4. Hagar represents the old covenant given on Mount Sinai, whereas Sarah represents the new covenant with the children of promise. The way in which God dealt with Sarah and Hagar is used as an allegory for the way in which God deals with Christians and Jews.

The other method of allegorical exegesis stemming from the Hellenistic philosophical schools was a method developed for interpreting the *Iliad* and the *Odyssey* of Homer. These ancient Greek epics were not only treated as literary classics, but as the embodiment of eternal truths. But how could poems that contained mostly folklore and myth and that often portrayed the gods as committing gross acts of immorality be regarded as the repository of eternal truths? In attempting to deal with this problem, the philosophers hit upon the notion that these poems must contain a hidden philosophical meaning behind the literal meaning of the text. This allegorical interpretation of Homer was already well established by the fourth century B.C. Allegory was especially associated with the Stoics, and it was primarily by way of Stoic writers that Hellenistic Jewish and Christian writers derived the allegorical method of exegesis.

The importance of biblical typology for the early theology of the sacraments is that it places the sacraments in the context of the history of salvation. The celebration of the sacraments in the early Church presupposed a whole biblical formation on the part of the people as a preparation for their participation in the liturgical rites. Participation in the sacramental rites evoked an association between the sacramental signs and the Old Testament types that prefigured them. This typological interpretation of the sacraments is evident both in early Christian art and in the catechetical homilies that come down to us from the early Church. A number of these catechetical homilies survive to us, particularly from the fourth century, notably those of Cyril of Jerusalem,

Ambrose, John Chrysostom, and Theodore of Mopsuestia.[88] In these sermons, which come from widely separated areas of the Church, we have a glimpse of the sacramental theology that was characteristic of the patristic age. Normally, the instruction on the sacraments was the last to be given, and the homilies that provided the commentary on them were only given during Easter week following the baptism and first communion of the new converts, which normally took place on Easter Eve. These homilies consisted of an exposition of the types of baptism and the eucharist in the Old Testament and a commentary on the liturgical rites.

The three principal types of the eucharist that the Church fathers found in the Old Testament were the offering of bread and wine by Melchisedech in Genesis 14:18–20, the feeding of the people of God with manna in the wilderness, and the eschatological meal traditions found in the Old Testament. The offering of bread and wine by Melchisedech was considered very early to be a type of the eucharist. Clement of Alexandria, for example, speaks of "Melchisedech, who offered bread and wine, the consecrated food as a figure (*typos*) of the eucharist."[89] Cyprian develops this idea in his sixty-third letter:

"In Melchisedech the priest, we see the sacrament of the sacrifice of the Lord prefigured according to the witness of Scripture, 'And Melchisedech, king of Salem, offered bread and wine.' . . . our Lord Jesus Christ . . . offered to the Father the same offering as Melchisedech, that is, bread and wine, which is to say, his body and his blood. . . . Thus . . . the figure of the sacrifice, consisting of bread and wine, has taken place in the past. And it is this figure that the Lord fulfilled and accomplished when he offered the bread and the chalice of wine mingled with water; he who is the fulfillment accomplished the reality of the figurative image."[90]

Ambrose also uses the Melchisedech typology in his catechetical homilies:

"Yesterday in our instructions we got as far as the sacraments of the sacred altar, and we learnt that a prefiguration of these sacraments was given in times past in the days of Abraham when the blessed Melchisedech, who had 'neither beginning of days nor end,' offered sacrifice."[91]

The eucharist was also associated with the miracles of the exodus, and in particular with the feeding of God's people with manna in the desert. The water that flowed from the rock at Horeb was sometimes considered a type of baptism and sometimes a type of the eucharist. Paul already employs this typology in 1 Corinthians 10:1–5.

"I want you to know, brothers and sisters, that our fathers were all under the cloud, and all passed through the sea, and all were baptized into Moses in the cloud and in the sea, and all ate the same spiritual food and all drank the same spiritual drink. For they drank from the spiritual Rock which followed them, and the Rock was Christ. Nevertheless with most of them God was not pleased; for they were overthrown in the wilderness."

Ambrose also refers to both the manna and the rock of Horeb as figures of the eucharist.

"The manna was a great marvel, the manna that God rained down on the fathers. The heavens nourished them with daily food, as it is written: 'Man ate angels' food' (Ps 78:25). And nevertheless, those who ate this bread died in the desert. But this nourishment that you receive, the bread descended from heaven, communicates to you the substance of eternal life. . . . It is the body of Christ. . . . As the light is greater than the shadow, the truth than the figure, so the body of the Creator is greater than the manna from heaven."[92]

". . . Moses touched the rock and it produced water in abundance, according to the word of the apostle: 'They drank of the spiritual Rock that followed them. And this rock was Christ.' . . . You too must drink, and Christ will accompany you. See the mystery. . . . the water flows; the people of God drink. The priest touches the chalice; the water flows into the chalice and springs up to eternal life for the people of God who receive the grace of God by drinking from it."[93]

A third example of typology is the use of Old Testament meal traditions as types of the eucharist. A number of texts in the Old

Testament are seen as types both of the eucharist and of the eschatological banquet. Didymus sees a eucharistic reference in Isaiah 55:1

"You who thirst, come to the waters, you who have no money, come and drink precious wine and eat good meats. By the water, he means the Holy Spirit and the spring of the baptismal pool. The wine and the meat stand for what was offered by the Jews in times past, and now for the immortal communion of the body and blood of the Lord."[94]

Likewise, Eusebius sees a reference to the eucharist in Isaiah 25:6

"The prophet announces to the nations the joy of the wine, prophesying by this the sacrament of the new covenant established by Christ, which today is visibly celebrated in all nations."[95]

Cyprian sees a figure of the eucharist in the banquet of wisdom in Proverbs 9:5

"Through Solomon also the Spirit shows us the figure of the sacrifice of the Lord. . . . Wisdom, he says . . . sends her servants in a loud voice inviting the guests to come and drink of her cup, saying: Come, eat my bread and drink the wine that I have mingled for you. Solomon speaks of the mingled wine, that is to say, he announces prophetically the chalice of the Lord mingled with water and wine."[96]

Psalm 23 was especially connected with the rites of Christian initiation in the early Church and was given a eucharistic interpretation. In some places, it was recited by the newly baptized as they processed from the baptistry to the church to participate in the Easter eucharist. Ambrose, for example, refers to it in his catechetical sermons:

"How often have you listened to the Twenty-third psalm without understanding it? See how fittingly it is applied to the heavenly sacraments. 'The Lord feeds me, I want for nothing. He has led me to a place of refreshment. He has brought me to the waters which refresh me, he has revived my spirit. He has led me by the paths of justice, for his name's sake. Though I should walk in the midst of death's shadow, I shall fear no evil, because you are with me. Your rod and your staff have comforted me. . . . You have prepared a table before me against them that trouble me. You have anointed my head with oil, and my over-flowing cup how glorious it is.' "[97]

These different typological strands that we find in the early Church tradition bring out different aspects of the patristic theol-ogy of the eucharist. The Melchisedech typology brings out the sacrificial character of the eucharist as an offering of bread and wine. The typology connected with the miracles of the Exodus bring out the aspect of the eucharist as the nourishment of the people of God on their pilgrimage from Exodus to promise. The strand of typology related to the Old Testament meal traditions brings out the eschatological perspective and views the eucharist as the anticipation of the eschatological meal in the kingdom of God. Whatever we may think of typology today as a method of exegesis, in the patristic period, biblical typology had a twofold importance. It kept the eucharistic theology of the early Church rooted in scripture, and because of the role it played in the catechetical tradition, it provided both a biblical foundation for participation in the liturgical rites and a sense of rootage in the whole history of salvation.

SYMBOL AND REALITY

Patristic thought represents a fusion of the biblical tradition and the Hellenistic world view. When we speak of the Hellenistic world view, we are speaking in the broadest sense of that vision of society, the world and reality as a whole that has its roots in the culture of classical Greece and that in the centuries immedi-ately preceding the Christian era penetrated throughout the area of the Mediterranean basin.[98] The highest intellectual expression of this culture was Greek philosophy.[99] In this fusion between the biblical tradition and Hellenistic culture, sometimes the one and sometimes the other predominates in the thought of individ-ual authors, and this is often true within the same passage or work. We have already seen the way in which early Christian writers appropriated the biblical tradition through the employ-ment of typology and allegory. We have now to see how the

Hellenistic world view served as a framework for their understanding of the sacraments.

Within the framework of biblical typology, the sacraments are understood in relation to their Old Testament types. We have here a model of understanding that we can describe as salvation-historical. Speaking metaphorically, we can say that this mode of understanding the sacraments is "horizontal," since it locates the present liturgical action within the framework of the historical action of God. The philosophical framework within which patristic thought operates has what we might call a "vertical" structure. Here the sacramental signs are related to a reality that "transcends" them. In the typological framework, the sacraments that are celebrated in the present are related to their types within the framework of historical revelation. In the philosophical framework, the sacraments are related as symbols to the reality that they signify. We can only understand early sacramental theology, therefore, when we place it against the background of the ancient world's view of the relationship between symbol and reality.[100]

The question of the nature and function of symbols is problematical in the modern world. The preoccupation of modern philosophers and social scientists with issues of language and symbol is one indication of this. With the collapse of old structures of meaning, the symbolic patterns that once informed the life of modern societies are called into question. In this situation, the question of the nature of symbols and of symbolic activity arises afresh. What are symbols? How do symbols and symbolic patterns arise? What causes symbols to lose their power?[101]

If we ask how the term "symbol" is understood in the modern world at the level of common usage, we could define a symbol as something that "represents," "signifies," or "points to" something in experience while not being identical with what it represents. According to modern popular understanding, a symbol functions as a pointer, directing our attention to that which it represents. Symbols are shared in common when we have a common understanding of what they represent. They cease to function as symbols when we no longer share that common understanding.

In the ancient world, a symbol had almost the opposite meaning to that which it has in modern culture. A symbol in ancient society is not primarily a pointer that represents something apart from the symbol. In ancient society, a symbol participates in that which it represents, so that it can almost be said to *be* that which it represents. Ancient thought does not distinguish in the way in which modern popular thinking does between symbol and reality. In antiquity, the symbol is the presence of that which it represents and mediates participation in that reality. Whereas the modern world is more aware of the distinction between symbol and reality, the ancient world was more aware of their identity. There is not a precise identity between symbol and reality in the ancient world, however. If this were the case, there would be no need for symbols. It was precisely through symbols that ancient societies participated in the mysterious reality that surrounded them.

Early Christian theologians shared the ancient world view and its understanding of symbols, and it is against this background that we must understand their conception of the sacraments. In patristic thought, the sacraments are symbols or signs, but we fatally misunderstand what was meant by this if we read the early texts against the background of the modern popular understanding of symbol. We can only understand the patristic texts if we place them in the context of the ancient world view within which they belong. This must constantly be borne in mind if we are to understand how the early Church understood the relation between the sacramental signs of bread and wine in the eucharist and the reality that they signify. Both Catholics and Protestants have constantly misunderstood early Christian thought in this respect by attempting to read the early texts against the background of the later distinction between a "realist" and a "symbolical" view of the sacraments. This distinction is based on an understanding of the relation between symbol and reality, which has moved away from the ancient understanding of a symbol as that which participates in the reality that it symbolizes. The distinction between a "realist" and a "symbolical" understanding of the sacraments is a distinction that would have had no meaning in the early Church. Harnack puts the matter precisely. In speaking of the patristic understanding of "the relation between the visible elements and the body of Christ," he says:

"So far as we are able to judge no one felt that there was a *problem* here, no one enquired whether this relation was realistic or symbolical. The symbol is the mystery and the mystery was not conceivable without a symbol. What we now-a-days understand by 'symbol' is a thing which is not that which it represents; at that time 'symbol' denoted a thing which, in some kind of way, really is what it signifies; but, on the other hand, according to the ideas of that period, the really heavenly element lay either in or behind the visible form without being identical with it. Accordingly the distinction of a symbolic and realistic conception of the Supper is altogether to be rejected. . . ."[102]

This ancient world view, which regarded the symbol as "participating" in the reality rather than simply "representing" it was appropriated by the Church fathers in a philosophical form, namely, Platonism.[103] Greek philosophy arose out of the symbolic world view that we have already described. In the religious life of the ancient world, the relation between symbol and reality was expressed primarily in myth.[104] Myth is simply a "bundle of symbols." It is a story told in symbolic form. It was through myth that ancient societies participated in the mysterious reality that surrounded them. Myth opened up a range of experience beyond that which could be perceived by the senses and gave structure, unity, and meaning to the world of sense-experience. Myth, therefore, provided the fundamental paradigm for the appropriation of reality and for the organization of sense-experience in the ancient world.

The myths, symbols, and ritual patterns of the ancient world were experienced and lived rather than reflected upon. The appearance of Greek Philosophy marks the beginning of rational reflection on the myth. The Greeks were the first to translate the mythological world view of the ancient world into a philosophical form. It was not, however, a complete translation, because there is always a surplus of meaning in the myth that cannot be adequately translated into other categories. This is evident, for example, in Plato's thought, where we find an overlap between myth and philosophy. Plato is often driven to express some of his deepest philosophical insights in a mythological form. Greek philosophy should not, therefore, be seen as a complete break with the ancient mythological world view, but as a partial translation of that world view into new categories.

Symbol, myth, and ritual were the ways in which ancient societies participated in the transcendent or the sacred, the world "behind" or "beyond" the world of ordinary sense-experience. The Greek philosophers sought to understand the relationship between the world of sense-experience and the transcendent world that lies "behind" or "beyond" it. Plato accepted the view that there are two "worlds," the world of ordinary sense-experience and a world "behind" or "beyond" sense-experience. Moreover, he considered the world beyond sense-experience as more real than the world of sense-experience. The world of sense-experience is the "image," "symbol," "sign," "figure," "type," "shadow," or "copy" of the real world lying behind it. Genuine knowledge is attained only through participation in the real world that transcends sense-experience. Plato called the world beyond sense-experience the world of the "forms" or "ideas." It is the world of the forms that gives unity and meaning to the world of sense-experience. In Platonism, these two "worlds" are not simply parallel to each other, but the relationship between them is conceived dialectically as one of "participation." This dialectical relationship between the world of the forms and the world of sense-experience means that the image or symbol cannot be thought of apart from the reality in which it participates. This means that the relationship between symbol and reality in Platonism is one of unity in distinction.

When early Christian writers attempted to give theological expression to their understanding of the sacraments, they used Platonism as a fundamental framework of interpretation. They distinguished two levels in the sacraments. There is, first of all, the level that can be perceived by the senses. In the case of the eucharist, that which can be perceived by the senses is the elements of bread and wine. The bread and wine are "symbols," "signs," "types," or "figures" that signify a reality at another level. This reality is the body and blood of Christ. This is the true reality that is present in the eucharist. It cannot, like the bread and the wine, be perceived by the senses, but can only be perceived by the mind and by faith. The sacramental signs or symbols, however, not only point to or represent the reality that they signify, they also participate in it and render it present. By participating in the symbols, therefore, those who participate in the sacramental rites participate in the reality that they signify. In the Platonic tradition, the transcendent world that lies behind the world of sense-experience is often spoken of as the "spiritual" or "heavenly" world, and the world of sense-experience is correspondingly spoken of as the "visible" or "earthly" or "material" world. When this language is applied to the sacraments, the reality signified by the sacramental signs is spoken of as a "spiritual" or "heavenly" reality, and the sacramental signs are spoken of as the "visible" or "material" elements. Irenaeus, therefore, can say that

" . . . the bread of the earth, receiving the invocation of God, is no longer common bread but eucharist, made up of two things, an earthly and a heavenly. . . . "[105]

Against the background of these presuppositions, early Christian writers could use three different kinds of language to describe the eucharist, which we can call "spiritualistic," "symbolical," and "realist." These kinds of language are often found side by side in the writings of the same author, so that we cannot speak of three different doctrines of the eucharist, but of three different modes of expression within the framework of common presuppositions. Spiritualistic language is language that describes the gifts given in the eucharist as "spiritual food and drink" and the manner of eating in the eucharist as a spiritual feeding on the body and blood of Christ by faith. This kind of language is already found in 1 Corinthians 10:3–4, where Paul uses the terms "spiritual food" and "spiritual drink" to speak of the manna that God provided for the Israelites in the wilderness and for the water that flowed from the rock of Horeb. According to E. Käsemann, the phrases "spiritual food" and "spiritual drink" were already traditional expressions for the eucharistic bread and cup, so that

Paul may have the eucharist in mind here as well.[106] The phrase "spiritual food and drink" is also found in the meal prayers in the *Didache*.[107] Ambrose, whose eucharistic language in general has a strongly realist character, can employ the same spiritualistic vocabulary.

"In that sacrament is Christ, because it is the body of Christ; therefore, it is not bodily food, but spiritual. Whence also the apostle says of the type of it that 'our fathers ate spiritual food and drank spiritual drink.' For the body of God is a spiritual body; the body of Christ is the body of a divine Spirit, because Christ is Spirit. . . . "[108]

Many examples of spiritualistic language are to be found in Augustine. Three examples will illustrate his thought:

" . . . the body and blood of Christ will be life to each one, if what is visibly received in the sacrament is spiritually eaten and drunk in very truth."[109]

"Jesus answered and said to them, 'This is the work of God, that you believe on him whom he has sent.' This then is to eat the food which does not perish but 'abides unto eternal life.' Why do you prepare teeth and stomach? Believe, and you have eaten."[110]

" 'This is the bread which comes down from heaven, that whoever eats of it may not die.' But that which belongs to the virtue of the sacrament, not that which belongs to the visible sacrament; whoever eats inwardly, not outwardly; the one who eats the sacrament in the heart, not the one who crunches it with the teeth. . . . "[111]

Alongside this spiritualistic language, we also find a symbolical mode of expression in the patristic writers. This kind of language is found, for example, in Tertullian.

" . . . (The Lord) called bread his body,"

says Tertullian,

"in order that you may understand him to have given the figure (*figuram*) of his body to the bread. . . . "[112]

And later in the same work he says,

"having taken the bread and given it to his disciples, he made it his body, saying, 'This is my body,' that is 'a figure of my body.' "[113]

Symbolic language is common among later patristic writers. Eusebius of Caesarea speaks of the "bread as the symbol (*symbolo*) of his own body" and of the "wine, which was the symbol (*symbolon*) of his blood."[114] Cyril of Jerusalem in his catechetical homilies says that "in the figure (*typo*) of bread is given to you the body, and in the figure (*typo*) of wine is given to you the blood."[115] Ambrose speaks of the contents of the chalice as the "likeness of the precious blood"[116] and testifies to the use of the term *figura* in the Eucharistic Prayer in the Church in Milan.

"Make this oblation to us approved, ratified, reasonable, acceptable, because it is the figure (*figura*) of the body and blood of our Lord Jesus Christ."[117]

Augustine has many examples of symbolical language:

"The Lord,"

he says,

"did not hesitate to say, 'This is my body,' when he gave the sign (*signum*) of his body."[118]

He also speaks of

"The supper, in which he committed and gave to his disciples the figure (*figuram*) of his body and blood."[119]

A realist strain is also present in the patristic tradition at an early point. Here such a close identification is seen between the sacramental signs and the reality that they signify that the bread and wine of the eucharist are said to *be* the body and blood of Christ. In the second and third centuries, realist language was used in an antidocetic and anti-Gnostic context. Writers such as Ignatius of Antioch and Irenaeus regarded the presence in the eucharist of the flesh of Christ in which he was crucified and raised as proof against docetic and Gnostic tendencies to undercut the full reality of Christ's humanity. Eucharistic realism is here closely related to Christological realism. Ignatius makes the following charge against the docetists:

"They abstain from eucharist and prayer because they do not acknowledge that the eucharist is the flesh of our Savior Jesus Christ which suffered for our sins, which the Father raised up by his goodness."[120]

In the same vein, warning the Philadelphians against schism through the infiltration of false (docetic) teaching, he exhorts:

"Be eager, therefore, to use one eucharist—for there is one flesh of our Lord Jesus Christ and one cup for union with his blood. . . ."[121]

Justin Martyr similarly describes the bread and wine of the eucharist in realist language. Justin's language also strongly reflects the antidocetic motif and the close relation between Christological and eucharistic realism.

"This food we call eucharist, of which no one is allowed to partake except one who believes that the things we teach are true, and has received the washing for the forgiveness of sins and for rebirth, and who lives as Christ handed down for us. For we do not receive these things as common bread or common drink; but as Jesus Christ our Savior being incarnate by God's word took flesh and blood for our salvation, so also we have been taught that the food consecrated by the word of prayer which comes from him, from which our flesh and blood are nourished by transformation, is the flesh and blood of that incarnate Jesus."[122]

The phrase "we have been taught" indicates that we have here a fragment of early Christian catechesis. This indicates that the teaching given here is not only determined by apologetic and polemical motives, but belongs to the tradition of faith handed down to those being prepared for baptism.

In the patristic period, the spiritualistic, symbolical, and realist modes of expression were not mutually opposing conceptions of the eucharist, but complementary ways of speaking about it. In the language of today, we could describe them as alternative theological models that are not exclusive but complementary ways of describing the eucharistic mystery. Spiritualistic language points to the spiritual reality that lies "behind" or "beyond" the visible elements of bread and wine, which is spiritually eaten by faith. Symbolic and realist language reflect the two sides of the ancient understanding of the relationship between symbol and reality. Because the symbol *is* the reality and yet is distinguished from it, both kinds of language could be used interchangeably, often by the same author. Eucharistic realism in the earliest period was also a safeguard of Christological realism.

The eucharistic thought of the Church fathers represents a fusion of biblical typology and Christian Platonism. Their thought, therefore, moved on two intersecting planes. From the perspective of biblical typology, the sacraments were seen within the framework of the history of salvation. The Old Testament presents them under the form of types or figures that point forward to their fulfillment in Christ. The sacraments are a prolongation of the works of God in the Old and New Testaments. This framework of biblical typology set the patristic theology of the eucharist firmly within the biblical tradition, so that the sacraments were viewed within the whole historical pattern of God's dealings with the people of God. In the patristic age, therefore, those who participated in the eucharistic celebration were kept alive to their biblical roots.

When viewed within the framework of Christian Platonism, the sacraments were seen as visible signs of invisible, heavenly realities. In patristic thought, therefore, to speak of the sacraments as signs, figures, or symbols is to evoke at once the whole world of the Bible and the whole invisible heavenly world. The eucharist is both a recapitulation of the history of salvation and an image of heavenly realities. Here the biblical and the Hellenistic world views intersect and unite.

In the course of the Middle Ages, the Platonic dialectic between symbol and reality was obscured and the salvation-historical perspective gave way to a greater preoccupation with metaphysical questions. This led to confusion regarding the relation of the sacramental signs to the reality that they signify. The source of this confusion lies in tendencies that are present in the theologies of

Augustine and Ambrose, which in the course of the Middle
Ages gave rise to a polarization between realist and symbolical
conceptions of the eucharist, which was unknown in the patristic
period. To these developments, we now turn.

AUGUSTINE AND AMBROSE

The eucharistic theologies of all the western churches have their
roots in the theology of St. Augustine, for it was Augustine who
developed the basic framework and the distinctive vocabulary of
the western theology of the sacraments. Augustine's theology of
the eucharist is of immense importance, because he held together elements that in the later history of theology became disas-
trously separated. Both the medieval and the reformation theologians appealed to him as the authority for their eucharistic doctrines, but neither did justice to the full measure of his thought.
Augustine is a restless thinker of tremendous creative power
who plumbed the depths of theological issues in the context of
the concrete life of the Church without ever bringing his reflections to rest in a thoroughly systematic fashion. His thought is
tantalizing and suggestive rather than finished and complete.
His eucharistic thought is no exception to this. We must try,
therefore, to grasp the characteristic features of his eucharistic
thought without destroying either the tensions between the elements that make it up or the unity of its outlook.

In his theology of baptism and the eucharist, Augustine developed further the North African tradition of Tertullian and Cyprian. It was Tertullian who first introduced the term *sacramentum*
into the vocabulary of the western Church as a way of describing
baptism and the eucharist.[123] In Tertullian, the term *sacramentum*
takes its meaning primarily from the background of Roman law.
Augustine took over the term *sacramentum* from Tertullian, but
developed its meaning within the framework of Christian Platonism. Augustine's theology of the sacraments, therefore, is a particular application of his Platonic theory of signs.[124] The terms
sacramentum and *signum* are virtually identical in meaning for Augustine. *Signum* is the general term for a sign or symbol. *Sacramentum* is the term used to describe those particular signs or

symbols that mediate the reality of Christ and salvation in the Christian community of faith.

Augustine's eucharistic thought is marked by a strong symbolic outlook. This is particularly true in his earlier writings. This symbolic outlook is related to two factors, his Platonism and his opposition to the Manicheans. As a Platonist, Augustine distinguishes between a sign (*signum*) and the reality (*res*) that it signifies. In line with the ancient understanding of symbols, a symbol not only represents that which it signifies, it also participates in that reality and mediates the reality to those who participate in the symbol. Symbolism, therefore, is not opposed to realism, but presupposes it. In opposition to the Manicheans, however, who held exaggerated physical conceptions of the presence of Christ, Augustine was careful to avoid any bold use of realist language when speaking about the eucharist. In his later anti-Pelagian writings, however, there are texts in which Augustine employs a more realist vocabulary. [125]

The relationship between symbol and reality operates on a number of different levels in Augustine's thought. In working out the relationship between sign and reality in his theology of the eucharist, Augustine employs the general vocabulary of his Platonic theory of signs. The *sacramentum* or *signum* is the outward visible sign; the *res* is the invisible reality that it signifies. [126] In the eucharist, the outward and visible signs are bread and wine, and the inward or invisible reality is Christ. The relationship between the signs and the reality signified by them is not an arbitrary one, but is understood through the concept of *similitudo*. A sign is only a sign in that it causes us to think of that which it signifies, because of a certain similitude or resemblance between the sign and the reality signified by it. It is this similitude, or resemblance between the signs and the reality signified by them, that justifies our giving to the signs the name of the reality signified by them. It is in this sense that we can speak of baptism as faith, or of the bread and wine as the body and blood of Christ.

"If the sacraments had not a kind of likeness to those things of which they are sacraments, they would not be sacraments at all. And from this likeness they generally receive the names of the things themselves. As therefore the sacrament of the body of Christ is, in a sense, the body of Christ, and the sacrament of Christ's blood is Christ's blood, so the sacrament of faith is faith."[127]

In line with his Platonism, Augustine distinguishes not only between the *sacramentum* or *signum* and the *res* in the sacraments, but also between the different ways in which we apprehend or receive them. The outward signs of bread and wine in the eucharist are perceived by the senses and eaten by the mouth. The invisible reality, however, is only attained by the mind and is only received by faith. There is, therefore, a double manner of eating in the eucharist. The outward signs of bread and wine are eaten in a physical manner. The *res*, or inward reality of the sacrament, however, which is Christ himself, is not eaten in a physical manner, but in a spiritual manner, i.e., by faith.[128] Christ is present in a bodily manner only at the right hand of the Father because he has ascended into heaven.

"Christ is always with the Father: in his *bodily* presence he is henceforth above the heavens, on the right-hand side of the Father; but in his presence of *faith*, he is in all Christians."[129]

" . . . he took flesh from the flesh of Mary. And he walked here in the flesh, and he gave this flesh to us to eat for our salvation, flesh which no one eats unless he has first adored. . . . But the Lord himself said, 'It is the spirit that gives life; the flesh is of no use.' . . . 'Interpret what I have said in a spiritual sense. It is not the body which you see which you are going to eat, you will not be drinking the blood which those who crucify me are to shed. I have entrusted you with something sacramental which, when spiritually understood, will give you life. Although it must of necessity be celebrated in visible form, it must still be understood invisibly.' "[130]

"Jesus answered and said to them, 'This is the work of God, that you believe on him whom he has sent.' This then is to eat the food which does not perish but 'abides unto eternal life.' Why do you prepare teeth and stomach? Believe, and you have eaten."[131]

In keeping with this symbolic and spiritualistic emphasis, Augustine places considerable emphasis not only on the relation between the sacraments and faith, but also on the relation between the sacraments and the word of God. Augustine took it for granted that the sacraments are celebrated in the context of the proclamation of the word of the gospel and in the context of a living community of faith. The sacraments are not only signs of faith, but visible words (*verbum visibile*). Proclamation and sacramental celebration, therefore, are intimately linked. This is brought out clearly in a famous text, where Augustine is speaking about baptism.

" 'Now you are clean through the word which I have spoken unto you.' Why does he not say, you are clean through the baptism with which you have been washed, but 'through the word which I have spoken unto you,' save only that in the water also it is the word that cleanses? Take away the word, and the water is neither more nor less than water. The word is added to the element, and there results the sacrament, as if itself also a kind of visible word. . . . And whence has water so great an efficacy . . . save by the operation of the word; and that not because it is uttered, but because it is believed? For even in the word itself the passing sound is one thing, the abiding efficacy another. 'This is the word of faith which we preach,' says the apostle, 'that if you shall confess with your mouth that Jesus is the Lord, and shall believe in your heart that God has raised him from the dead, you shall be saved. For with the heart we believe unto righteousness, and with the mouth confession is made unto salvation.' . . . The cleansing, therefore, would on no account be attributed to the fleeting and perishable element, were it not for that which is added, 'by the word.' "[132]

Schillebeeckx interprets this passage succinctly against its background in earlier patristic thought:

" . . . The Fathers thought of the sacraments as the bringing together of an earthly and a heavenly element, which was manifested externally in the liturgical action and a prayer of petition or *epiclesis*. The sacraments . . . were considered to consist of 'matter and spirit'; of an element or a thing (water, oil, bread, the laying on of hands), and the *pneuma* of the *Logos* which, in the power of the *epiclesis*, came down upon the material element. 'Accedit verbum ad elementum et fit sacramentum,' as St. Augustine so concisely formulated it—'A word comes to an element and a sacrament is there.' This word is a confession of faith, a *verbum fidei*. It is, that is to say, Christ's own proclamation of the word, made known by means of the Gospel, accepted through the faith of the Church, and confessed with regard to the sacramental action in a *verbum fidei*, a word of faith."[133]

As well as speaking of the *res*, or reality, of the sacrament, Augustine also speaks of the *virtus* (virtue), or grace, of the sacrament. The introduction of the notion of the *virtus* of the sacrament into his eucharistic theology reflects the profound orientation of the whole of Augustine's theology toward the reality of divine grace. Augustine's theology is both a theology of faith and a theology of grace, and these two aspects cannot be played off against each other. The sacraments are signs of faith. They are also means of grace.

" 'This is the bread which comes down from heaven, that whoever eats of it may not die.' But that which belongs to the virtue of the sacrament, not that which belongs to the visible sacrament; whoever eats inwardly, not outwardly; the one who eats the sacrament in the heart, not the one who crushes it with the teeth. . . . "[134]

How does Augustine understand the relationship between the *res* and the *virtus* of the sacrament? Are they identical or are they to be distinguished, and, if so, in what way? This may appear to be a matter of hairsplitting, but in the subsequent history of sacramental theology in the West, this proved to be the key point in Augustine's thought where his interpreters divided. The issue at stake is whether those who receive the sacrament unworthily, i.e., without faith, receive the body and blood of Christ, or whether they receive only the outward signs of bread and wine (i.e., the *sacramentum*).

The medieval theologians clearly distinguished between the *res* and the *virtus* of the sacrament. Both those who receive the sacrament worthily and those who receive the sacrament unworthily receive the body and blood of Christ (i.e., the *res* of the sacrament). Those who receive the sacrament worthily receive it for their salvation (i.e., they also receive the *virtus* or grace of the sacrament); those who receive the sacrament unworthily, receive it to their condemnation. The Swiss and the English reformers tended to identify the *res* and the *virtus* of the sacrament and to argue that since Christ can only be received by faith, the unworthy receive only the outward signs of bread and wine. Luther supported the medieval view. Augustine nowhere explicitly works out his own understanding of the relationship between the *res* and the *virtus* of the sacrament.

The tension can be seen in the following two texts where Augustine deals with the question of the unworthy reception of the sacrament:

" 'Whoever eats my flesh, and drinks my blood, dwells in me, and I in them.' This it is, therefore, for anyone to eat that meat and to drink that drink, to dwell in Christ, and to have Christ dwelling in them. Consequently, whoever does not dwell in Christ, and in whom Christ does not dwell, doubtless neither eats his flesh [spiritually] nor drinks his Blood [although they may press the sacrament of the body and blood of Christ carnally and visibly with their teeth], but rather they eat and drink the sacrament of so great a thing to their own judgment, because being unclean, they have presumed to come to the sacraments of Christ, which no one takes worthily except those who are pure. . . ."[135]

"For as Judas, to whom the Lord gave a morsel furnished a place within himself for the devil, not by receiving an evil thing but by receiving evilly, so whoever receives unworthily the sacrament of the Lord does not cause that it is evil because they themselves are evil or that they have received nothing because they have not received to salvation. For it was none the less the body of the Lord and the blood of the Lord even to those of whom the apostle said, 'Those who eat unworthily, eat and drink damnation to themselves.' "[136]

The most obvious reading of the second of these texts suggests a distinction between the *res* and the *virtus* of the sacrament. Judas did not receive "nothing" even though he did not receive "to salvation." It is "none the less the body of the Lord and the blood of the Lord" even to those who receive unworthily. This interpretation of the text coheres with the ancient understanding of the relationship between symbol and reality, where participation in the symbol requires participation in the reality. The first text, on the other hand, seems to imply fairly clearly that those who receive the sacrament unworthily receive only the *sacramentum* and not the *res*. This would imply an identity between the *res* and the *virtus* of the sacrament. This coheres with the other line of thought in Augustine, which insists that the *res* of the sacrament is only received by faith. Because there is a tension in Augustine's own thought, those who followed him resolved the tension in different ways.

When we have spoken of the relation between symbol and reality and of the relation between the sacraments and the word of God and faith, we have still not reached the heart of Augustine's understanding of the eucharist, which is only attained when we have brought out his profoundly ecclesial understanding of the eucharist.[137] Augustine stands squarely in the tradition of Paul. Like Paul, he interprets participation in the body of Christ in both its Christological and ecclesiological senses. The ultimate gift of the eucharist is the building up of the community of believers into union with Christ their head in a unity of peace and love. The *res*, or reality that is signified by the sacramental signs, is not simply an individual relationship with Christ attained by faith, but community in love between Christ and all the members of his body. Augustine brings this out in a marvelous homily addressed to the newly baptized:

"If you wish to understand the body of Christ, listen to the Apostle's words: 'You are the body and the members of Christ.' If you are the body and members of Christ, it is your mystery which is placed on the Lord's table; it is your mystery you receive. It is to that which you are that you answer, 'Amen,' and by that response you make your assent. You hear the words 'the body of Christ'; you answer, 'Amen,' Be a member of Christ, so that the 'Amen' may be true. Why then is he in bread? Let us not put forward any suggestion of our own, but listen to the repeated teaching of the Apostle; for he says, speaking of this sacrament: 'We are many, but we are one loaf, one body.' Understand and rejoice: unity, truth, goodness, love. 'One loaf.' What is that one loaf? 'We many are one body.' Remember that the bread is not made from one grain of wheat, but of many. When you were exorcized you were, in a manner, ground; when baptized you were, in a manner, moistened. When you received the fire of the Holy Spirit you were, in a manner, cooked. . . . Many grapes hang in a cluster, but their juice is mixed in unity. So the Lord has set his mark on us, wished us to belong to him, has consecrated on his table the mystery of our peace and unity. If anyone receives the sacrament of unity, but does not 'keep the bond of peace,' they do not receive a sacrament for their benefit, but evidence for their condemnation."[138]

Augustine's ecclesial interpretation of the eucharist is also reflected in his description of the eucharist as a sacrifice. There is no new sacrifice of Christ in the eucharist. The sacrifice of Christ on the cross is unique. In the eucharist, what is celebrated is the sacramental memorial (*anamnesis*) of Christ's sacrifice. Augustine understands the eucharistic *anamnesis* in the biblical sense. It is neither the mental recollection of a past event nor a repetition of the sacrifice of Christ offered once for all for our salvation. It is the sacramental or liturgical celebration of that which took place once for all in the past in order that the present community of believers can participate in its redemptive reality.

"Before the coming of Christ, the flesh and blood of this sacrifice were foreshadowed in the animals slain; in the passion of Christ the types were fulfilled by the true sacrifice; after the ascension of Christ, this sacrifice is commemorated in the sacrament."[139]

It is primarily within the context of his ecclesial conception of the eucharist, however, that the sacrificial aspect of the eucharist takes on its full meaning for Augustine. The sacrifice that is offered in the eucharist is the Church itself, the body of Christ, in union with its head:

"Such is the sacrifice of Christians. 'We, the many, are one body in Christ.' This is the sacrifice, as the faithful understand, which the church continues to celebrate in the sacrament of the altar, in which it is clear to the church that she herself is offered in the very offering she makes to God."[140]

Augustine does not restrict the meaning of sacrifice, however, to the act of offering. The sacrificial action is not complete until it is consummated in the act of communion. The model that lies in the background of Augustine's thought is that of a communion-sacrifice in which the participants share in the offering as part of a sacrificial meal:

"Christians also make the memorial of this sacrifice in the holy offering and partaking of the body and blood of Christ."[141]

Augustine's theology of the eucharist developed primarily within the framework of a Platonic understanding of the relationship between sign and reality. As we saw in an earlier section, an alternative way of speaking about the relationship between the sacramental signs of bread and wine and the reality signified by them began to appear among the fourth-century Greek fathers. Here the relationship between the elements of bread and wine and the presence of Christ signified by them began to be expressed in terms of a "change" in the elements of bread and wine. Cyril of Jerusalem, referring to the epiclesis of the Holy Spirit in the Eucharistic Prayer, speaks of the Holy Spirit coming upon the gifts of bread and wine

"that he may make the bread the body of Christ, and the wine the blood of Christ; for everything that the Holy Spirit has touched, has been sanctified and changed."[142]

This way of speaking of the relationship between the elements of bread and wine and the reality signified by them is often referred to as a "conversionist," "transformationist," or "metabolic" view of the eucharistic presence of Christ, since it conceives of the presence of Christ through a change in the elements by means of their consecration, rather than through a dialectical relationship between the sacramental signs and the reality signified by them.

This conversionist conception of the eucharistic presence was transmitted to the West by Ambrose, who was the first to introduce the language of change into the eucharistic vocabulary of the western Church. Ambrose, like Augustine, uses the terms *sacramentum* and *signum*, but he can also speak of the sacramental signs as "transformed into the flesh and blood through the mystery of the holy prayer."[143] At the time of the consecration, therefore, a change takes place in the "natures" of the elements by the word of Christ, although this is not yet called "transubstantiation."

". . . cannot the word of Christ, then, which was able to make out of nothing that which was not, change those things which are into what they are not? For it is not a less matter to give new natures to things than to change their natures."[144]

The metabolic interpretation of the relationship between the elements of bread and wine and the reality signified by them is not opposed by Ambrose to a symbolic interpretation of their relationship. Metabolic and symbolic languages exist side by side in his writings. Indeed, in the Eucharistic Prayer that was in use in Milan in Ambrose's day, the eucharistic offering is referred to explicitly as "the figure of the body and blood of . . . Christ."[145] Ambrose still uses the language of symbol and reality, but through his use of conversionist language, the *signum* and the *res* are more closely identified than they are in the thought of Augustine. Before the consecration, one reality is signified, bread and wine; after the consecration, another reality is signified, the body and blood of Christ. Moreover, Ambrose identifies the body of Christ that is present in the sacrament primarily as the body of Christ in the Christological sense rather than the body of Christ in the ecclesiological sense.

" . . . this body which we consecrated is that which was born of the Virgin . . . it was certainly the true flesh of Christ, which was crucified, which was buried: truly therefore it is a sacrament of that flesh. . . . The Lord Jesus himself proclaims, 'This is my body.' Before the blessing of the heavenly words another kind of thing is named; after the consecration the body is signified. He himself speaks of his blood. Before consecration it is called another thing; after consecration it is named 'blood.' "[146]

There is no trace in Ambrose, however, of any materialistic or physical conception either of the eucharistic change or of the sacramental eating of Christ. Both are conceived in the same spiritualistic language that Augustine uses. The manner of the presence is spiritual and the manner of eating is spiritual. This is brought out in a passage that we quoted earlier:

"In that sacrament is Christ, because it is the body of Christ; therefore it is not bodily food, but spiritual. Whence also the apostle says of the type of it that 'our fathers ate spiritual meat and drank spiritual drink.' For the body of God is a spiritual body; the body of Christ is the body of a divine Spirit, because Christ is Spirit. . . ."[147]

The alternative conceptions of the eucharistic presence found in the writings of Augustine and Ambrose were not in competition with each other, any more than symbolist, realist, and spiritualistic language were in competition with each other throughout the patristic period. There is no hint of controversy between Augustine and Ambrose over the eucharist. Indeed, Ambrose was Augustine's teacher who prepared him for baptism. Their writings simply reflect two different theological models for interpreting the relationship between the elements of bread and wine and the reality signified by them that were able to coexist quite happily in the fourth century. In the course of the Middle Ages, however, the conversionist view of Ambrose came to predominate over the symbolic conception of Augustine and eventually took the form of the doctrine of transubstantiation.

NOTES

1. For a form-critical study of the *berakah* prayer form, see Joseph Heinemann, *Prayer in the Talmud* (New York: Walter de Gruyter, 1977), 77–103.

2. Cf. Finkelstein, "The Birkat Ha-Mazon," 211–262.

3. Translation in R. C. D. Jasper and G. J. Cuming, *Prayers of the Eucharist: Early and Reformed*, 3d ed., rev. and enl. (New York: Pueblo Publishing Co., 1987), 23–24, hereafter cited as *PEER*.

4. For the origins and development of the eucharistic prayer, see Louis Ligier, "From the Last Supper to the Eucharist," in Lancelot Sheppard (ed.), *The New Liturgy* (London: Darton, Longman & Todd, 1970), 113–150; *idem*, "The Origins of the Eucharistic Prayer: From the Last Supper

to the Eucharist," *Studia Liturgica,* 9 (1973): 161–185; Thomas Talley, "The Eucharistic Prayer: Tradition and Development," in Kenneth Stevenson (ed.), *Liturgy Reshaped* (London: SPCK, 1982), 48–64; *idem,* "The Eucharistic Prayer of the Ancient Church According to Recent Research: Results and Reflections," *Studia Liturgica,* 11 (1976): 138–158 (a slightly expanded version of this article appeared as "From *Berakah* to *Eucharistia:* A Reopening Question," *Worship,* 50 [1976]: 115–137); *idem,* "The Literary Structure of the Eucharistic Prayer," *Worship,* 58 (1984): 404–420; Alan Bouley, *From Freedom to Formula: The Evolution of the Eucharistic Prayer from Oral Improvisation to Written Texts* (Washington, DC: Catholic University of America Press, 1981).

5. *PEER,* 10.

6. Talley, "Tradition and Development," 49–52.

7. *PEER,* 23–24.

8. Best edition of Hippolytus is Bernard Botte (ed. and trans.), *La tradition apostolique de Saint Hippolyte: essai de reconstitution* (Münster Westfalen: Aschendorffsche Verlagsbuchhandlung, 1963). English translation in Geoffrey J. Cuming (ed.), *Hippolytus: A Text for Students,* Grove Liturgical Studies, no. 8 (Bramcote, Notts.: Grove Books, 1976).

9. Ligier, "Last Supper to Eucharist," 129ff.

10. *PEER,* 34–35.

11. *Ibid.,* 42–44. See also Bryan D. Spinks (ed.), *Addai and Mari—The Anaphora of the Apostles: A Text for Students,* Grove Liturgical Studies, no. 24 (Bramcote, Notts.: Grove Books, 1980).

12. Louis Bouyer, *Eucharist: Theology and Spirituality of the Eucharistic Prayer* (Notre Dame: University of Notre Dame Press, 1968), 147.

13. William F. Macomber, "The Oldest Known Text of the Anaphora of the Apostles Addai and Mari," *Orientalia Christiana Periodica,* 32 (1966): 335–371.

14. *PEER,* 46–51.

15. Talley, "Recent Research," 154.

16. Hedegard, 152, cited in Talley, "Recent Research," 155.

17. H. Engberding, "Zum anaphorischen Fürbittgebet des ostsyrischen Liturgie Addaj und Mar(j)," *Oriens Christianus* 41 (1957): 102–124. Cf. also E. J. Cutrone, "The Anaphora of the Apostles: Implications of the Mar Esa'ya Text," *Theological Studies,* 43 (1973): 636–640.

18. Cutrone, 640–641.

19. Geoffrey Cuming, "The Anaphora of St. Mark: A Study in Development," *Le Muséon*, 95 (1982): 115–129; *idem*, "Four Very Early Anaphoras," *Worship*, 58 (1984): 168–172. See also H. A. J. Wegman, "Une Anaphore Incomplète?" in R. van den Broek and M. J. Vermaseren (eds.), *Studies in Gnosticism and Hellenistic Religions* (Leiden: E. J. Brill, 1981), 432–450; *idem*, "Généalogie hypothétique de la prière eucharistique," *Questions Liturgiques*, 61 (1980): 263–278; Bryan D. Spinks, "A Complete Anaphora? A Note on Strasbourg Gr. 254," *Heythrop Journal*, 25 (1984): 51–55.

20. *PEER*, 53–54. Liturgy of St. Mark (final form), *ibid.*, 57–66.

21. *Didache* 14.3; Justin Martyr *Dialogue with Trypho* 41.2; Irenaeus *Against Heresies* 4.17.5.

22. *PEER*, 104–113.

23. *Ibid.*, 90–99.

24. *Ibid.*, 131–134.

25. *Ibid.*, 116–123.

26. *Ibid.*, 70–73.

27. Cf. John H. McKenna, *Eucharist and Epiclesis: The Eucharistic Epiclesis in Twentieth Century Theology*, Alcuin Club Collections, no. 57 (Great Wakering: Mayhew-McCrimmon, 1975), 24, 29.

28. Ligier, "Origins," 182–185.

29. For a discussion of the non-Roman western rites, see Bouyer, 315–337. For the Roman rite, see Joseph A. Jungmann, *The Mass of the Roman Rite*, 2 vols. (New York: Benziger, 1951–1955).

30. *PEER*, 144–146.

31. Ralph A. Keifer, "The Unity of the Roman Canon: An Examination of its Unique Structure," *Studia Liturgica*, 11 (1976): 39–58.

32. Keifer, 54.

33. Ligier, "Last Supper to Eucharist," 140–141.

34. Cf. Bryan D. Spinks, "The Consecratory Epiklesis in the Anaphora of St. James," *Studia Liturgica*, 11 (1976): 25–26.

35. Geoffrey J. Cuming (ed.), *Essays on Hippolytus*, Grove Liturgical Studies, no. 15 (Bramcote, Notts.: Grove Books, 1978), 48.

36. Aidan Kavanagh, "Thoughts on the Roman Anaphora," *Worship*, 39 (1965): 528–529.

37. Bouyer, 74.

38. *PEER*, 24.

39. *Ibid.*, 77.

40. *Ibid.*, 80.

41. *Ibid.*, 71.

42. *Ibid.*, 120.

43. *Ibid.*, 43.

44. See Paul V. Marshall in Gregory Dix, *The Shape of the Liturgy*, with additional notes by Paul V. Marshall (New York: Seabury Press, 1982), 771–772.

45. Cf. Edward Kilmartin, "A Modern Approach to the Word of God and Sacraments of Christ: Perspectives and Principles," in Francis A. Eigo (ed.), *The Sacraments: God's Love and Mercy Actualized* (Villanova, PA: Villanova University Press, 1979), 64ff.

46. Gregory Dix, "The Origins of the Epiclesis," *Theology*, 28 (1934): 189.

47. *Against Noetus* 4.16.

48. McKenna, 20.

49. *PEER*, 35.

50. *Ibid.*, 43.

51. *Ibid.*, 140.

52. Aidan Kavanagh, "Thoughts on the Roman Anaphora," *Worship*, 40 (1966): 6–7.

53. *PEER*, 70–72.

54. For a study of the verbs in the early epicleses, see especially P. Dinesen, "Die Epiklese im Rahmen altkirchlicher Liturgien," *Studia Theologica*, 16 (1962): 42–107.

55. Cf. Albert Houssiau, "The Alexandrine Anaphora of St. Basil," in Sheppard, 239–241.

56. Cf. e.g., Bouyer, 246–250 and Bouley, 249–250.

57. *PEER*, 65–66.

58. *Ibid.*, 93.

59. *Ibid.*, 119–120.

60. *Ibid.*, 133.

61. *Ibid.*, 85–86. Cf. Adolph Harnack, *History of Dogma,* 7 vols. (New York: Dover Publications, 1961), 2:293–297; and R. J. Halliburton, "The Patristic Theology of the Eucharist," in Cheslyn Jones, Geoffrey Wainwright, and Edward Yarnold (eds.), *The Study of Liturgy* (New York: Oxford University Press, 1978), 207–208.

62. *PEER,* 29.

63. 1 Cor. 10:14–22. Cf. Frances M. Young, *The Use of Sacrificial Ideas in Greek Christian Writers from the New Testament to John Chrysostom,* Patristic Monograph Series, no. 5 (Cambridge, MA: Philadelphia Patristic Foundation, 1979), 241–242.

64. Cf. G. D. Kilpatrick, *The Eucharist in Bible and Liturgy,* (Cambridge, England: Cambridge University Press, 1983), 45–58.

65. Cf. Young, 239–284.

66. Gustaf Dalman, *Jesus-Jeshua: Studies in the Gospels* (New York: KTAV Publishing House, 1971), 116.

67. For the following discussion, see esp. Roland de Vaux, *Ancient Israel* (New York: McGraw-Hill, 1961), 415–456; and Young, 35–73.

68. Lv 17:11.

69. de Vaux, 451.

70. See pages 29–30 above.

71. Is 1:11–17; Jer 7:21–23; Hos 6:6; Am 5:21–24; Mi 6:6–8.

72. Pss 40:6–8; 50:7–15; 51:16–19.

73. See Young, 79ff.

74. See Edward J. Kilmartin, "Sacrificium Laudis: Content and Function of Early Eucharistic Prayers," *Theological Studies,* 35 (1974): 268–287.

75. *Didache* 14:1–3.

76. Irenaeus, *Against Heresies* 4.19.6.

77. *Ibid.*, 4.17.5.

78. *PEER,* 35.

79. *Ibid.*, 43.

80. Keifer, 53–55. For a detailed study of the way in which the sacrificial theme developed in both eastern and western liturgies, see Kenneth

Stevenson, *Eucharist and Offering* (New York: Pueblo Pu[
1986).

81. Cyprian, *Letter* 63.14.

82. *Ibid.*, 63.17.

83. Chrysostom, *Homilies on Hebrews* 17.6

84. Theodore of Mopsuestia, *Baptismal Homilies* 5. Translation in A. Mingana (ed.), *Woodbrooke Studies*, vol. 6 (Cambridge, England: W. Heffer & Sons, 1933), 79–80.

85. *City of God* 10.6.

86. *Against Faustus* 20.18.

87. For the following discussion, see esp. G. W. H. Lampe and K. J. Woollcombe, *Essays on Typology* (London: SCM Press, 1957); and Jean Danielou, *The Bible and the Liturgy* (Notre Dame: Notre Dame University Press, 1956).

88. See Edward Yarnold, *The Awe-Inspiring Rites of Initiation: Baptismal Homilies of the Fourth Century* (Slough, England: St. Paul Publications, 1972).

89. *Miscellanies* 4.25.

90. 63.4.

91. *On the Sacraments* 5.1.

92. *On the Mysteries* 47, 49.

93. *On the Sacraments* 5.3.

94. *On the Trinity* 2.127, cited by Danielou, 159.

95. *Proof of the Gospel* 1.39, cited by Danielou, 159.

96. *Letter* 63.5.

97. *On the Sacraments* 5.13.

98. For the Hellenistic background of early Christianity, especially as it relates to the sacraments, see Arthur D. Nock, *Early Gentile Christianity and its Hellenistic Background* (New York: Harper and Row, 1964).

99. For an introduction to Greek philosophy and its relation to early Christian thought, see A. H. Armstrong, *An Introduction to Ancient Philosophy*, 3d ed. (London: Methuen & Co., 1959).

100. For the role of symbols in the ancient world, see Mircea Eliade, *Images and Symbols* (New York: Sheed & Ward, 1962).

. For modern approaches to symbols, see Chapter Seven.

102. Harnack, 2:144–145.

103. See Armstrong, Chaps. 4 and 5.

104. See Mircea Eliade, *Myth and Reality* (New York: Harper & Row, 1963).

105. *Against Heresies* 4.18.5.

106. Käsemann, *Essays*, 113–114.

107. *PEER*, 23–24.

108. *On the Mysteries*, 58.

109. *Sermon* 131.1.

110. *Homilies on John* 25.12.

111. *Homilies on John* 26.12.

112. *Against Marcion* 3.19.

113. *Ibid.*, 4.40.

114. *Proof of the Gospel* 8.1.

115. 4.3.

116. *On the Sacraments* 4.20.

117. *Ibid.*, 4.21.

118. *Against Adimantus* 12.3.

119. *On the Psalms* 3.1.

120. *Smyrneans* 7.

121. *Philadelphians* 4.

122. *1 Apology* 66.1, 2.

123. See Kilmartin, "Sacraments . . . Perspectives and Principles," 98–101 and D. Michaélidès, *Sacramentum chez Tertullien* (Paris: Etudes Augustiniennes, 1970).

124. See C. P. Mayer, *Die Zeichen in der geistigen Entwicklung und in der Theologie Augustinus*, 2 vols. (Würzburg: Augustinus-Verlag, 1969–1974).

125. See P. Th. Camelot, "Réalisme et Symbolisme dans la doctrine eucharistique de S. Augustin," *Revue des Sciences Philosophiques et Théologiques*, 36 (1947): 394–410.

126. See H. M. Féret, "Sacramentum. Res. dans la langue théologique de S. Augustin," *Revue des Sciences Philosophiques et Théologiques*, 29 (1940): 218–243.

127. *Letter* 98.9.

128. Cf. C. W. Dugmore, *The Mass and the English Reformers* (London: Macmillan, 1958), 14–18.

129. *Sermon* 361. See G. Martelet, *The Risen Christ and the Eucharistic World* (London: Collins, 1976), 124–128.

130. *On the Psalms* 99.8.

131. *Homilies on John* 25.12.

132. *Ibid.*, 80.3.

133. Edward Schillebeeckx, *Christ the Sacrament of the Encounter with God* (New York: Sheed & Ward, 1963), 92.

134. *Homilies on John* 26.12.

135. *Ibid.*, 26.18.

136. *On Baptism* 5.9.

137. See Wilhelm Gessel, *Eucharistische Gemeinschaft bei Augustinus* (Würzburg: Augustinus-Verlag, 1966).

138. *Sermon* 272.

139. *Against Faustus* 20.21.

140. *City of God* 10.6.

141. *Against Faustus* 20.18.

142. *PEER*, 86.

143. *On the Christian Faith* 4.125.

144. *On the Mysteries* 52.

145. *PEER*, 145.

146. *On the Mysteries* 53, 54.

147. *Ibid.*, 58.

CHAPTER THREE

The Eucharist in the Middle Ages

EARLY MEDIEVAL EUCHARISTIC CONTROVERSIES

During the Middle Ages, a number of fundamental changes took place in the understanding of the eucharist and in its celebration that have had far-reaching effects on the eucharistic faith and life of all the western Churches. The eucharistic traditions of Augustine and Ambrose were transmitted to the early Middle Ages initially through Isidore of Seville (ca. 560–636). Isidore combined these two traditions in his own thought. He spoke about the bread and wine of the eucharist becoming the body and blood of Christ through transformation, but his basic outlook was Augustinian. In the ninth century, however, these two traditions came into conflict with each other for the first time in a controversy that broke out between Paschasius Radbertus and Ratramnus, two monks of the monastery of Corbie. The controversy was renewed in a different form in the eleventh century between Berengar of Tours and Lanfranc.[1]

These early medieval controversies reflect two fundamental liturgical and cultural shifts that had taken place since the fourth century. In the first place, the unity between symbol and reality, which was characteristic of the ancient world, is beginning to dissolve. The symbol is no longer seen as the means of participating in the reality, but is on the way to becoming a mere sign or pointer that is separated from the reality that it signifies. It is against the background of this fundamental cultural shift that symbolical and realist language run into conflict with each other. As long as the symbol is the means by which the community participates in the reality that it signifies, there is no problem in using symbolical and realist language simultaneously. Once the unity between the symbol and the reality begins to dissolve, however, the presence of the reality seems to be threatened when symbolical language is used.

The other fundamental change that is beginning to take place in the ninth century is the loosening of the unity between the Christological and the ecclesiological meanings of the "body of Christ." In Paul and in Augustine, the body of Christ in the eucharist is understood in both its Christological and its ecclesiological senses. Participation in the eucharist means both participation in Christ himself and participation in his body the Church. H. de Lubac has shown the way in which a complete transformation took place in the meaning of the term "body of Christ" between the patristic period and the Middle Ages. In the patristic period, the term "body of Christ" meant primarily the Church, in the tradition of Paul and Augustine. In the Middle Ages, the term "body of Christ" came to mean primarily the sacramental presence of Christ in the elements of bread and wine on the altar.[2]

Nathan Mitchell has shown how this reflects a fundamental change in liturgical sensibility. The eucharist is no longer perceived as a community celebration but as a ritual drama enacted by the priest at the altar, and the congregation become merely spectators. Similarly, the bread and wine of the eucharist are no longer seen as the symbols of participation in the risen Christ through the sharing of a meal, but as sacred objects on the altar.[3] In this context, the focus of eucharistic piety becomes the presence of Christ in the elements on the altar, and the central questions for eucharistic theology become the questions of how Christ is present in the elements and what the relationship is between the outward signs of bread and wine and the inward reality of the body and blood of Christ that they contain. These are precisely the questions that are raised in the ninth-century controversy between Radbertus and Ratramnus.

Radbertus approaches these questions by insisting on the realism of Christ's presence in the elements, and in the tradition of Ambrose, asserts a change in the elements at the consecration into the body and blood of Christ. Moreover, he insists on a strict identity between the sacramental body of Christ and the historical body of Christ:

". . . and since he willed to remain, though under the figure of bread and wine, we must believe that after the consecration these are nothing else at all but the flesh and blood of Christ. . . . And, that I may speak more marvelously, (this flesh) is in no way at all distinct from that which was born of Mary and suffered on the cross and rose from the tomb. . . ."[4]

At the same time, Radbertus uses an Augustinian vocabularly and operates with Augustinian presuppositions. He acknowledges that there is both "figure" or "image" and "truth" in the sacrament. Moreover, Christ's body is not physically present in the eucharist (although he sometimes quotes with approval popular stories that suggest a physical presence of Christ under the sacramental signs). The natural body of Christ remains in heaven and only those who receive the sacrament spiritually by faith receive the flesh of Christ. The unworthy receive only the outward signs of bread and wine. At the same time, it is the "truth" of the sacrament rather than the "figure" that really matters for Radbertus:

". . . if we look at the matter correctly, we can see that (the eucharist) is simultaneously image and truth. What is experienced externally (in this sacrament) is an image or figure of truth; but what is rightly believed or understood internally about this (sacrament) is truth. . . ."[5]

Ratramnus, on the other hand, does not totally exclude metabolic language in speaking of the eucharistic presence, but his characteristic language is Augustinian and Platonic. He is one of the last representatives of an exclusively Augustinian interpretation of the eucharist at a time when conversionist categories were gaining increasing acceptance by theologians. Ratramnus does not reject the real presence of Christ in the sacrament, but he wants to understand it exclusively in spiritualistic and symbolical categories. Where he allows a change in the elements, this is understood in a purely spiritual sense. Ratramnus prefers, however, to speak of "figure" and "truth" in connection with the eucharist rather than of a change in the nature of the elements.

For him, Christ's body and blood are present in the eucharist "in figure" and not "in truth" (i.e., literal truth). This use of language caused him to be accused of denying the real presence of Christ in the sacrament. Ratramnus is not denying the real presence here, but reaffirming the Augustinian tradition that the body of Christ is present in the eucharist not to the senses but to the mind and to faith. The elements are perceived by the senses, but the reality that they image is only received by faith.

"Faith does not receive what the eye sees but what it believes, because this is a spiritual food and a spiritual drink, spiritually feeding the soul and giving the life of eternal satiety."[6]

Radbertus and Ratramnus lived at a time when the Church could still tolerate within its ranks theologians who inclined in their theological interpretation of the eucharist either toward the metabolic realism of Ambrose or toward the symbolic realism of Augustine. At the same time, they represent a period when the unity between symbol and reality is beginning to break down, and where the older Augustinian vocabulary is giving way to a more realist conception of the eucharist. Subsequently, the work of Ratramnus was lost and was only rediscovered in the sixteenth century, when it was translated and eagerly read by the Reformers as evidence for a Catholic tradition of the eucharist before the rise of the doctrine of transubstantiation.[7]

From the ninth century onwards, the realist tradition represented by Radbertus became increasingly aggressive and received cruder expression as time went on, so that the older Augustinian tradition came to be no longer generally understood even by theologians. The idea of a physical miracle in the mass now gained increasing ground in popular piety. It is in this context that the earlier ninth-century protest of Ratramnus against extreme realism was renewed in the eleventh century by Berengar.

Berengar came into open conflict with Lanfranc, afterwards Archbishop of Canterbury, who represented the realism of Radbertus in a heightened form.[8] As a result, Berengar was summoned to a series of councils where he was forced to assent to statements concerning the eucharistic presence of a strongly realistic character, the most extreme of which was the confession of faith forced on him by the synod of Rome in 1059:

"The bread and wine which are placed on the altar are after consecration not only a sacrament but also the real body and blood of our Lord Jesus Christ, and that with the senses not only by way of a sacrament but in reality these are held and broken by the hands of the priest and are crushed by the teeth of the faithful."[9]

The idea of a physical presence of Christ in the elements had now gained approval even at the level of official authority.

In his theology of the eucharist, Berengar accepts Augustine's distinction between the outward sign (*signum* or *sacramentum*) and the reality signified by it (*res*). Following Augustine, he holds that the outward sign is perceived by the senses, whereas the reality is only attained by the mind and by faith. This reflects a Platonic vision of reality in which the invisible reality of the body and blood of Christ is symbolized by the outward visible sign. The nature, essence, or substance of bread and wine is not changed in the eucharist, but they signify another invisible, heavenly reality, the body and blood of Christ. Berengar, like Augustine, believed that the risen and glorified body of Christ is in heaven in view of the ascension and cannot be physically present on the altar. It can only be present in the eucharist in a sacramental manner.

Lanfranc, on the other hand, taking Ambrose's metabolic realism rather than Augustine's symbolic realism as his starting point, affirms that there is a real change in the nature, essence, or substance of the bread and wine at the consecration. Rather than distinguishing between the *signum* and the *res*, Lanfranc distinguishes between the outward appearances of bread and wine and the *substance* or reality of the body and blood of Christ that lies behind them.

"We believe that through the ministry of the priest, the earthly substances on the Lord's table are sanctified by divine power in a manner that is unspeakable, incomprehensible, marvelous; and that (these substances) are changed into the essence of the

Lord's body, even though the appearances of earthly elements remain. . . ."[10]

Already we have the appearance in this text of the distinction that will later be made between "substance" and "accidents" in the doctrine of transubstantiation.

The particular significance of the debate between Berengar and Lanfranc is that the conflict between symbolism and realism now begins to take a philosophical form, and the concept of "substance" is introduced into the discussion for the first time.[11] We are also beginning to see a shift taking place from a predominantly Platonic to an Aristotelian outlook. In the ninth-century controversy between Radbertus and Ratramnus, the issue had been between a metabolic and an Augustinian conception of the eucharist. At that time, the concept of "substance" was not employed to explain the change that takes place in the elements at the consecration. The concept of "substance" is the new factor in the eleventh-century debate, and from now on, it becomes the central issue for eucharistic theology. The term "transubstantiation," however, does not appear until the twelfth century.

During the eleventh century, the works of Boethius were disseminated throughout the libraries of Europe. Boethius was a sixth-century philosopher who wrote on philosophical and theological subjects. His works included translations and commentaries on some of the works of Aristotle, especially his logic.[12] These translations and commentaries were the principal source for the knowledge of Aristotle prior to the thirteenth century, when the metaphysics of Aristotle became known. The importance of Boethius' works is that they introduced into medieval Europe for the first time an Aristotelian world view, which now begins to make itself felt in theology, and by the thirteenth century, made a strong bid to replace the Platonic world view as the framework within which theology was done.

The most important among the ideas that Boethius' works contained were the concepts of "substance" and "accidents," the philosophical concepts in which the later doctrine of transubstantiation came to be expressed. In common usage up to this time, the concept of "substance" had been used in two ways, only one of which was strictly theological. It was used first of all as a commonsense equivalent for what would be spoken about in ordinary experience as a "thing." A book, a chair, a table, a person, any individual entity in the world is a "substance." In theology, the term was employed in the doctrine of the Trinity, where God was confessed as three persons in one substance. The word had not previously been used in connection with the eucharist. The question that lay behind the debate between Berengar and Lanfranc was whether and in what respect the substance of Christ's body is present in the elements.

R. W. Southern has pointed out that Berengar entered the controversy as a scholar whose principal training was in the discipline of grammar. While Berengar was no stranger to the logic of Boethius, Lanfranc was preeminently the dialectician.[13] The implication is that for Lanfranc when the concept of substance is applied to the eucharist, the logic of the sentences "This is my body" and "This is my blood" is that an essential or substantial change takes place in the elements of bread and wine at the time of the consecration. To Berengar the grammarian, on the other hand, such a dialectical argument ignores the plain function of words and is self-contradictory. Sentences are made up of subjects and predicates. No sentence can stand if the subject of the sentence is denied, destroyed, or contradicted by its predicate. If applied to the eucharist, this means that the sentence "This is my body" would be self-contradictory if the subject were denied or ceased to exist. For Berengar, subject = substance. The assertion that the substances of bread and wine are changed or cease to exist at the time of the consecration is self-contradictory. Berengar, by a purely grammatical argument, claims to refute the assertion of a change of substance in the eucharist.

While these simple arguments by no means exhaust the thinking of Berengar and Lanfranc on the eucharist, they illustrate the way in which new intellectual methods and concepts were being applied in the eleventh century to the solution of theological problems. In the succeeding period, the concept of substance became central in eucharistic theology, and as the term entered into more common usage, the attempt was made to give it a more precise philosophical meaning in order to explain the change that was held to take place in the elements of bread and wine at the consecration.

THOMAS AQUINAS AND THE DOCTRINE OF TRANSUBSTANTIATION

By the twelfth century, the application of philosophical methods to the understanding of the sacraments becomes more rigorous and systematic. From now on, theologians use philosophical reason as a primary means for understanding the operation of the sacraments and the manner of Christ's presence in the eucharist. It is for this reason that the theologians of the High Middle Ages are commonly referred to as "scholastics" or "schoolmen." The greatest of the scholastics was Thomas Aquinas (ca. 1225–1274).[14]

Aquinas' sacramental theology is found both in his theological writings and in his liturgical compositions.[15] As well as producing voluminous theological tomes, he also wrote the propers for the new feast of *Corpus Christi* and composed a number of hymns. In the *Summa Theologiae*, his systematic theology, he gives his definition of a sacrament, which is derived from Augustine:

". . . to define the special sense in which the term sacrament is being used in our present discussion of the sacraments—it is applied to that which is a sign (*signum*) of a sacred reality (*res*) inasmuch as it has the property of sanctifying human beings."[16]

This definition is extremely important, because it affects everything that Thomas has to say about the eucharist. As we shall see, it is crucial for his interpretation of the eucharist as a sacrifice.

In their character as signs, the sacraments have a threefold signification.[17] They celebrate the *anamnesis* of the death of Christ, they are an offer of present grace, and they are a pledge of participation in the kingdom of God.

". . . as a sign a sacrament has a threefold function. It is at once a remembrance of that which has gone before, namely the passion of Christ, a demonstration of that which is brought about in us through the passion of Christ, namely grace, and a promise, i.e., a pledge of future glory."[18]

The counterpoint between these themes is reflected in the antiphon to the Magnificat for the second Vespers of *Corpus Christi:*

"O sacred banquet in which Christ is received, the memorial of his passion is renewed, the soul is filled with grace, and a pledge of future glory is given to us, Alleluia!"[19]

Following both Paul and Augustine, Thomas interprets the *res* that is signified by the eucharist in both its Christological and its ecclesiological sense:

". . . the apostle says, 'For we being many are one bread, one body, all we who share in one bread and one cup.' This text shows clearly that the eucharist is the sacrament of the church's unity."[20]

". . . in the sacrament of the altar the reality signified is twofold, namely, as Augustine tells us, the true and the mystical body of Christ."[21]

". . . Christ's actual body . . . (and) Christ's mystical body . . . are respectively the reality signified (*res et sacramentum*) and the ultimate reality (*res tantum*) in the eucharist."[22]

In another place, Thomas reformulates the threefold signification of the sacrament in a way that incorporates the ecclesial perspective.

"This sacrament signifies three things. It looks back to the past: in this sense it commemorates the passion of our Lord. . . . In regard to the present, there is another thing to which it points. This is the unity of the church, into which human beings are drawn together through this sacrament. Because of this it is called '*communio*' or '*synaxis*.' As Damascene says, 'it is called "communion" because by it we are joined to Christ and because we share his flesh and his Godhead, and because we are joined and united to one another by it.' It has a third significance with regard to the future. . . ."[23]

The grace of the eucharist is not only for the sanctification of the individual, but for the building up of the unity of the body of Christ, the Church.

The Prayer over the Gifts for *Corpus Christi* is a direct reflection of Augustine's ecclesial perspective:

"O Lord, graciously bestow upon your church the gifts of unity and peace, which are symbolized in this sacrifice we offer you."[24]

Thomas employs a spiritualistic vocabulary both to describe the manner of Christ's presence in the elements and the manner of eating and drinking the body and blood of Christ in the eucharist:

". . . Christ's body [is not present in the eucharist] . . . in the way that is natural for a body to be present, that is visibly in its normal appearance. . . . [The presence is] a spiritual, non-visible presence, in the way of a spirit and by the power of the Spirit. For this reason Augustine says, 'if you have understood in a spiritual way' the words of Christ about his flesh, 'they are spirit and life for you; if you have understood them in a carnal manner, they are still spirit and life, but not for you.' "[25]

"The sacraments of the church are ordained to serve the spiritual life of human beings. . . . the eucharist . . . is . . . spiritual food. . . . It is our spiritual refreshment."[26]

"Its purpose is to refresh us spiritually, as bodily nourishment does physically. . . . [It is] spiritual food and spiritual drink. . . ."[27]

"Christ is taken under the species of bread and wine as spiritual refreshment, and not as common food and drink, in a horrible and cannibal manner."[28]

The role that faith and the Word of God play for Thomas in relation to the sacrament comes out in a wonderful way in his hymn *Adoro Te Devote*:

"Humbly I adore thee, Verity unseen,
Who thy glory hidest 'neath these shadows mean;

Lo, to thee surrendered, my whole heart is bowed,
Tranced as it beholds thee, shrined within the cloud.

"Taste, and touch, and vision, to discern thee fail;
Faith, that comes by hearing, pierces through the veil.
I believe whate'er the Son of God hath told;
What the Truth hath spoken, that for truth I hold.

"O memorial wondrous of the Lord's own death;
Living Bread, that givest all thy creatures breath,
Grant my spirit ever by thy life may live,
To my taste thy sweetness never failing give.

"Jesus, whom now veiled, I by faith descry,
What my soul doth thirst for, do not, Lord, deny,
That thy face unveiled, I at last may see,
With the blissful vision blest, my God, of thee."[29]

While Aquinas defines the sacraments as "signs" of grace, following Augustine, he also speaks of them as "causes" of grace.[30]
There are two reasons for this. In the first place, as a result of
the early medieval controversies over the eucharist, Thomas is
aware of the way in which the concept of "sign" has been weak-
ened in common usage, so that its use in connection with the
eucharist seems to suggest that the elements of bread and wine
are "mere" signs that do not convey the reality that they signify.
The other reason is that Thomas opts for an Aristotelian rather
than a Platonic framework in which to work out his theology of
the sacraments.

Whereas Platonism has a "two-storey" vision of reality in which
the visible world perceived by the senses is a reflection of the
invisible world of reality perceived by the mind, Aristotle understands reality as the interaction of causal relationships between
substances. When these two philosophical world views are applied to an understanding of the sacraments, the sacramental theologies that result look rather different. In the Platonic world
view, the relationship between visible sign and invisible reality is
one of "participation" rather than "causality." As long as the traditional Platonic framework formed the general background for

theological reflection on the sacraments, no need was felt for a causal principle to explain "how" the visible sign conveys the invisible reality that it signifies and represents. To say that sacraments "signify" something is at the same time to say that they "convey" something. That is what "signs" are. The idea that a sign could be a "mere" sign could only arise in a radically changed intellectual climate. Such was the climate of the thirteenth century. It is not enough now to say that the sacraments are "signs" of grace without also saying that they "cause" grace. Once the notion of "participation," essential to an understanding of the relation between sign and reality in the Platonic tradition has been lost, the language of "figure," "sign," and "symbol" appears to evacuate the sacraments of their reality. Thomas Aquinas was filling an evident theological vacuum, therefore, when he applied the Aristotelian principle of causality to explain the relationship between the sacramental signs and the reality that they signify. Thomas employs the principle of causality not in order to negate the symbolic character of the sacraments, but in order to make clear in the medieval context what was obvious in the patristic context, namely, that the sacraments as signs participate in the reality that they signify and are not "mere" signs.

For Aquinas, the sacraments are true causes of grace, but they are "instrumental" causes. The sacraments do not cause grace through their own power. God is the principal or primary cause of grace. The sacraments are secondary causes or "instruments" through which Christ's saving power is conveyed:

". . . neither the sacraments nor any other creature can be the principal causes of grace, which is produced solely by divine power, but . . . they are instrumental causes."[31]

". . . the principal efficient cause of grace is God himself, to whom the humanity of Christ is related as a conjoined instrument, whereas the sacrament is related as a separate instrument. Consequently, the saving power in the sacraments must be derived from the divinity of Christ through his humanity."[32]

The term "transubstantiation" was first introduced during the first half of the twelfth century.[33] The first writer to use the word *transubstantiare* was Stephen of Beaugé, bishop of Autun (1139–1140). The term *transubstantiatio* was first used by Roland Bandinelli (later Pope Alexander III) in his *Sentences,* written between 1140 and 1150. The term represents an attempt both to affirm the reality of the eucharistic presence and to give the conversionist understanding of it a more precise formulation. After its appearance, it quickly established itself as the major theological interpretation of the doctrine of the real presence. It was defined as the official teaching of the Church at the Fourth Lateran Council in 1215, and was later reaffirmed as a dogma of the Roman Catholic Church at the Council of Trent.

Throughout the Middle Ages and long after it had been first defined by the Fourth Lateran Council, theologians continued to discuss it. Particularly during the fourteenth and fifteenth centuries and right up to the time of the Council of Trent, while it was universally accepted as a doctrine of the Church, theologians continued to ask whether it was the best or the only possible way of affirming and understanding the doctrine of the real presence. At least in theory, therefore, the doctrine of transubstantiation was understood as a particular way of affirming and interpreting the doctrine of the real presence and was not understood to be identical with the doctrine of the real presence itself.

Although by the sixteenth century, the term had become so well established that it was virtually identified with the doctrine of the real presence, this process was still not complete. Luther, well aware of the medieval debates on the question, is only reflecting the opinions of the fourteenth- and fifteenth-century schools when he argues that the doctrine of transubstantiation came to be connected with the doctrine of the real presence because it was defined by the Church, not because there is an inner connection between them. This outlook is still reflected in the debates at the Council of Trent when the aptness of the term and the wisdom of including it as a dogmatic formulation of the eucharistic presence of Christ was still an open question. After Trent, the doctrine of the real presence and the doctrine of transubstantiation were so closely identified in the Roman Catholic tradition that they could no longer be distinguished in practice.

It is extremely difficult for modern persons brought up in
empirically oriented culture even to understand what the do
trine of transubstantiation means. It is small comfort that the
term was a source of confusion during the medieval period itsel
The term was intended to function at a metaphysical level, not at
an empirical level. All the great scholastic theologians, including
Thomas Aquinas, understood it in this sense. The problem is
that these two levels were often confused in practice both at the
level of popular piety and at the level of theological discussion,
where the doctrine was widely misunderstood in a physical or
materialistic sense. Thomas Aquinas' explanation of the doctrine
explicitly excludes the idea of a material, physical, or local presence of Christ in the elements, but not all theologians were as
careful as Thomas.

". . . it is clear that the body of Christ does not begin to exist in
this sacrament by being brought in locally . . . because it would
thereby cease to be in heaven. . . ."[34]

"The body of Christ is not in this sacrament in the way a body is
in place. . . . Christ's body is here in a special way that is proper
to this sacrament. For this reason we say that the body of Christ
is on different altars, not as in different places, but as in a sacrament."[35]

The term "substance" does not refer to a material substance. It
refers to the inner reality (= substance) present in the eucharist,
i.e., Christ himself. The term "transubstantiation" was formulated to answer two questions. The first question is: What is the
reality that is present on the altar after the consecration? The
answer is: (the substance of) Christ himself. The second question
is: How does this reality come about? The answer is: through a
change (i.e., a trans-substantiation) of the elements, so that their
inner reality is no longer the "substance" of bread and wine, but
the substance or reality of Christ himself. This does not mean
that the empirical signs of bread and wine are annihilated. Their
material qualities and chemical properties do not change. In the
language of Aristotelian metaphysics in which Thomas Aquinas
explained the doctrine, the "substance" (i.e., the reality that un-

ments) changes, while the "accidents"
irical qualities) remain. The Reformers'
tion represents an attack both on the ma-
he doctrine that was common in popular
osophical subtlety that had been ex-
val theologians. In their attack, they
pirical and the metaphysical levels of
so doing, they reflected a confusion that they
found in the medieval church.

In the light of the storm that the doctrine of the sacrifice of the
mass generated in the sixteenth century, it may appear surprising that Thomas devotes only one article in the *Summa* to an
explicit consideration of the eucharist as a sacrifice, whereas he
devotes twenty-four to the doctrine of transubstantiation. The
sacrifice of the mass had not yet become a controversial issue.
Thomas is entirely in line with Augustine and the patristic tradition in his interpretation of the eucharistic sacrifice. He connects
the eucharist with the sacrifice of Christ primarily by way of the
eucharistic memorial. The eucharist is not a new sacrifice, nor is
it in any sense a repetition of the sacrifice of the cross. It is
called a sacrifice because it celebrates the *anamnesis* of Christ's
death.

"This sacrament . . . commemorates the passion of our Lord,
which was the true sacrifice. . . . Because of this it is called 'sacrifice.' "[36]

The theme of the memorial of the passion is almost a refrain in
his writings:

". . . this sacrament is called the memorial of the passion of our
Lord, according to the text of Matthew, 'Do this for a commemoration of me.' "[37]

"This sacrament was instituted at the last Supper that it might in
the future be a memorial of the passion when that had been
accomplished."[38]

The eucharistic memorial is the central theme of the collect for
Corpus Christi:

"O God, who in a wonderful sacrament has left us a memorial of your passion: grant us so to venerate the sacred mysteries of your body and blood that we may know within ourselves the fruit of your redemption."[39]

In the article in which he specifically discusses the sacrificial aspect of the eucharist, Thomas gives two reasons why the eucharist is called a sacrifice. First of all, it is called a sacrifice because in the eucharist, we have an "image" of Christ's passion. Second, it is called a sacrifice because in the eucharist, we participate in the redemptive effects of Christ's death.

"For two reasons is the celebration of this sacrament called the sacrifice of Christ. First, because, as Augustine writes, 'Images are called by the names of the things of which they are images. . . .' Now, as we have said, the celebration of this sacrament is a definite image representing Christ's passion, which is his true sacrifice. Hence Ambrose writes on Hebrews, 'In Christ was offered once a sacrifice powerful for eternal salvation. What do we do? Is it not to offer it every day, yet for the recalling of his death?' Second, in respect of the effect of Christ's passion. By this sacrament we are made sharers of the fruit of the Lord's passion. Hence in a Sunday secret prayer it is said, 'Whenever the commemoration of this sacrifice is celebrated the work of our redemption is carried on.' "[40]

It is quite clear from this passage that Christ's sacrifice on the cross was offered once for all and cannot be repeated. Nevertheless, because in the eucharist we have an "image" or sacramental sign of Christ's passion, the image can be called by the name of the reality that it signifies. Here Thomas is following Augustine, for whom the sacramental sign is the image of the reality signified. The eucharist is the sacramental sign of Christ's sacrifice. As he puts it in another place, ". . . we have the following statement of Augustine, 'The visible sacrifice is the sacrament, i.e., the sacred sign, of the invisible sacrifice.' "[41] Furthermore, the quotation from Ambrose (actually John Chrysostom[42]) and the reference to the secret prayer for the ninth Sunday after Pentecost make it clear that the passion of Christ is present in the eucharist not by way of repetition, but by way of *anamnesis*.

While the theological discussion was going on concerning the nature and mode of Christ's presence in the eucharist, parallel developments were taking place in eucharistic piety. Already by the end of the patristic period, in both East and West, the practice of attending the eucharist without receiving communion had become the rule rather than the exception. This had taken place due to a profound change in the perception of the eucharist by priest and people alike. The eucharist was no longer viewed primarily as the common action of the people of God in which all shared. It was viewed rather as a sacred action done by the priest and that inspired awe rather than participation on the part of the people. The elements were regarded with such reverence that the fear of receiving such "holy things" unworthily led to infrequent communion. The people regularly participated in the eucharistic celebration, but received communion only occasionally. All of this led in the Middle Ages to a situation in which the role of the people in the celebration of the eucharist became that of witnessing what the priest did at the altar. The mass was no longer the action of the whole people of God. It was an action that the priest did on behalf of the people while the people watched as spectators. Moreover, the priest recited the mass in Latin and frequently in an inaudible voice, so that the people could not hear or join in the prayers. This led to the practice among the devout of saying their own private prayers while the priest celebrated the mass at the altar. These private prayers proliferated in the later Middle Ages and were compiled in popular prayer books for those who could read. The people, therefore, ceased to pray the liturgy itself and substituted their own private prayers for the prayers of the mass.[43]

The focus of eucharistic piety, which had long since ceased to be the act of receiving communion, now became the act of seeing the consecrated host and chalice that were solemnly elevated by the priest after the recital of the words of consecration in the canon of the mass. This shift in focus from receiving communion to seeing the consecrated host became so deeply rooted in the popular piety of the Middle Ages that the Fourth Lateran Council in 1215 was forced to enact legislation requiring the reception of communion at least once a year at Easter. In the mystical tradition of the later Middle Ages, there developed a deep mystical devotion to the sacramental presence of Christ in the consecrated host. The custom had long been observed of reserving the consecrated elements for the sick and dying. Indeed, the practice of the deacons taking the consecrated elements to the sick after the eucharistic celebration is attested as early as the middle of the second century.[44] There was, however, no cultus of the reserved sacrament during the patristic period. In the later Middle Ages, however, there was a dramatic increase in public and private devotion to the Blessed Sacrament outside the time of mass. This was an extension of the practice of the adoration of Christ in the sacrament at the time of the elevation of the host in the mass itself. The institution of the feast of *Corpus Christi* in 1264 gave a new impetus to this kind of devotion. Processions of the Blessed Sacrament through the streets, the custom of exposing the host on the altar for adoration in a transparent vessel called a monstrance, and Benediction of the Blessed Sacrament gained increasing popularity from the latter part of the thirteenth century onward.[45]

A further change in eucharistic piety is related to the sacrificial character of the mass rather than to the real presence. While the theologians of the late Middle Ages continued to teach that the mass is not a new sacrifice, but is called a sacrifice because in it the memorial of Christ's passion is made by means of the sacramental signs of bread and wine, late medieval eucharistic practice moved in a direction that tended to give the mass the value of a sacrifice independent of the sacrifice of Christ on the cross. In the ninth century, Amalarius of Metz had given an allegorical interpretation of the ceremonies of the mass, which had turned the mass into a dramatic passion play. This kind of interpretation was continued by the twelfth-century commentators on the mass and fostered the development of a medieval passion mysticism.[46] In the popular imagination, the mass was seen as a new Calvary, and in practice if not in theory, the mass came to be seen as a sacrifice somehow added to the cross. This also became linked in the later Middle Ages with a theology of the "fruits" of the mass. This is related to a kind of quantitative thinking that attributes a limited "worth" to each mass.[47] In this case, two masses are better than one. This led to a dramatic increase in the number of masses celebrated and "private" masses were offered for all kinds of individual needs.[48] The custom grew of endowing chantries or chapels and providing priests with stipends to offer "votive" masses (i.e., masses for particular intentions or needs) for both the living and the dead.

"There were votive Masses of the twenty-four patriarchs or elders; of the fourteen, fifteen, and more 'holy helpers'; of the seven joys and sorrows of Mary; votive Masses against sicknesses, including one against pestilence, one of Holy Job against syphilis, one of St. Christopher against sudden death, one each of Saint Roch and Saint Sebastian against pestilence, one of Saint Sigismund against fever; votive Masses for special requests: in honor of the Archangel Raphael or of the Three Magi for a safe journey; a Mass to keep away thieves and to recover stolen property, a Mass before a duel or ordeal, one against Hussites and Turks and against witches; the seven-day, thirteen-day, or thirty-day Masses of emergency, which had to be offered by one priest for seven, thirteen, or thirty days respectively, at the end of which interval guaranteed liberation from sickness and distress was expected, and in addition the three Masses of Saint Nicholas for needs."[49]

Rightly or wrongly, the reformers saw the root of these practices in the doctrine of the sacrifice of the mass itself, which they interpreted as a new "sin-offering" (propitiatory sacrifice) offered on behalf of the living and the dead independently of Christ's sacrifice on the cross. This they regarded as blasphemous and idolatrous, because it underminded the all-sufficiency of Christ's sacrifice on the cross as the full atonement for human sin. Luther, therefore, regarded the sacrifice of the mass as the evil that lay at the root of medieval religious piety; it was a "good work" by which people sought to justify themselves before God. The reformers, therefore, ended up opposing the ideas of "sacrifice" and "memorial" rather than understanding the eucharist as a sacrifice precisely because it is the *anamnesis* of Christ's sacrifice on the cross.

While the medieval theologians themselves rejected the idea that the eucharist is a sacrifice in its own right independent of the sacrifice of Christ on the cross, nevertheless, in the context of medieval eucharistic praxis, the mass functioned practically as an independent sacrifice. Only in the context of a different liturgical praxis and with the recovery of the biblical concept of *anamnesis* by both Catholics and Protestants does a reassessment of sacrificial language and theological consensus on the eucharist become possible. This has awaited both the liturgical and the ecumenical movements of our own time.[50]

NOTES

1. For these developments, see especially Joseph R. Geiselmann, *Die Abendmahlslehre an der Wende der christlichen Spätantike zum Frühmittelalter. Isidor von Seville und das Sakrament der Eucharistie* (Munich: M. Hueber, 1933); idem, *Die Eucharistielehre der Vorscholastik* (Paderborn, 1926); Jaroslav Pelikan, *The Growth of Medieval Theology (600–1300)*, vol. 3 of *The Christian Tradition: A History of the Development of Doctrine* (Chicago: University of Chicago Press, 1978), 74–80, 184–204; Kilian McDonnell, *John Calvin, the Church, and the Eucharist* (Princeton, NJ: Princeton University Press, 1967), 46–55.

2. Henri de Lubac, *Corpus Mysticum: L'Eucharistie et l'Eglise au Moyen Age*, 2d rev. ed. (Paris: Aubier, 1949).

3. Nathan Mitchell, *Cult and Controversy: The Worship of the Eucharist Outside Mass* (New York: Pueblo, 1982), especially Chaps. 2 and 3.

4. Radbertus, *On the Body and Blood of the Lord* 1.2.

5. *Ibid.*, 4.2.

6. Ratramnus, *On the Body and Blood of the Lord* 101.

7. See J. N. Bakhuizen van den Brink, "Ratramn's Eucharistic Doctrine and its Influence in Sixteenth-Century England," in Geoffrey J. Cuming (ed.), *Studies in Church History*, vol. 2 (London: Thomas Nelson & Sons, 1965), 54–77.

8. For the historical context of the dispute, see Margaret Gibson, *Lanfranc of Bec* (Oxford: Clarendon Press, 1978), Chap. 4. For a theological analysis, see Jean de Montclos, *Lanfranc et Bérengar; La Controverse eucharistique du XIe siècle*, Spicilegium sacrum Lovaniense. Etudes et documents, 37 (Louvain, 1971).

9. Denzinger-Schonmetzer, *Enchiridion Symbolorum* 690.

10. Lanfranc, *On the Body and Blood of the Lord* 18.

11. Richard W. Southern, "Lanfranc of Bec and Berengar of Tours," in R. W. Hunt *et al.* (eds.), *Studies in Medieval History presented to Frederick Maurice Powicke* (Oxford: Clarendon Press, 1948), 34.

12. See Margaret Gibson (ed.), *Boethius: His Life, Thought and Influence* (Oxford: Blackwell, 1981).

13. Southern, 28ff.

14. For twelfth-century developments, see Gary Macy, *The Theologies of the Eucharist in the Early Scholastic Period* (Oxford: Clarendon Press, 1984). Macy shows that eucharistic theology during this period is by no means monolithic but manifests considerable variety.

15. For St. Thomas' liturgical compositions, see W. D. Loring, "Altar and Throne: A Study of Eucharistic Theology and the Vision of God in St. Thomas Aquinas," *Anglican Theological Review*, 52 (1970): 97–102.

16. *Summa Theologiae* 3a. 60,2.

17. See J. M. R. Tillard, "La triple dimension du signe sacramentel," *Nouvelle Revue Théologique*, 83 (1961): 225–254.

18. *Summa Theologiae* 3a. 60,3.

19. The Latin text of the propers for *Corpus Christi* may be found in Thomas Aquinas, *Opera Omnia*, repr. Parma ed., 25 vols. (New York: Musurgia, 1950), 15: 233–238. The antiphon referred to is on p. 236.

20. *Summa Theologiae* 3a. 73,2.

21. *Ibid.*, 3a. 60,3.

22. *Ibid.*, 3a. 73,1. Cf. also 73,3.

23. *Ibid.*, 3a. 73,4.

24. Thomas Aquinas, *Opera Omnia* 15:238.

25. *Summa Theologiae* 3a. 75,1 ad 4.

26. *Ibid.*, 3a. 73,1.

27. *Ibid.*, 3a. 73,2.

28. *De Rationibus Fidei* 8. *Opera Omnia* 16:93. Translation in Thomas Gilby (ed.), *St. Thomas Aquinas: Theological Texts* (London: Oxford University Press, 1955), 620.

29. English version from *The Hymnal of the Protestant Episcopal Church in*

the United States of America (New York: Church Pension Fund, 1940), Hymn 204.

30. See Kilmartin, "Sacraments . . . Perspectives and Principles," 61–62, 71–73.

31. *De Veritate* 27, 4. *Opera Omnia* 9:420–421. Gilby, 596.

32. *Summa Theologiae* 3a. 62,5.

33. For the history of the doctrine of transubstantiation, see James F. McCue, "The Doctrine of Transubstantiation from Berengar through Trent: The Point at Issue," *Harvard Theological Review*, 61 (1968): 385–430; Hans Jorissen, *Die Entfaltung der Transubstantiationslehre bis zum Beginn der Hochscholastik* (Münster: Aschendorff, 1965).

34. *Summa Theologiae* 3a. 75,2.

35. *Ibid.*, 3a. 75,1 ad 3.

36. *Ibid.*, 3a. 73,4.

37. *Ibid.*, 3a. 73,5.

38. *Ibid.*, 3a. 73,5 ad 3.

39. Thomas Aquinas, *Opera Omnia* 15:233, 237.

40. *Summa Theologiae* 3a. 83,1.

41. *Ibid.*, 3a. 60,1.

42. *Homilies on Hebrews* 17.6.

43. See Dix, 589–598.

44. Justin, *1 Apology* 65.

45. For these developments, see Mitchell, 163–186.

46. See Mitchell, 49–62; Jungmann, 1:115–117.

47. See Edward J. Kilmartin, "The Sacrifice of Thanksgiving and Social Justice," in Mark Searle (ed.), *Liturgy and Social Justice* (Collegeville, MN: The Liturgical Press, 1980), 63–64; *idem*, "The One Fruit and the Many Fruits of the Mass," *Catholic Theological Society of America* (*Proceedings*), 21 (1966): 43–50.

48. See Hubert Jedin (ed.), *Handbook of Church History*, 10 vols. (New York: Herder & Herder, 1965–1981), vol. 4 (1970), 572–574.

49. Jedin, 574.

50. See Chapter Seven.

CHAPTER FOUR

Luther and Zwingli

Luther's understanding of the Lord's Supper is a reflection of his understanding of the gospel. This explains both the positive and the negative elements in his eucharistic teaching. On the one hand, we find in Luther's writings a vigorous polemic against the medieval understanding of the mass. On the other hand, we find a positive eucharistic doctrine that represents the working out in the sphere of the sacraments of the fundamental principles of the Reformation: the sole sufficiency of grace, the primacy of the Word of God, and justification by faith.

Luther's early eucharistic thought has a strong Augustinian flavor. There is an emphasis on the sacramental signs and on the relationship between the sacramental signs and the Word of God and faith. The ecclesial interpretation of the eucharist, which we have found in both Paul and Augustine, is strongly emphasized at this stage of Luther's thought. All of this is clearly evident in his earliest treatise on the eucharist, *The Blessed Sacrament of the Holy and True Body of Christ, and the Brotherhoods* (1519). His writing at this stage is pastoral rather than polemical, and still moves within the broad sphere of Catholic tradition. He follows Augustine's definition of a sacrament. A sacrament is an outward sign that has an inward significance. He adds, however, a third part to the definition of a sacrament, namely, faith. It is faith that "must make both of them together [i.e., the *sacramentum* and the *res*] operative and useful."[1] The *res* or inward significance of the sacrament is, as it was for Augustine, the unity of the church:

"The *significance* or effect of this sacrament is fellowship of all the saints. From this it derives its common name *synaxis* [Greek] or *communio* [Latin], that is fellowship."[2]

". . . this sacrament [of the Body of Christ] . . . signifies the complete union and the undivided fellowship of the saints. . . ."[3]

Luther develops the ecclesial interpretation of the sacrament under the figure of a city and its citizens in a wonderful passage that is clearly reminiscent of Augustine:

". . . Christ and all saints are one spiritual body, just as the inhabitants of a city are one community and body, each citizen being a member of the other and of the entire city. . . .

"This fellowship consists in this, that all the spiritual possessions of Christ and his saints are shared with and become the common property of him who receives this sacrament . . . all sufferings and sins also become common property; and thus love engenders love in return and [mutual love] unites. . . .[4]

"When you have partaken of this sacrament, therefore, or desire to partake of it . . . your heart must go out in love and learn that this is a sacrament of love. As love and support are given you, you in turn must render love and support to Christ in his needy ones. . . .[5]

". . . in times past this sacrament was so properly used, and the people were taught to understand this fellowship so well, that they even gathered food and material goods in the church, and there—as St. Paul writes in 1 Corinthians 11—distributed among those who were in need. . . . Christians cared for one another, supported one another, sympathized with one another, bore one another's burdens and affliction. This has all disappeared, and now there remains only the many masses and the many who receive this sacrament without in the least understanding or practicing what it signifies.

". . . They will not help the poor, put up with sinners, care for the sorrowing, suffer with the suffering . . . risk . . . [their own] life. . . .[6]

"To signify this fellowship, God has appointed such signs of this sacrament as in every way serve this purpose and by their very form stimulate and motivate us to this fellowship. For just as the bread is made out of many grains ground and mixed together, and out of the bodies of many grains there comes the body of one bread, in which each grain loses its form and body and takes upon itself the common body of the bread; and just as the drops of wine, in losing their own form, become the body of one common wine and drink—so it is and should be with us, if we use this sacrament properly. Christ with all saints, by his love, takes upon himself our form [Phil 2:7], fights with us against sin, death, and all evil. This enkindles in us such love that we take on his form, rely upon his righteousness, life, and blessedness. And through the interchange of his blessings and our misfortunes, we become one loaf, one bread, one body, one drink, and have all things in common. O this is a great sacrament, says St. Paul, that Christ and the church are one flesh and bone. Again, through this same love, we are to be changed and to make the infirmities of all other Christians our own; we are to take upon ourselves their form and their necessity, and all the good that is within our power we are to make theirs, that they may profit from it. That is real fellowship, and that is the true significance of this sacrament. In this way we are changed into one another and are made into a community by love."[7]

While this passage is full of promise for a social interpretation of the eucharist in the emphasis that it places on the love and support that are to be rendered to Christ in his needy ones by those who partake of the sacrament, Luther does not develop this line of thought in his later writings. Under the pressure of controversy, he gave primary emphasis to the real presence of Christ in the sacrament.

In the early part of 1520, Luther begins to lay the foundations for a distinctively Reformation theology of the sacraments that centers around the key conceptions of Gospel, Word, Promise, Testament, Sign, and Faith. This is developed in his *A Treatise on the New Testament, that is, the Holy Mass*. The words of institution now come to the center of the stage in Luther's thought and remain central in all of his subsequent writings. It is the words of institution that primarily interpret the meaning of the Supper for Luther from now on. In this treatise, Luther also launches his first attack on the sacrifice of the mass. At the same time, he allows an understanding of the eucharist as a sacrifice in a manner that is reminiscent of Augustine's conception of the eucharist as the offering of the members of the body in union with Christ their Head, although all of this is expressed in a Reformation key. Nevertheless, the controlling thought for Luther from now on is that the mass is the very opposite of a sacrifice, i.e., something offered to God. It is rather a gift that is received from God. This is entirely in line with the primacy of grace and justification by faith, which are the central tenets of his theology. The sacraments are grounded in the divine initiative of grace, not in human works:

"If a man is to deal with God,"

says Luther,

"and receive anything from him, it must happen in this manner, not that man begins and lays the first stone, but that God alone—without any entreaty or desire of man—must first come and give him a promise. This word of God is the beginning, the foundation, the work, upon which afterward all works, words and thoughts of man must build. This word man must gratefully accept. . . . This trust and faith is the beginning, middle, and end of all works and righteousness."[8]

The Word of God, then, comes to us first of all as a promise. This promise comes to us in the form of a testament that Christ left us before his death. This testament is the Lord's Supper, the meaning of which is contained in the words of institution that sum up the whole gospel:

"What is the whole gospel but an explanation of this testament? Christ has gathered up the whole gospel in a short summary with the words of this testament or sacrament. For the gospel is nothing but a proclamation of God's grace and of the forgiveness of sins, granted us through the sufferings of Christ, as St. Paul proves in Romans 10 and as Christ says in Luke 24 [:46–47]. And this same thing, as we have seen, is contained in the words of this testament."[9]

The great treasure that is bequeathed to us in this sacrament, the forgiveness of sins, can only be received by faith:

131

"But who will love Christ unless he tastes the riches of this testament of Christ, bequeathed to poor sinners out of pure mercy and without cost? This taste comes by the faith which believes and trusts the testament and promise. If Abraham had not believed the promise of God, he would never have amounted to anything. Just as certainly, then, as Abraham, Noah, and David accepted and believed God's promises to them, so certainly must we also accept and believe this testament and promise."[10]

It is important, however, to place this text alongside the previous one. Luther is by no means suggesting here that the reality of the sacrament is created by the faith of the believer. On the contrary, Luther is insistent on the divine initiative of grace in the sacraments. The reality of the sacrament is dependent on the Word and the promise of God, but the grace of the sacrament cannot be received without faith.

The importance, for Luther, of establishing the foundation of the sacraments on the word of promise, the testament, and faith is that without this foundation, the mass becomes the opposite of what Christ instituted it to be. When the mass ceases to be a testament responded to in faith, it becomes a work. This is the heart of Luther's attack on the sacrifice of the mass that he first makes in this treatise and hammers home in *The Babylonian Captivity of the Church*. The mass is not a good work that we offer to God; it is a gift that we receive from God.

Luther does not altogether reject the idea of sacrifice in the mass, provided it is understood rightly. He allows that in the mass, we offer ourselves and we offer a sacrifice of praise and thanksgiving, but these can only be offered rightly if they are offered in union with Christ:

". . . we do not offer Christ as a sacrifice, but . . . Christ offers us. And in this way it is permissible, yes, profitable, to call the mass a sacrifice; not on its own account, but because we offer ourselves as a sacrifice along with Christ. That is, we lay ourselves on Christ by a firm faith in his testament and do not otherwise appear before God with our prayer, praise, and sacrifice except through Christ and his mediation."[11]

He can even go so far as to say that we offer Christ in the mass in the highly qualified sense that through faith we believe that Christ accepts us and our prayer and praise and presents them to God:

"Through [faith], we offer ourselves, our need, prayer, praise, and thanksgiving in Christ and through Christ; and thereby we offer Christ to God, that is, we move Christ and give him occasion to offer himself for us and to offer us with himself."[12]

With the publication of *The Babylonian Captivity of the Church* (1520), Luther launches a frontal attack on the medieval mass. Although this work is of great importance for the progress of the Reformation, it marks no further advance in Luther's thought except in one very important respect, namely, the position that he now takes concerning the real presence of Christ in the elements. His fundamental conception of the sacrament and his position on the sacrifice of the mass are the same as those that he developed in *A Treatise on the New Testament, that is, the Holy Mass*. With regard to the real presence of Christ in the sacrament, Luther says that he went through a period of intense doubt before espousing the position he now holds. He now puts forward a belief in the real presence of Christ in the elements of bread and wine. From now on, this becomes the hallmark of Luther's eucharistic teaching, which he will later defend vigorously against the spiritualistic and symbolical positions of Carlstadt and the Swiss reformers.

Luther bases his belief in the real presence of Christ in the elements on the words of institution at the Last Supper. Christ said, "This is my body," and Luther accepts this in its straightforward grammatical sense. In his writings from now on, this is his constant point of departure and the point to which he returns again and again in his arguments with Zwingli. What is involved here is Luther's fundamental understanding of religious authority. The fundamental issue at stake is the authority of scripture and the kind of hermeneutic employed in its interpretation. For Luther, scripture is the ultimate authority for Christian faith. Only that which is based on the authority of scripture can be made an article of faith:

"For what is asserted without the Scriptures or proven revelation may be held as an opinion, but need not be believed."[13]

Moreover, the words of scripture

". . . are to be retained in their simplest meaning as far as possible. Unless the context manifestly compels it, they are not to be understood apart from their grammatical and proper sense. . . ."[14]

The words of institution are to be taken in their grammatical sense, and no arguments put forward by the Swiss could budge Luther from that position.

Because of the position that he takes up on the authority of scripture, Luther will not allow reason or philosophy to determine the content of Christian faith. It is on this basis that he rejects the doctrine of transubstantiation while retaining the doctrine of the real presence of Christ in the elements. Since the doctrine of transubstantiation is a philosophical explanation of the real presence it cannot be made an article of faith. It is often asserted that Luther held the doctrine of "consubstantiation." While it is true that Luther's view, expressed in philosophical terms, comes closest to the view known as "consubstantiation," neither Luther himself nor the Lutheran confessions teach a doctrine of consubstantiation. To replace transubstantiation by consubstantiation would be to substitute one philosophical explanation of the real presence for another. Luther's point is that no philosophical explanation can be made an article of faith. Neither transubstantiation nor consubstantiation are found in scripture. The real presence is; therefore, the real presence must be confessed, but its philosophical expression can be left as an open question:

"For my part, if I cannot fathom how the bread is the body of Christ, yet will I take my reason captive to the obedience of Christ [2 Cor 10:5], and clinging simply to his words, firmly believe not only that the body of Christ is in the bread, but that the bread is the body of Christ. My warrant for this is the words which say: 'He took bread, and when he had given thanks, he broke it and said, "Take, eat, this (that is, this bread, which he had taken and broken) is my body." ' "[15]

For Luther, to deny the real presence of Christ in the sacrament is to deny the gospel itself, for the whole gospel is summed up in these words of Jesus at the Last Supper. These are

". . . words of life and of salvation, so that whoever believes in them has all his sins forgiven through that faith; he is a child of life and has overcome death and hell. Language cannot express how great and mighty these words are, for they are the sum and substance of the whole gospel."[16]

Luther's defense of the real presence of Christ in the Supper, therefore, was a defense of the gospel itself. To confess the real presence is to confess that the gift given in the supper is Jesus Christ himself in all his saving power.

With the publication of *The Babylonian Captivity of the Church*, the main outlines of Luther's position concerning the sacrament had been worked out vis-à-vis Rome. His writings from 1520–1526 do not mark any essential advance in his views. In 1526, however, we enter a new phase in Luther's thinking, for he is now forced to defend his position against the Zurich reformer Huldrych Zwingli.[17]

W. P. Stephens has recently put Zwingli's sacramental thought in clearer historical perspective in his book *The Theology of Huldrych Zwingli*.[18] Stephens clarifies the underlying theological presuppositions of Zwingli's thought and shows how the distinctive emphases of his eucharistic theology reflect these presuppositions. At the heart of Zwingli's theology and piety is his unshakeable conviction that Christ alone is the cause of our salvation. In this, he does not differ from Luther, but from the same presupposition Luther and Zwingli draw different conclusions. For Luther, this means that Christ must be really present in the sacrament. For Zwingli, it means that faith must cleave to Christ alone and not to outward things. This leads Zwingli to make a sharp distinction between the sacramental signs and the reality signified by them. This distinction is strengthened by Zwingli's conviction concerning the freedom of God in relation to all created things. God may choose to use created realities, such as the sacraments, but God does not need to use them and is by no means bound by them. The role of the Spirit is also central here for Zwingli. The sacraments do not cause or convey grace. It is from Christ through the Spirit alone that we receive grace and faith. In all of this, Zwingli is attempting to safeguard the fundamental Reformation principle that salvation is by grace alone, by faith alone, and that grace is the free gift of God through Jesus Christ in the power of the Holy Spirit. Faith must place its whole trust in God, not in the sacraments.

These convictions are reinforced by Zwingli's exegesis of John 6, which determines his interpretation of the eucharist, and by his Platonism, which is mediated primarily through Augustine. His Platonism leads him to see a sharp distinction between the sacramental signs and the reality signified by them rather than to stress the participation of the signs in the reality signified. His exegesis of John 6 also leads him to make a sharp distinction between Spirit and flesh. "Eating Christ" in John 6 means believing in him. It is the flesh of Christ as slain for us, and not as eaten by us, that is food for the soul. The key text, for Zwingli, is John 6:63, "It is the spirit that gives life, the flesh is of no avail; the words that I have spoken to you are spirit and life." This means that Christ is neither present in a bodily manner in the eucharist nor eaten in a bodily way. Christ is present in the eucharist only through the Spirit and only eaten spiritually by faith. What then is the role of the sacraments? The sacraments testify to our faith, unite us in the community of the body of Christ, and are acts of thanksgiving and remembrance for the saving death of Christ.

While Zwingli's spiritualistic and symbolical interpretation of the eucharist can already be found in his earlier writings, it is only after his reception of a letter from the Dutch humanist Cornelis Hoen in 1524 that he interprets the words of institution, "This is my body," to mean "This signifies my body." Hoen's basis for this exegesis is a spiritualistic interpretation of John 6. To eat Christ's body and to drink his blood means to eat and drink Christ by faith. Moreover, according to Hoen, Paul in 1 Corinthians 10:16 does not call the bread the body of Christ, but communion in Christ's body. Hoen also regards the sacraments as signs or tokens of the promise of God rather than as means of grace. According to Hoen, the eucharist is a visible pledge added by

Christ to the promise of the gospel. It is like a wedding ring given as a token of love and as a reminder of the promises given. Zwingli also employs this analogy in his interpretation of the sacraments.[19]

Zwingli dislikes the word "sacrament" and wishes that it had never become a part of the theological vocabulary of the Church. To his mind, the word lends a numinous quality to the elements that they do not possess. From an exegetical point of view, he believes that the spiritualistic interpretation of the Supper as a feeding on Christ by faith is the authentic biblical understanding, which later became overladen with a sacramental interpretation from which it ought now to be detached. From an historical point of view, Zwingli argues that the word *sacramentum* derives from secular history. In antiquity, the *sacramentum* was the token laid upon the altar by men going into battle. Those who were victorious returned to reclaim their tokens. The word also had the meaning of an oath. The *sacramentum* was not regarded as something holy or sacred in itself in pre-Christian usage. The term *sacramentum* took on a sacred quality when it came to be used in theological writings as a translation of the Greek word *mysterion*, which has a completely different background.

Zwingli is prepared to adopt the term sacrament in its ancient secular meaning as a pledge or oath. To receive it is to enlist in Christ's forces and to receive a token or reminder of the victory won by Christ through his saving death on the cross. The inner reality of the eucharist, however, is the transaction of faith between Christ and believers. The sacrament is a visible token of this transaction in the context of the community of faith, the Church. The bread and wine are symbols. They have no sacramental character in the sense in which that term was used in the patristic and medieval Church. They are not, however, empty symbols. They are symbols of the body and blood of Christ. They point to Christ, who alone brings salvation. They function, however, in a representative rather than in a realistic manner. The Platonic dialectic between the sign and the reality signified is broken. The real symbol becomes the representative symbol. Historically, therefore, Zwingli represents the point at which the symbolical and spiritualistic traditions in eucharistic thought threaten to become antirealist and even antisacramental. This does not mean that for Zwingli the eucharist is unimportant. It means that the tension is now broken between two strains in the eucharistic tradition, which up to this point had belonged together. It was in this way that the Zurich reformer sought to safeguard the Reformation principle of justification by faith alone. No visible sign can bring salvation. Only Christ brings salvation. Is Christ's flesh of no avail, then, asks Zwingli? "I answer," he says, "that Christ's flesh avails a great deal. It avails through his death, not through our eating."[20] It is faith, and faith alone that embraces salvation.

In Zwingli's eucharistic thought, the themes of "thanksgiving" and "memorial" come into the foreground in stark contrast to the idea of the mass as a sacrifice. For Zwingli, the eucharist is a joyful thanksgiving meal celebrated as a memorial of Christ's saving death on the cross. G. Locher thinks that the idea of "memorial" here means more than a mere mental recollection of the death of Christ. According to Locher, Zwingli derived it from the passover tradition. The model Zwingli had in mind is that of the passover as a public feast of remembrance and thanksgiving for past deliverance and the covenant relationship, and he interprets the *anamnesis* formula in the New Testament institution accounts against this background. This is refracted, however, through Platonic–Augustinian categories:

"*Memoria*, as understood by Augustine (like *anamnesis* in Plato) describes the soul's power of realization and of consciousness in general; it often means the same as *conscientia*. According to this tradition, remembrance does not denote our ability to set ourselves back into the immediate or the remote past, but the way in which the past is brought into our present time, becoming contemporary with us and effective in us. Zwingli thinks in the categories of this Platonist–Augustinian anthropology; though for him the power to 'render present' the death of Christ as our salvation does not lie within our soul, but in the Holy Spirit, on the basis of the eternal efficacy of the Lord's sacrifice; the organ by which it is received is faith, or rather the conscious contemplation of faith."[21]

The eucharistic *anamnesis*, therefore, is not simply a mental recollection of the past, but the effective realization by faith in the souls of believers of the presence of Christ and the power of his atoning death, through the power of the Holy Spirit.

One of the most significant results of Zwingli research is a new appreciation of the ecclesial dimension of Zwingli's eucharistic theology. A proper appreciation of Zwingli's eucharistic thought requires that we place in juxtaposition to each other his exegesis of John 6 and his exegesis of 1 Corinthians 10:16–17. Whereas his exegesis of the former led him to a purely symbolical understanding of the relation between the body and blood of Christ and the elements and to a spiritualistic understanding of the acts of eating and drinking that take place in the eucharist, his exegesis of the latter led him to a realism with respect to the Church that he denied with respect to the elements. The body of Christ that is eaten spiritually by faith transforms the community that receives it into the body of Christ, the Church. The body of Christ is not in the bread, but in the Church. The importance, indeed the necessity of the eucharist, for Zwingli, lies not in the sacramental eating and drinking of the body of Christ, but in the formation of the community of believers into the body of Christ:

". . . they who here eat and drink are one body, one bread; that is, all those who come together to proclaim Christ's death and eat the symbolical bread, declare themselves to be Christ's body, that is, members of his church; and as this church holds one faith and eats one symbolical bread, so it is one bread and one body."[22]

The ecclesial dimension of the eucharist is essential for Zwingli. The celebration of the memorial of the Lord's death in thanksgiving for the salvation won for us is an act of community. To participate by faith in the salvation that Christ alone brings is to be formed into a community that together confesses his name.

"Paul seems to say clearly [in 1 Cor 10:17] . . . that those who eat this bread and drink this cup unite in one body with the rest of the community, which indeed is the body of Christ, because the body of Christ is the community of those who believe that Christ's flesh was slain and his blood shed for them."[23]

If we are saved by Christ alone and by faith alone, we are not saved alone, but as members of Christ's body. The bread and wine of the eucharist, which are the symbols of Christ's body and blood, are the tokens of our common faith in Christ and of our salvation through his death.

The ecclesial aspect of Zwingli's eucharistic thought reflects a wider social dimension in his thought. To worship God "in spirit and in truth," which was Zwingli's watchword, implies the transformation of social and political life. The true service of God is not the liturgy as such, but the service of the neighbor.

"Where the Spirit of God is, there one knows well . . . that the highest service of God in the faith is to do good to one's neighbor. Wherever one trusts in God, there is God. Where God is, there is also careful diligence in all that is good. . . . Here I could, indeed, speak of men, whose names I prefer not to mention, who are progressing excellently—eternal praise and thanks to God!—in love to God, in peace with their neighbor, in the knowledge of the Gospel, in simplicity of life, in godly wisdom, in giving alms and help to the poor, in humbling their pride, in forgiving their enemies, in concern for the teaching of Christ, in concern for the prisoners of Christ and in concern for the whole of Christ's people. And though kindling lights, burning incense, making offerings (for the rich priests, I say), babbling prayers, vigils, wailing chants, the sound of masses, dazzling temples, the hoods of the theologians, the colorful robes of the monks and the well-cut coats of the parsons . . . are not to their liking, they do take pleasure in everything that is pleasing to God. They reduce the rents of their tenants, they pay the laborer more than he dares to demand, they invite the poor and wretched into their homes, they do not indulge in gaming, cursing, buffoonery and all the vanity of the age, and they strive to prepare themselves for eternal life."[24]

The issues between Luther and Zwingli concerning the real presence come out in Luther's later writings from 1526 on,[25] and from Luther's point of view, they come down to two essential points: the relation between reason and revelation, and Christology. In these writings, Luther lumps Zwingli in with Carlstadt (the German anti-Lutheran reformer) and Oecolampadius (the Swiss reformer from Basel) and calls them all "fanatics." For Luther, the Swiss attempt to "measure God's will and work by human reason."[26] They reject the real presence of Christ in the elements because they find it unreasonable. For Luther, this is to exalt reason over scripture and to destroy the mystery of Christian faith. If reason is the measuring rod, then the incarnation, the cross, the mystery of creation itself, and the presence of Christ in the human heart by faith would not be worthy of belief, because they far transcend the limits of human reason. For Luther, God does not have to justify his ways before the bar of human reason. On the contrary, faith must cleave to the clear words of Christ, and these words proclaim the real presence. To Luther, the Swiss are essentially rationalists. They cannot conceive how Christ can be present in the sacrament; therefore, they interpret scripture to suit their own preconceptions. For Luther, on the other hand, faith means obedience to the Word of God. The crucial text here, for Luther, is 1 Corinthians 1:18 ff., where Paul contrasts human wisdom with the wisdom of God. Luther is speaking from the standpoint of a theology of the cross. Human wisdom is not the arbiter of God's works, but the wisdom of God that is disclosed in the cross of Christ, while foolishness to the world, is the power of God and the wisdom of God to those who believe.

Not only do Luther and Zwingli operate from different positions on the relation between revelation and reason,[27] they also operate with different Christologies.[28] In the classical Christology of the early Church, Christ is understood to have two natures, a divine nature and a human nature, united in one person. The Alexandrian theologians emphasized the unity of the person of Christ, whereas the Antiochene theologians emphasized the distinction between the natures.[29] This same difference in emphasis is evident in the Reformation controversies over the Lord's Supper. Luther holds to the Alexandrian Christology, which stresses the unity of the person of Christ, whereas Zwingli emphasizes the distinction of natures. The Alexandrian theologians held that the attributes of each nature are communicated to the other nature because of the unity of the person of Christ. Luther takes up this position and develops it in his own way. What it means for Luther in relation to the doctrine of the real presence is that the attribute of "omnipresence" or "ubiquity" (i.e., the capacity to be in many places [*ubique* = everywhere] at once) that belongs to the divine nature of Christ is communicated to the human nature of Christ. This means that the human nature of Christ is not confined to a physical space "at the right hand of God," but can dwell in many hearts and can be present in many places in the sacrament of the altar. Zwingli, and the Swiss theologians generally, held that since Christ is ascended into heaven, his human nature is in heaven and cannot also be present in the sacrament. The body of Christ remains in heaven, and cannot, therefore, also be in the bread. This presupposes a Christology in which the divine attribute of ubiquity is not communicated to the human nature because of the distinction of the natures in Christ. Different philosophical presuppositions also lie behind these positions. Zwingli is working with the Aristotelian notion that a body is by definition that which occupies a place. Since the human nature of Christ is in heaven, it cannot also be in the bread. Against this, Luther brought the Occamist view that the power of God is not limited by the constraints of nature, and that a body can be present in different modes.[30]

The differences between Luther and Zwingli, however, are at bottom theological not philosophical. These fundamental theological visions are supported and nourished by different Christologies, by different understandings of the relationship between revelation and reason, and by different philosophical presuppositions. The whole cast of Zwingli's thought is spiritualistic, emphasizing the distinction between the creature and the Creator. Zwingli's theological vision is supported exegetically by his interpretation of John 6:63, "It is the spirit that gives life, the flesh is of no avail," and by his Platonic humanism that leads him to see an absolute distinction between the spiritual and heavenly world of the divine and the visible world of the senses, and an absolute distinction between body and soul in his doctrine of human nature. In the sphere of the sacraments, this leads him to place an absolute distinction between the sign and the reality signified, between the symbol and the reality. For Zwingli, faith can have no earthly thing for its object. To trust in the sacraments is idolatry. Zwingli's protest against Luther's sacramental realism stems both from his Christology and from this dualism between flesh and spirit. Zwingli feared that Luther's sacramental realism threatened the sole sufficiency of Christ's death. It tempted faith to cling to what is visible rather than to Christ. For Zwingli, however, the controversy is not about whether Christ is present in the Supper, but how he is present. He agrees with Luther that Christ is present in the Supper, but present in the souls of the believers by faith, not in the elements.

On the other hand, the whole cast of Luther's thought is incarnational, emphasizing the entrance of God into human history. In the incarnation, God has taken our nature and in the eucharist feeds our whole bodily–spiritual nature with the body of Christ. Luther does not draw the Johannine distinction between "spirit" and "flesh" or the Platonic distinction between the heavenly and the earthly, the divine and the human, body and soul, matter and spirit, but the Pauline distinction between "spirit" and "flesh." Spirit is not opposed to the bodily and the earthly, but the realm of "spirit" is the sphere of God's activity in Christ through the power of the Spirit. "Flesh" does not mean the bodily and the earthly, but human life under the dominion of sin and death. For Luther, therefore, the incarnation is the paradigm for the sacraments. Luther's Christological realism led him in the sphere of the sacraments to a corresponding sacramental realism. God uses earthly means by which to come to us. Faith does not trust in the sacraments themselves, but in the Word of God, which declares that through this means, Christ gives himself to us. The sacraments, therefore, are means of grace, because by means of the sacrament, we partake of Jesus Christ himself. Luther attempted to support his sacramental realism by the theory of ubiquity, but the heart of the matter does not lie there. The real presence is not a metaphysical affirmation, but a religious affirmation grounded in the words of institution, that Christ has bound himself to these earthly means. The real presence of Christ in the sacrament is not a materialistic presence or a metaphysical presence, but the presence in grace of the saving word of God. It is the presence of the God–man Jesus Christ in all his saving power.

In their reforms of the liturgy for the mass, both Zwingli and Luther attacked the canon of the mass. Zwingli attacks the canon because it teaches that the mass is a sacrifice, whereas for him it is not a sacrifice, but a memorial of Christ's sacrifice and a pledge of our redemption through Christ. In his first revision of the liturgy in 1523, Zwingli replaced the canon by four prayers of his own composition,[31] but in 1525, these were dropped and replaced by the words of institution from the Last Supper alone.[32] Zwingli also decided that the eucharist should be celebrated four times a year, at Easter, Pentecost, once during the autumn, and at Christmas.

Luther undertook the reform of the liturgy in accordance with the doctrine of justification by faith and his eucharistic theology.[33] While keeping the basic structure of the old mass, at the heart of the liturgy, he replaced the Roman canon with the words of institution, which in his *Deutsche Messe* of 1526,[34] he instructed should be sung in the same tone that was used for singing the gospel in the liturgy of the Word.[35] Since the words of institution were for Luther a summary of the whole gospel, it was fitting that they should be proclaimed in the same manner as the gospel reading for the day. Luther's justification for replacing the canon of the mass with the words of institution alone was that the canon taught that the mass was a sacrifice, whereas, for Luther the mass is the very opposite of a sacrifice. It is a testament of what God offers to us, namely, the forgiveness of sins.

"As far as Luther was concerned, in emphasizing the words of institution he was replacing the canon with the gospel itself, and in the gospel it is God who does something for us [not we who offer something to God]. . . ."[36]

Luther interpreted the canon of the mass as an expression of what he understood to be the medieval doctrine of the sacrifice of the mass. He, therefore, rejected it outright as the antithesis of the Reformation principle of justification by faith. In our study of the history of the Eucharistic Prayer, we have seen that the text of the Roman canon of the mass attained its final form by the sixth century, long before the medieval developments that we traced in the last chapter. It, therefore, preserves a much older theology of eucharistic sacrifice than Luther supposed. As a result of Luther's abolition of the canon, the tradition of the Eucharistic Prayer was lost in the Lutheran tradition, and has only been recovered today in recent revisions of the Lutheran liturgy.[37]

NOTES

1. LW 35.49. References to Luther's works are to the American edition: Jaroslav Pelikan and Helmut T. Lehmann (eds.), *Luther's Works*, cited as LW by volume and page.

2. LW 35.50.

3. LW 35.50.

4. LW 35.51.

5. LW 35.54.

6. LW 35.57.

7. LW 35.58.

8. LW 35.82.

9. LW 35.106.

10. LW 35.89.

11. LW 35.99.

12. LW 35.102.

13. LW 36.29.

14. LW 36.30.

15. LW 36.34.

16. LW 36.277.

17. The classic study of the controversy between Luther and Zwingli is Walther Köhler, *Zwingli und Luther. Ihr Streit über das Abendmahl nach seinen politischen und religiösen Beziehungen*, 2 vols. (Leipzig, 1924; Gütersloh, 1953). See also Hermann Sasse, *This is My Body: Luther's Con-*

tention for the Real Presence in the Sacrament of the Altar, rev. ed. (Adelaide, South Australia: Lutheran Publishing House, 1977).

18. (Oxford: Clarendon Press, 1986), 180–193 (on the sacraments); 218–259 (on the eucharist).

19. The precise influence of Hoen's letter on Zwingli is difficult to determine (see Stephens, 227–228). Köhler had argued that Zwingli's symbolical view of the eucharist dates only from the reception of Hoen's letter and that before that time, Zwingli held a view of the sacrament similar to that of Erasmus. Stephens argues for continuity rather than discontinuity in Zwingli's view of the eucharist throughout the different stages of his development, with only differences in emphasis and expression in his early, middle, and later writings (Stephens, Additional Note 2, 256–257).

20. Z 3.782.26–32. References to Zwingli's works are to the modern critical edition: Emil Egli et al. (eds.), Huldreich Zwinglis Sämtliche Werke, cited as Z by volume, page, and line.

21. Gottfried W. Locher, Zwingli's Thought: New Perspectives (Leiden: E.J. Brill, 1981), 222–223.

22. Z 3.802.30–35.

23. Z 3.348.11–17.

24. Z 2.47.30ff., quoted by Locher, 4–5.

25. The two most important treatises are That These Words of Christ, "This Is My Body," etc., Still Stand Firm Against the Fanatics, 1527 (LW 37.4–150) and Confession Concerning Christ's Supper, 1528 (LW 37.151–372). The Marburg Colloquy (1529), the public debate between Luther and Zwingli, is a rerun of established positions and arguments. For a reconstruction of the debate (based on Köhler), see Sasse, 173–220.

26. LW 36.345.

27. Köhler held that Zwingli followed Thomas Aquinas on the relation between revelation and reason, but see Stephens, 6–7, on Zwingli's relation to scholasticism. Zwingli has often been portrayed as a rationalist, but this needs revision in the light of modern Zwingli research (see Locher, 59). For the philosophical presuppositions of Zwingli's eucharistic theology and his hermeneutics, see E. M. Henning, "The Architectonics of Faith: Metalogic and Metaphor in Zwingli's Doctrine of the Eucharist," Renaissance and Reformation, n.s., 10 (1986): 315–365.

28. See Stephens, 112–117.

29. See Jaroslav Pelikan, The Emergence of the Catholic Tradition (100–600),

vol. 1: *The Christian Tradition: A History of the Development of Doctrine* (Chicago: University of Chicago Press, 1971), Chap. 5.

30. "Luther's statement that "the right hand of God" does not denote a place, but rather omnipotence . . . [is] a piece of late scholastic philosophy, as Luther himself was well aware. . . . According to William of Occam, divine omnipotence can cause a substance (in this case, the body of Christ) to be so condensed as to be without dimensions, like a mathematical point; and it can at the same time confer upon it the possibility of ubiquity. This was the idea that was taken up by Luther" (Locher, 225, n. 366).

31. See *PEER*, 183–186.

32. *PEER*, 187–188.

33. See Bryan Spinks, *Luther's Liturgical Criteria and his Reform of the Canon of the Mass*, Grove Liturgical Studies, no. 30 (Bramcote, Notts.: Grove Books, 1982).

34. *PEER*, 197–199.

35. Spinks, *Luther's Liturgical Criteria*, 34.

36. *Ibid.*

37. See *Lutheran Book of Worship* (Minneapolis: Augsburg Publishing House, 1978), 68–70.

CHAPTER FIVE

Calvin

When we think of the Reformed tradition, we think of Calvin
and Calvinism, and, clearly, it is Calvin above all who shaped
the doctrine of the eucharist in the Reformed tradition.[1] Calvin is
a second-generation reformer. He came on the scene after the
first round of the Reformation contest over the eucharist was
over. Luther and Calvin never corresponded and Luther never
gained a full impression of Calvin's position. Calvin, for his part,
although he had a high personal regard for Luther and had read
at least his earlier eucharistic writings, differed from Luther in
his understanding of the relationship between the real presence
and the elements and developed his eucharistic teaching along
independent lines. On the other hand, Calvin tended to agree
with Luther's estimate of Zwingli, so that his eucharistic teaching evolved in contradistinction to both Luther's and Zwingli's
as well as in opposition to Rome.[2] Calvin's eucharistic thought,
like Zwingli's, has a strong spiritualistic strain, but it is also bal-
anced by a realist strain. Calvin is a theological giant and his
eucharistic thought derives from a number of sources. Through
his own theological genius, he forged these elements into a distinctive mold that placed an indelible stamp on the Reformed
tradition.

Calvin studied in Paris, where he came under the influence of
the Scotist and Occamist traditions in philosophy[3] and the *devotio
moderna*.[4] From the Scotist and Occamist schools, Calvin inher-
ited some of the more important presuppositions of his theological system. The central place that the sovereignty of God and the
absolute freedom of the divine will have in his theology and his
understanding of the relationship between revelation and reason
all reflect a Scotist–Occamist background. The *devotio moderna*

was a late form of the medieval mystical tradition. This tradition developed a deep eucharistic piety that is reflected, for example, in the *Imitation of Christ* by Thomas à Kempis. Calvin evidently read this work, and the piety of the *devotio moderna* undoubtedly contributed to the spiritualistic tendency in his eucharistic thought. During his student years, Calvin also became acquainted with the early Church fathers and particularly with Augustine.[5] In his writings, Calvin quotes Augustine more frequently than any other early theologian and he regards his own eucharistic teaching as nothing else but a defense of Augustine's.

As his studies progressed, Calvin became more and more influenced by humanism, which turned him away from the scholastics and toward classical authors.[6] During this period, he apparently came into contact with Platonism. The extent and character of this influence is difficult to determine, but whether the influence came directly or by way of Augustine, there is an underlying Platonic structure to Calvin's eucharistic thought.[7] Platonism never assumes the role of a consciously adopted philosophical system. It is always subordinate to revelation and scripture and represents an underlying leitmotif rather than a set of deliberately chosen categories.

A Platonic outlook is reflected in Calvin's sacramental theology in several basic respects. It contributes to the dialectical structure of his sacramental thinking. For Calvin, there is a dialectical relationship between the sacramental signs and the reality signified by them rather than the causal relationship characteristic of a sacramental theology that is developed under the influence of Aristotelian categories. Platonism also contributes to the spiritualistic strain in Calvin's eucharistic thought. On the other hand, Platonism contributes to Calvin's sacramental realism. Through the visible signs, the Christian believer participates in an invisible and spiritual reality. Unlike Zwingli, Calvin maintained both the distinction and the unity between the sacramental signs and the reality signified by them.

In order to understand Calvin's eucharistic teaching, we need to understand it not only against the background of his intellectual formation, but also in relation to his primary theological motivations. The fundamental theological principle governing Calvin's thought is his affirmation of the sovereignty and the glory of God. This is simply the obverse side of the Reformation principle of justification by faith. Salvation is due entirely to the free operation of God's grace accepted in faith. It is independent of any human action or merit. This presupposes God's absolute sovereignty and freedom with respect to creation.[8] Even in using created signs as instruments of grace, God is in no way bound by them nor is the divine freedom in relation to them in any way diminished:

"It is our duty to put no confidence in other creatures which have been destined for our use by God's generosity and beneficence, and through whose ministry he lavishes the gifts of his bounty upon us; nor to admire and proclaim them as the causes of our good. In the same way, neither ought our confidence to inhere in the sacraments, nor the glory of God be transferred to them."[9]

We can only understand Calvin's eucharistic thought if we see it against this background. The effect of this principle is the repudiation of any doctrine that would make the sacraments causes of grace in their own right. Calvin regards such an understanding of the sacraments as idolatrous since it ties God's grace to created things and makes them independent causes of our salvation. In Calvin's view, the medieval Church had interposed the sacramental system between God and humanity, thereby abrogating the freedom of God and undermining the role of Jesus Christ as the sole mediator of salvation. The mass had become the supreme idolatry. The doctrine of transubstantiation had bound God's grace to the material signs, and the sacrifice of the mass had replaced the saving work of Christ on the cross as the real cause of our salvation.

It requires an effort of historical imagination on the part of twentieth-century Christians to reconstruct the picture of the medieval mass and the practices and doctrines connected with it that Calvin has in mind in his lurid polemics, but only by such an act of historical imagination can we appreciate both the real object of his attack and the positive thrust of his eucharistic doctrine. He believed that in practice, the doctrine of transubstantiation had turned the real presence of Christ into an object on the altar that placed it at the disposal of human beings. This is simply blasphemy for Calvin. God is never at our disposal. We are always at God's disposal. This is the deepest theological motivation for his rejection of any understanding of the eucharistic presence that would tie it too closely to the elements. Calvin affirms the real presence, but he wants to preserve the freedom of God in relation to the material signs. In doing so, he is not opposing either sacramental objectivity or sacramental realism. He does not make the eucharistic presence dependent on the faith of the recipient, nor does he regard the sacraments as empty signs. The sacraments are true signs through which God really gives grace to those who receive them in faith, but the sacraments do not contain grace and they are not causes of grace in their own right.

The central axis around which Calvin's eucharistic theology revolves is his understanding that the goal of the eucharist is union with Christ.[10] All the other themes in Calvin's eucharistic theology are organized around this center. The relationship between the eucharist and faith is a fundamental theme in Calvin's theology, but faith itself has union with Christ as its aim. Faith, he says, ". . . does not reconcile us to God at all unless it joins us to Christ."[11] However, while union with Christ is the goal of the eucharist, union with Christ is not dependent on the eucharist, but upon grace received through faith. Here Calvin's Reformation posture comes through clearly. Only on such an understanding is the absolute sovereignty of God and the primacy of justification by faith maintained. The eucharist is not the cause of our union with Christ; it is the pledge of that union, the strengthening of a union that takes place first through faith.

Does this mean then that the reality or gift given in the eucharist is dependent on faith? At this point, we are open to a fundamental misunderstanding of Calvin's position. While for Calvin the sacraments are not causes of grace in their own right, they are divine gifts that are constitutive of the Church's life. They belong to the very existence of the Church, which announces and realizes through them its union with Christ. We can only really understand Calvin at this point if we keep in mind that he develops his eucharistic theology in opposition both to Rome and to Zwingli. As over against Rome, on the one hand, Calvin maintains the primacy of grace and justification by faith against any attempt to regard the sacraments as independent causes of grace. On the other hand, over against Zwingli, he maintained that the sacraments are means of grace and not only signs of the life of faith. Only if we remain conscious of Calvin's aim in rejecting both the positions of Rome and Zwingli, as he understood them, can we appreciate the true contours of his sacramental thought.

Following Paul and Augustine, Calvin understands union with Christ in an ecclesial and not in a individualistic sense.[12] Union with Christ means being grafted into Christ's body, the Church. For Calvin, the eucharist is always an act of the Church, the community of believers. The eucharist unites with Christ by uniting the members of Christ's body with one another and with Christ their head. Calvin's teaching concerning the ecclesial character of the eucharist is rooted in his doctrine of election.[13] The sovereign God, who transcends all created things and is determined by none, elects in accordance with the absolute freedom of the divine will. This election, however, takes place in Christ, the one mediator, so that election and union with Christ are bound up together. Election in Christ forms the basis of the Church, since ". . . the elect are so united in Christ that as they are dependent on one Head, they also grow together into one body. . . ."[14]

Calvin's grounding of the Church in the divine election is important for two reasons. In the first place, it means that the individual believer's union with Christ does not take place apart from membership in the Church, and it means that the Church, like the sacraments, stands under the Lordship of Christ, who remains the sole cause of our salvation.[15] The Church, therefore, like the sacraments, is not an independent instrument of salvation. It is through Christ alone that the people of God are elected. The word and the sacraments are constitutive of the Church because it is through them that election in Christ and union with him is continually appropriated by Christian believers.

The primacy of union with Christ as the goal of the eucharist and its essential character is well brought out in the following passage:

"For the Lord so communicates his body to us there [in the eucharist] that he is made completely one with us and we with him. Now, since he has only one body, of which he makes us all partakers, it is necessary that all of us also be made one body by such participation. The bread shown in the sacrament represents this unity. . . . I prefer to explain it in Paul's words: 'The cup of blessing which we bless is a communicating of the blood of Christ; and the bread of blessing which we break is a participation in the body of Christ. . . . Therefore . . . we . . . are all one body, for we partake of one bread.' "[16]

Despite his disagreement with Luther and Zwingli over the nature of the eucharistic presence, Calvin is at one with them in his affirmation of the ecclesial character of the eucharist.

We need to turn now to a consideration of Calvin's understanding of the real presence. In his controversy with Westphal, his principal adversary in the eucharistic controversy with the Lutherans, he says, "Westphal insists on the presence of the flesh of Christ in the Supper: we do not deny it. . . ."[17] Calvin affirms the doctrine of the real presence. Where he differs from the Lutherans and the Roman Catholics is in his understanding of the mode of the presence. If we are to understand Calvin's view of the real presence, we have to keep in mind his polemic against the Lutherans and the Roman Catholics on the one hand and his opposition to the Zwinglians on the other. Above all, however, we have to understand the dialectical method of his theology.[18]

Against the Lutherans and the Roman Catholics, Calvin rejects the idea of a bodily presence, a local presence, or a substantial presence. He rejects this understanding of the eucharistic presence on three grounds. In the first place, he agrees with Zwingli and the other Swiss reformers that since the body of Christ is in heaven in virtue of the Ascension, it cannot also be in the elements.[19] In the second place, a bodily, local, or substantial presence of Christ in the eucharist threatens the sovereignty of God and puts the presence of Christ at our disposal. Closely connected with this is Calvin's third ground for rejecting a bodily, local, or substantial presence of Christ in the eucharist, namely, that such an understanding of the eucharistic presence makes the presence of Christ into an object, whereas Christ is always present in the eucharist as subject. Christ cannot be contained, carried about, or disposed of. We can only appreciate Calvin's point of view here if we remember that he is writing against the background of medieval eucharistic practice, where the host was an object of adoration and was carried about in procession through the streets. If we cannot find a doctrine of the real presence in Calvin that enables us to confine it and determine it in relation to the elements, this is because Calvin expressly excludes such an understanding of the real presence.

On the other hand, over against the Zwinglians, Calvin wants to maintain the reality of the eucharistic presence in relation to the sacramental signs. While rejecting the bodily, local, or substantial presence of Christ in the eucharist, Calvin wants to avoid allowing the bread and the wine to become mere tokens or symbols of a reality that is essentially unrelated to them. There is a real relationship between the signs and the reality that they signify, but this relationship is neither a relationship of identity (Rome and the Lutherans) nor a relationship of absolute distinction (the Zwinglians). It is a dialectical relationship modeled on Calvin's Christology and the Platonic relationship between symbol and reality. In adopting such an understanding of the eucharistic presence, Calvin believes he is being faithful both to scripture and to the early Church and that he stands in the tradition of Augustine. For Calvin, the relationship between the sign and the reality signified is never either one of simple identity or one of absolute distinction. It is always a unity in distinction; otherwise, the eucharistic presence is made to depend entirely upon our faith (the Zwinglians), or placed at our disposal (Rome), or bound to the elements (Rome and the Lutherans), thus threatening the freedom of God.

How then does Calvin understand this dialectical relationship between the presence of Christ and the sacramental signs? We have indicated that Calvin's point of departure here is his Christology. Calvin, like Zwingli, maintains a clear distinction between the two natures of Christ, although he also stresses the unity of person in Christ.[20] Like Zwingli, however, and unlike Luther who argued that the attribute of omnipresence that belongs to the divinity of Christ has been conferred on his humanity, so that Christ can be bodily present in many places at the same time, Calvin argued that the humanity of Christ can be bodily present only in heaven because of the distinction between the divine and human natures in Christ. Calvin rejects the attribution of divine characteristics to the human nature of Christ on the ground that this implies a docetic Christology. Moreover, any "descent" of the human nature of Christ into the elements implies a threat to Christ's sovereignty and freedom in relation to all earthly creatures.

Following Augustine, Calvin posits an exchange of names between the sacramental signs and the reality signified by them because of the "similitude" or analogy that exists between a sign and the reality that it signifies. On this basis, the name of Christ's body is given to the bread. The technical term for this exchange of names is "metonymy."

". . . on account of the affinity which the things signified have with their symbols, the name of the thing was given to the symbol. . . . I say that this expression is a metonymy, a figure of speech commonly used in Scripture when mysteries are under discussion. . . . For though the symbol differs in essence from the thing signified (in that the latter is spiritual and heavenly, while the former is physical and visible), still, because it not only symbolizes the thing that it . . . represent(s) . . . but also truly exhibits it, why may its name not rightly belong to the thing?"[21]

Does this mean that the relationship between the sign and the reality signified by it is a linguistic relationship only and not a real one? Calvin replies:

"There is no reason for anyone to object that this is a figurative expression by which the name of the thing signified is given to the sign . . . (for) by the showing of the symbol the thing itself is also shown. For unless a person means to call God a deceiver, they would never dare assert that an empty symbol is set forth by him. Therefore, if the Lord truly represents the participation in his body through the breaking of the bread, there ought not to be the least doubt that he truly presents and shows his body. And the godly ought by all means to keep this rule: whenever they see symbols appointed by the Lord, to think and be persuaded that the truth of the thing signified is surely present there. For why should the Lord put in your hand the symbol of his body, except to assure you of a true participation in it? But if it is true that a visible sign is given us to seal the gift of a thing invisible, when we have received the symbol of the body, let us no less surely trust that the body itself is also given to us."[22]

The sacramental signs, therefore, not only represent what they signify, they also give what they signify.

While he rejects transubstantiation and a "substantial" presence of Christ in the elements, Calvin nevertheless acknowledges that it is the substance of Christ's body that is received by means of the sacramental signs.

". . . all benefit which we ought to seek from the Supper is annulled, unless Jesus Christ be there given to us as substance and foundation of all . . . the communion which we have with the body and blood of our Lord . . . is . . . symbolized by visible signs . . . but in such a way that it is not a bare figure, but joined to its reality and substance . . . the sacraments of the Lord ought not and cannot at all be separated from their reality and substance. To distinguish them so that they be not confused is not only good and reasonable but wholly necessary. But to divide them so as to set them up the one without the other is absurd."[23]

In a letter to the Italian reformer Peter Martyr, Calvin deplores the fact that the arguments of John à Lasco (a Zwinglian) always end up in the assertion ". . . that the natural body of Christ is not given us to eat. As though we could gain life from any other source than the natural body of Christ."[24] Calvin is as insistent as Luther that it is the body of Christ itself that we receive in the eucharist.

Calvin, however, not only speaks of the "substance" or "reality" of Christ's body, but like Augustine, he also speaks of the "virtue" or "power" of Christ's body and, to confuse matters, he sometimes identifies the "power" of Christ's body with the "substance" of Christ's body. This has sown confusion among his interpreters. The difficulty lies in the fact that Calvin uses the term "substance" in three different ways in his writings and doesn't always make clear which meaning he intends.[25] We can distinguish these meanings as follows:

1. In some contexts, Calvin uses the term "substance" to refer to the presence of Christ's natural body in the elements. In this sense, he denies that the substance of Christ's body is present in the eucharist, because the natural body of Christ is in heaven:

". . . we say that the body and the blood of Christ are presented to us truly and effectively, but not naturally. By that we mean that this is not the substance itself of the body, nor the true and natural body of the Christ that is given us there, but all the benefits that Christ offers us in his body."[26]

2. In other contexts, the term "substance" means Christ himself, who is the reality present in all the sacraments:

"I say that Christ is the matter or (if you prefer) the substance of all the sacraments; for in him they have all their firmness, and they do not promise anything apart from him."[27]

It is in this sense that he insists against the Zwinglians that it is the substance of Christ's body that is given in the sacrament and not only his redemptive benefits.

3. In a third sense, Calvin can use the term "substance" to refer to the life, the benefits, or the "power" that proceeds from Christ's body. He insists, however, that the communication of Christ's benefits can never be separated from the communication of his person, as the following text makes clear:

"I . . . maintain that it is only after we obtain Christ himself, that we come to share in the benefits of Christ. And I further maintain that he is obtained, not just when we believe that he was sacrificed for us, but when he dwells in us, when he is one with us, when we are members of his flesh, when, in short, we become united in one life and substance (if I may say so) with him . . . for Christ does not offer us only the benefit of his death and resurrection, but the self-same body in which he suffered and rose again . . . the body of Christ is really, to use the usual word, i.e., truly, given to us in the supper, so that it may be health-giving food for our souls. I am adopting the usual terms, but I mean that our souls are fed by the substance of his body, so that we are truly made one with him; or, what amounts to the same thing, that a life-giving power from the flesh of Christ is poured into us through the medium of the Spirit, even although it is at a great distance from us, and is not mixed with us."[28]

By denying that the "substance" of Christ's body is present in the eucharist in the first meaning of the term, Calvin intends to exclude any local or physical presence of Christ in the Supper. Calvin sees no opposition, however, beween the second and the third meaning of the term "substance," between the assertion that we receive the very body of Christ in the Supper and the assertion that "a life-giving power from the flesh of Christ is poured into us through the medium of the Spirit." The tension in these texts is a reflection of Calvin's dialectical method. The heavenly and the earthly reality stand in a real but dialectical relationship to each other. The substance of Christ's body is really given and received in the eucharist, but the natural body of Christ remains in heaven. The mode of Christ's presence in the eucharist is that of a personal or relational presence, not that of a natural object. Christ is present in the Supper not as an object on the altar, but as the Lord of the Church for the purpose of nourishing his people and uniting them to himself. Union with Christ, therefore, and not real presence remains the dominant motif in Calvin's eucharistic theology.

If Christ is really present in the Lord's supper in a personal and relational manner rather than in a substantialist manner, how is this presence effected and how is its virtue communicated to us? Calvin revives the patristic tradition that it is the Holy Spirit who effects the presence of Christ in the sacrament and sanctifies believers through it. The tradition of the epiclesis surfaces again in Calvin, although in a theological rather than a liturgical form.

For Calvin, it is the Holy Spirit who effects the presence of Christ in the sacrament and also communicates the body of Christ to believers. Unlike the Roman Catholics and the Lutherans who explained the eucharistic presence along substantialist lines, Calvin explains the presence of Christ in the eucharist and the efficacy of the sacrament for believers in terms of the agency and power of the Holy Spirit.[29] It is through the Holy Spirit that believers are united to the ascended Christ.

It is important for Calvin that the Holy Spirit be understood not only as the agent of the presence of Christ, but also as the agent through which his presence and life are communicated to us. This double agency of the Holy Spirit safeguards the realism and the objectivity of the eucharistic gift. There was always the danger, once the objectivity of a substantialist position was abandoned, of making the eucharistic presence dependent on the subjective faith of the recipient. Calvin guards against this kind of subjectivism by his doctrine of the double agency of the Holy Spirit. The Holy Spirit is both the agent of the presence of Christ and the one who gives the gift of faith by which it is received. Faith itself, therefore, is the effect of the divine action of the Holy Spirit. The Holy Spirit provides the objective bond between the presence of Christ in the eucharist and the subjective response of the believer in faith.

In Chapter Eighteen of Book Four of the *Institutes*, Calvin attacks the sacrifice of the mass. Calvin's polemic against the sacrifice of the mass is no less biting than Luther's. It is a blasphemous doctrine because it replaces the sacrifice of Christ offered once for all as the cause of our salvation. The eucharist, therefore, is not a sacrifice. Calvin, however, like Luther, does not altogether reject the sacrificial character of the eucharist.[30] While he chides the early Christian writers for calling the eucharist a sacrifice because it laid the foundation for the medieval doctrine, he professes agreement with what was intended by the term in the early Church.

". . . the ancient writers . . . use the word 'sacrifice'; but at the same time they explain that they mean nothing else than the remembrance of that one true sacrifice which Christ, our sole

Priest (as they everywhere proclaim), made upon the cross . . . Augustine [says that] '. . . Christians, by the most holy offering and partaking of the body of Christ, celebrate the remembrance of a sacrifice already made.' . . . in his writings you will repeatedly find that the Lord's Supper is called a sacrifice for no other reason than that it is a memorial, an image, and a testimony of that singular, true, and unique sacrifice by which Christ has atoned for us. . . . Chrysostom also speaks in the same sense . . . [and] we do not deny that the sacrifice of Christ is so shown to us there that the spectacle of the cross is almost set before our eyes—just as the apostle says that Christ was crucified before the eyes of the Galatians when the preaching of the cross was set before them."[31]

The relation between the real presence, the ecclesial aspect of the eucharist, union with Christ, the agency of the Holy Spirit, and the sacrificial aspect of the eucharist is brought out in a remarkable way in the following passage in Calvin:

"The cup and also the bread must be sanctified . . . in order that the wine may be a figure of the blood of our Lord Jesus Christ and the bread of his body, in order to show that we have truly fed upon him, and being as it were grafted into him may have a common life, and that by virtue of the Holy Spirit may be united to him, in order that the death and passion that he has undergone may belong to us and that that sacrifice, by which we are reconciled to God, may be attributed and imputed to us now as if we had offered it ourselves in person."[32]

Because of his polemic against the mass, the sacrificial aspect of the eucharist remains at the periphery rather than at the center of Calvin's eucharistic theology, but it is there and it remains as a pregnant source for theological reflection in a more ecumenical age.

Calvin's reform of the liturgy was an adaptation of Martin Bucer's Strasbourg liturgy, which was in turn based on the German mass of Diebold Schwarz, the first reformed liturgy to be used in Strasbourg after the Reformation. Bucer rewrote the canon entirely in three versions and placed the words of institution immediately after it.[33] The words of institution were now treated as a scripture reading directed toward the congregation and providing a warrant for the Supper rather than as a formula of consecration directed toward the elements. Bucer's new "eucharistic prayers" bear no obvious resemblance in language or structure to any of the classical Eucharistic Prayers, except that like the Roman canon, they contain intercessions. They are essentially intercessions followed by a prayer of approach to the table rather than prayers of thanksgiving for creation and redemption on the *berakah* model. In Geneva, Calvin adopted the structure of Bucer's rite, but placed the words of institution before the "canon." Calvin's "canon" is an exhortation followed by a reminder of the promises of Christ and a prayer for the worthy reception of the sacrament.[34]

Both Bucer and Calvin desired that the Lord's Supper be celebrated as the normal Sunday service of worship in which word and sacrament would complement each other. In Strasbourg, Bucer managed to retain a weekly celebration in the cathedral, but in the parish churches, a monthly celebration became the norm. It was no part of Calvin's purpose to replace the eucharistic worship of the Church by a service of the preaching of the word alone. On the contrary, his deepest desire was to restore the unity of word and sacrament, which he believed had been destroyed by the medieval system:

"To imagine that Calvin wished to replace sacramental worship by a preaching service is to completely misunderstand his mind and work and to ignore all that he taught and did. His aim was twofold: to restore the eucharist in its primitive simplicity and true proportions—celebration and communion—as the central weekly service, and, within this service, to give the Holy Scriptures their authoritative place. The Lord's Supper, in all its completeness, is the norm he wished to establish.[35]

The Genevan council, however, would allow only a quarterly celebration and Calvin had to bow his will.[36]

NOTES

1. But for Calvin's indebtedness to Bucer, see François Wendel, *Calvin: The Origins and Development of his Religious Thought* (London: Collins,

1963), 137–144 and 332, and Kilian McDonnell, *John Calvin, the Church, and the Eucharist* (Princeton NJ: Princeton University Press, 1967), 75–85.

2. For Calvin's relationship to Luther, see Wendel, 131–134 and 329–331, and McDonnell, 59–74; to Zwingli, see Wendel, 135–137 and 333–334, and McDonnell, 85–95; to Rome, see McDonnell, Chap. 3.

3. See McDonnell, 7–22.

4. *Ibid.*, 25–27.

5. See Wendel, 123–125 and 313, and McDonnell, 40–46.

6. See McDonnell, 27–32.

7. *Ibid.*, 32–37.

8. *Ibid.*, 160–169.

9. Calvin, *Institutes* 4.14.12. References to Calvin's *Institutes of the Christian Religion* are to the edition in John T. McNeill (ed.) and Ford L. Battles (trans.), *Library of Christian Classics,* vols. 20 and 21 (Philadelphia: Westminster Press, 1960), by book, chapter, and section.

10. See *Institutes* 4.17.2; McDonnell, 177–181.

11. *Institutes* 3.20.30.

12. See *Comm.* 1 Cor 216–217. References cited as *Comm.,* followed by biblical book and page, are to David W. Torrance and Thomas F. Torrance (eds.), *Calvin's Commentaries,* (Edinburgh, various dates). See also McDonnell, 181–196.

13. See McDonnell, 169–172.

14. *Institutes* 4.1.2.

15. See McDonnell, 172–176.

16. *Institutes* 4.17.38. Cf. Calvin's *Short Treatise on the Lord's Supper,* in J. K. Reid (ed.), *Calvin: Theological Treatises,* Library of Christian Classics, vol. 22 (Philadelphia: Westminster Press, 1954), 151 (hereafter cited as *Short Treatise* by page in LCC edition).

17. *Second Defence of the Faith Concerning the Sacraments,* in Henry Beveridge (trans.), *Tracts and Treatises,* repr. with intro. by Thomas F. Torrance, 3 vols. (Grand Rapids, MI: Eerdmans, 1958), 2:281.

18. See McDonnell, 156–160.

19. See *Institutes* 4.17.26ff.

20. See McDonnell, 212–220.

21. *Institutes* 4.17.21.

22. *Institutes* 4.17.10. Cf. *Comm.* 1 Cor 245 and *Comm.* Harmony of the Gospels, 134–136.

23. *Short Treatise,* 146–148.

24. CR 15.388, quoted by McDonnell, 242. References to Calvin's untranslated writings are to the edition in the *Corpus Reformatorum,* cited as CR by volume and page.

25. See Wendel, 341–342; McDonnell, 232–234 and 241–248.

26. CR 1.123, quoted by Wendel, 341.

27. *Institutes* 4.14.16.

28. *Comm.* 1 Cor 246.

29. See *Institutes* 4.17.12,33; McDonnell, 249–279.

30. See McDonnell, 282–286.

31. *Institutes* 4.18.10,11.

32. CR 49.665, quoted by McDonnell, 284.

33. See *PEER,* 206–211.

34. *Ibid.,* 215–218.

35. William D. Maxwell, *A History of Christian Worship: An Outline of Its Development and Forms* (Grand Rapids, MI: Baker Book House, 1982), 112. See *Institutes* 4.17.43,44,46.

36. Maxwell, 116–117.

CHAPTER SIX

Anglican, Puritan, and Methodist Traditions

THOMAS CRANMER AND THE BOOK OF COMMON PRAYER
The English Reformation was in its beginnings a political rather
than a religious reformation.[1] Of course, it was true for Europe
as a whole as well as for England in this period that Church and
state were two aspects of a single Christian society, so that the
direct action of the state was necessary in the implementation of
reform. The separation of Church and state is something still in
the future. In England, however, this common European fact
took on a particular character.

When the Reformation began in England after the severing of
the ties with Rome, there was at first no discernible change in
the character of English Church life. When change did eventually come, it took a liturgical rather than a doctrinal form.
Moreover, no single reformer determined the character of the English reformation in the way in which Luther and Calvin determined the course that the reformation took in Europe. Therefore,
even when the doctrinal questions that were inevitably bound
up with the reform of the liturgy came to play their part in the
progress of the English reformation, they were settled by the English genius for compromise rather than by confessional agreement. Even the Articles of Religion,[2] which together with the
Book of Common Prayer set forth the doctrinal standards of the
Church of England, were never regarded as confessional statements in the same sense as the confessional documents of the
continental reformation. They represent the settlement of religion in England agreed to by the legitimate authorities of Church
and state. Anglicanism, therefore, never developed a doctrine of
the eucharist bearing the distinctive stamp either of a single

great reformer or of common confessional agreement. Rather, within the broad framework of the Anglican settlement, there grew up a spectrum of doctrinal opinion that represented a *via media* between Rome and the continental reformed Churches. This *via media* was based on a broad appeal to scripture, the early Church, reason, and experience, which became characteristic of the Anglican ethos. This peculiar character of the English reformation accounts for the extraordinary difficulty that historians have had in determining what the position of the Church of England was on the eucharist at any given stage of its history. It also accounts for the vastly different estimates that have been made of the eucharistic opinions of the English reformers. This is particularly true for Cranmer himself, the principal author of the Book of Common Prayer.

During the reign of Henry VIII, no major reforms took place in doctrine or practice in the Church of England. Henry himself defended both the doctrine of the sacrifice of the mass and the doctrine of transubstantiation in his *Assertio Septem Sacramentorum* written against Luther's attack on the mass in his *On the Babylonian Captivity of the Church*, and he received the title "Defender of the Faith" for his efforts from Pope Leo X. The second phase of the English reformation took place during the reign of Edward VI. It was marked by the drawing up of the Book of Common Prayer in its first two editions in 1549 and 1552, and by the beginning of reform in doctrine. Close relations developed during this period between the English divines and the continental reformers, a number of whom came to England as refugees.

In 1549, the first edition of the Book of Common Prayer appeared.[3] It was Archbishop Cranmer who had the main hand in producing it. As far as the eucharistic rite is concerned, it was a halfway measure that followed the traditional Roman mass quite closely as far as order and structure are concerned. It is impossible to be certain, however, concerning the doctrine of the eucharist that it was intended to convey. By the middle of 1548, three schools of thought had emerged among the English bishops in the matter of eucharistic doctrine.[4] One party held to the doctrine of transubstantiation or at least to a doctrine of the bodily presence of Christ in the eucharist. Stephen Gardiner, with whom Cranmer carried on a lively controversy, was the major spokesman for this position. A center party represented chiefly by Nicholas Ridley favored a position similar to that of Ratramnus. A third party favored the position in some form of the reformers of the Zurich school, Zwingli, and Bullinger (Zwingli's successor in Zurich), or of the Basel reformer Oecolampadius.

The debate in the House of Lords, which preceded the publication of the book and the manner in which the book was received afterwards by all parties, reflects this lack of unanimity among the bishops.[5] In the debate itself, Cranmer took up a position that sided very largely with the opinions of the Zurich school. The party that held to a belief in the bodily presence of Christ in the eucharist opposed the book in parliament, but afterwards argued that it could be interpreted to teach transubstantiation and even the doctrine of the sacrifice of the mass. The "Zurich" party, on the other hand, while able to use the book, was unhappy with it because in their view it had not gone nearly far enough in repudiating Roman errors and in embodying reformed teaching.

The 1549 Prayer Book was a compromise book. It proved capable of accommodating the variety of opinions that were actually present in the Church in England at that time without giving express sanction to any of them. It was a moderate revision of the old mass, which shows its greatest departure from the doctrine of the older rite in the revisions that were made in the canon of the mass.[6] The structure of the old canon was followed, but the theological emphasis was placed squarely on the sacrifice of Christ "once offered" on the cross. All references to the mass as a sacrifice in any other sense than that of a commemoration of the sacrifice of the cross, a sacrifice of praise and thanksgiving, or the sacrifice of "ourselves, our souls, and bodies," were carefully excluded. The whole prayer was more clearly oriented around the theme of thanksgiving in line with the early anaphoras. The anamnesis is restored to a position of central prominence, and an epiclesis is introduced that invokes both the Word and the Holy Spirit on the gifts in view of their reception in communion.

However one judges Cranmer's eucharistic opinions, there is no doubt that he was a liturgical scholar with few peers in his own or any age.

The subject of Cranmer's eucharistic opinions is one that has aroused considerable controversy among historians. Dom Gregory Dix held that Cranmer was a Zwinglian.[7] G. B. Timms, on the other hand, thought that his doctrine stands closer to that of Calvin and Bucer.[8] C. W. Dugmore countered that he got his doctrine not from the continental reformers but from the ancient fathers and in particular from Augustine and Ratramnus.[9] More recently, Peter Brooks has tried to reassess the influence of the continental reformers on the development of his eucharistic thought.[10]

In the wake of these studies, Cyril Richardson attempted to get beyond the question of Cranmer's sources to the underlying structure of his thought.[11] According to Richardson, there is an underlying conflict in Cranmer's thought between realism and nominalism. Cranmer is a realist in his understanding of the incarnation and in his understanding of the union between Christ and believers (a realism derived from his biblical and patristic roots), but his eucharistic ideas are developed against the background of late medieval nominalism. There is a real substantial union between the divine and human natures in Christ (although the distinction of natures prohibits the transfer of properties such as ubiquity from the divine to the human nature) and a real substantial union and mutual indwelling between Christ and Christian believers. Cranmer's nominalism, however, prevents him from asserting a real substantial union between the body of Christ and the elements even in a spiritual and nonlocal manner, since it is contrary to the nature of a body to be present in two places at once even in different modes. This is clear from his controversy with Gardiner, who held, like Aquinas, that the mode of Christ's substantial presence in the elements was spiritual and not physical or material. For Cranmer, however, the body of Christ is present only in heaven and cannot, therefore, also be in the elements. On this point, Cranmer is entirely at one with the Swiss reformers and against Luther.

If Richardson is right, then there is a fundamental inconsistency, not to say incoherence, in Cranmer's sacramental theology between two sets of unconscious underlying presuppositions, realist and nominalist. This would explain the conflict of interpretation among historians, some arguing that Cranmer is consistently "Zwinglian" and others producing texts to show that there is a strain of realism in his sacramental thought. These texts could simply indicate that Cranmer's religious instincts, nourished by scripture and the early Church, are more realist than his intellectual presuppositions. Richardson's thesis goes a long way toward helping to explain the origins of Anglican "receptionism."

During the period of Henry's reign up to 1546, Cranmer still held to a doctrine of the bodily presence of Christ in the sacrament as he believed it to have been taught by the theologians of the early Church. During this time, he made himself acquainted with the writings of both the early fathers and the continental reformers. It is probably asserting too much to say that he passed through a Lutheran phase during this period, but he certainly made a careful assessment of Luther's position before finally swinging away from a bodily view of the eucharistic presence to take up a position of the Augustinian-Reformed type. It was Nicholas Ridley who in 1546 persuaded him to change his mind:

"I grant that then I believed otherwise than I do now; and so I did, until my lord of London, doctor Ridley, did confer with me, and by sundry persuasions and authorities of doctors drew me quite from my opinion."[12]

Ridley himself, on his own admission, had been converted from belief in transubstantiation and the doctrine of the mass as a propitiatory sacrifice by reading Ratramnus' treatise *On The Body and Blood of the Lord*. He now persuaded Cranmer to adopt a similar position. Ratramnus taught that there is a change in the elements at the consecration, but that the nature of the change is spiritual. While Christ's natural body is in heaven, the sacrament is the very body of Christ inwardly, spiritually, in a figure, by the power of God. The senses perceive only the natures of bread and wine. The spiritual presence of Christ is perceived by the inward mind and by faith. How closely Ridley's own position is to this can be discerned from his statement at the Oxford disputation just prior to his execution.

". . . in the sacrament is a certain change, in that the bread, which was before common bread, is now made a lively presentation of Christ's body, and not only a figure, but effectuously representeth his body; that even as the mortal body was nourished by that visible bread, so is the internal soul fed with the heavenly food of Christ's body, which the eyes of faith see, as the bodily eyes see only bread. Such a sacramental mutation I grant to be in the bread and wine, which truly is no small change, but such a change as no mortal man can make, but only that omnipotency of Christ's word . . . the true substance and nature of bread and wine remaineth: with which the body is in like sort nourished, as the soul is by grace and Spirit with the body of Christ."[13]

In 1546, Cranmer seems to have adopted a position very much like that of Ridley's, which is to say very much like that of Ratramnus. C. Dugmore thinks that Cranmer adopted Ratramnus' doctrine from Ridley and remained with it to the end of his life except for a brief Zwinglian phase prior to the publication of the first Prayer Book. Dix, on the other hand, maintained that he became a Zwinglian from 1547 onwards. P. Brooks points out rightly that the term "Zwinglian" is an anachronism after the publication of the *Consensus Tigurinus* in 1551, which marked the agreement reached between the Zurich and the Genevan reformers on the eucharistic question.[14]

When we compare Ridley's language concerning the eucharist with that of Cranmer, Ridley's exhibits a greater degree of objective realism in regard to the eucharistic presence. This lends some support to the view that while Cranmer may have followed Ratramnus in 1546, he was by no means uninfluenced by the Swiss reformers in the following years. Nevertheless, on balance, however much he may have veered toward the views of the Zurich school, he has a grasp on the realism of the sacramental gift that is lacking in Zwingli himself, but this is clearly related to reception by faith and not to the elements.

Cranmer's view can only be understood from the perspective of the purpose for which he understood the eucharist to have been instituted. This purpose is the spiritual nourishment of the bodies and souls of Christian believers by Christ himself in his Supper. Cranmer's aim is to reorient eucharistic doctrine around the act of communion rather than around a change in the nature of the elements. His doctrine can perhaps best be described as a doctrine of the real partaking of the body and blood of Christ in the eucharist rather than as a doctrine of the real objective presence of Christ in the eucharist. The sacramental signs are connected with the reality that they signify through their use rather than in an objective manner. Such a standpoint represents an attempt to retain sacramental realism in relation to the faithful believer rather than in relation to the elements:

"And therefore, in the book of the holy communion, we do not pray absolutely that the bread and wine may be made the body and blood of Christ, but that unto us in that holy mystery they may be so; that is to say, that we may so worthily receive the same, that we may be partakers of Christ's body and blood, and that therewith in spirit and in truth we may be spiritually nourished."[15]

Like Augustine, Ratramnus, and the Swiss reformers, Cranmer denies a bodily presence of Christ in the eucharist. Christ is present in his natural body only in heaven. Like Calvin, therefore, he has often been thought to teach that it is only the effect of Christ's body and not the very substance of his body that is received with the sacramental signs. In the disputation with his Roman opponents at Oxford in 1555, he expressly denies this:

Chedsey: "By this your interpretation which you have made upon the first conclusion, this I understand; the body of Christ to be in the sacrament only by the way of participation, insomuch as we communicating thereof, do participate the grace of Christ; so that you mean hereby only the effect thereof. . . ."

Cranmer: "This you gather upon my answer, as though I did mean of the efficacy, and not of the substance of the body; but I mean of them both, as well of the efficacy as of the substance."[16]

The role of faith is central in all eucharistic doctrines of the Augustinian-Reformed type, and Cranmer's is no exception. His eucharistic thought moves within a theological framework that gives the primacy to justification by faith. For Cranmer, therefore, "eating" Christ's body means feeding on Christ spiritually by faith. "The sacrament," he says, "(that is to say, the bread) is corporally eaten and chewed with the teeth in the mouth: the very body is eaten and chewed with faith in the spirit."[17] Unlike Zwingli, however, who regarded the sacramental signs as outward tokens of this inward spiritual feeding upon Christ by faith, Cranmer also regards the sacraments as "effectual signs of grace"[18] for faithful receivers:

"And although the sacramental tokens be only significations and figures, yet doth Almighty God effectually work, in them that duly receive his sacraments, those divine and celestial operations which he hath promised, and by the sacraments be signified."[19]

Cranmer's doctrine is a doctrine of the Augustinian-Reformed type without being precisely identical with that of Augustine, Ratramnus, or the Swiss reformers. Cranmer could learn from all of them, but his doctrine bears the marks of his own independence of mind, of long study, and of controversy. As Cranmer himself says:

"I have seen almost everything that has been written and published either by Oecolampadius or Zwingli, and I have come to the conclusion that the writings of every man must be read with discrimination."[20]

By 1551, the more extreme reform party was in the ascendancy and was demanding a more radical version of the Book of Common Prayer. In 1552, the second edition of the Prayer Book appeared.[21] The 1552 eucharistic rite is a much more drastic revision of the old mass than 1549.[22] The title of the rite of the 1549 book was "The Supper of the Lord, and the holy Communion, commonly called the Mass." The new title is now simply, "The order for the administration of the Lord's Supper or holy Communion." The structure of the rite was also fundamentally reordered. Cranmer's 1549 canon had had three sections. The first section contained intercessions and commemorations adapted from the Roman canon; the second section contained the thanksgiving for redemption, the epiclesis, and the words of institution; and the third section contained the anamnesis followed by the offering of "ourselves, our souls, and bodies," and concluded with the doxology.

The presence of intercessions in the first section of the canon and the presence of sacrificial language in the third section enabled Stephen Gardiner to interpret the mass as a propitiatory sacrifice for the living and the dead. Gardiner likewise interpreted the presence of an epiclesis over the gifts in the second section together with the words for the administration of communion, which were, "The body of our Lord Jesus Christ which was shed for thee, preserve thy body and soul unto everlasting life," and "The blood of our Lord Jesus Christ which was shed for thee, preserve thy body and soul unto everlasting life," as teaching transubstantiation. In order to exclude such interpretations, Cranmer divided the 1549 canon. The first section was moved to a point earlier in the service, immediately after the offertory. The third section became an optional prayer after communion. The epiclesis was removed from the middle section, so that all that remained of the Eucharistic Prayer in 1552 was the thanksgiving for redemption and the words of institution. This was followed immediately by the words for the administration of communion, which now read, "Take and eat this, in remembrance that Christ died for thee, and feed on him in thy heart by faith, with thanksgiving," and "Drink this in remembrance that Christ's blood was shed for thee, and be thankful." Whether these changes also reflect a definite plan on Cranmer's part to produce a Zwinglian rite is a disputed question.[23] At any rate, the Church of England did not feel bound by Cranmer's interpretation of the rite and in all subsequent Anglican revisions of the Prayer Book, the eucharistic rite has been revised, however slightly, in the direction either of restoring one or more elements from the 1549 rite or of bringing the rite more clearly into line with the early liturgies.

With the death of Edward VI in 1553 and the accession of Mary Tudor, Roman Catholicism was temporarily restored in England. The Prayer Book was suppressed, and the old Latin mass was restored. Cranmer, Latimer, and Ridley were martyred, and a number of the other leading English reformers fled to the continent.

ELIZABETHAN ANGLICANISM

The accession of Elizabeth I in 1558 ushered in a new era in the history of the English Church. It provided the signal for the return of the English exiles, a number of whom were in a short time raised to positions of authority in the established Church. In 1559, the 1552 Prayer Book was restored with minor but significant changes.[24] The words for the administration of communion in the 1549 and 1552 rites were combined, and the notorious "Black Rubric" inserted in the 1552 book by royal authority, and denying any "real and essential presence of Christ" in the eucharist was dropped.[25] These changes opened the way at least for a broader spectrum of opinion concerning the eucharistic presence than that envisioned by the 1552 rite. The predominant characteristics of the Elizabethan period were the long struggle with Puritanism and the gradual emergence of a distinctively Anglican tradition.

The leading theologians in Elizabeth's reign were John Jewel and his younger contemporary and protégé Richard Hooker. Jewel is typical, and one of the best representatives of the eucharistic thought of the early Elizabethan period. He was closely associated with the early Anglican reformers and had acted as notary to Cranmer and Ridley at their trial in 1554. His own eucharistic theology is close to Cranmer's in both thought and spirit. He had studied under Peter Martyr during Edward's reign and kept up a regular correspondence with the Italian reformer until the latter's death in 1563.[26] As an exile during Mary's reign, he lived for a time in Frankfurt, Strasbourg, and Zurich, and was in close touch with the reformers there. At Frankfurt, he allied himself with the Prayer Book party over against the supporters of John Knox and the nascent Genevan Service Book.

Jewel was deeply read in the Greek and Latin fathers as well as in the reformers. His eucharistic doctrine coincides with that of Peter Martyr and the moderate Swiss reformers, but like the reformers themselves, he defends it through an extensive appeal to the fathers. This appeal to the Church fathers played a prominent role in his major work, *An Apology for the Church of England*, in which he sought to show that the doctrine of the Church of England was no novelty, but rooted in scripture and the consensus of the patristic Church before the rise of the doctrine of transubstantiation.

Jewel had a lively sense of the sacraments as "holy mysteries,"[27] which is ultimately rooted in the Greek fathers. He amasses an array of patristic texts to show that the fathers spoke of the elements as "figures," "signs," and "tokens" of the body of Christ. From Augustine, he draws the definition of a sacrament as an outward and visible sign of an invisible grace:

"A sacrament is an outward and visible sign, whereby God sealeth up his grace in our hearts, to the confirmation of our faith. St. Augustine saith . . . : 'A sacrament is a visible sign of grace invisible.' "[28]

He also draws on the reformers. Luther had sought to ground the sacraments in the divine word of promise. Calvin had emphasized the sacraments as seals that confirm the divine promise for faith. Jewel incorporates both these perspectives in his definition of a sacrament:

"Christ hath ordained . . . [the sacraments], that by them he might set before our eyes the mysteries of our salvation, and might more strongly confirm the faith which we have in his blood, and might seal his grace in our hearts. As princes' seals confirm and warrant their deeds and charters; so do the sacraments witness unto our conscience that God's promises are true, and shall continue for ever."[29]

Jewel clearly belongs to the symbolic and spiritualist streams of eucharistic tradition. The Augustinian distinction between the *signum* and the *res* is firmly maintained and the language of representation and signification is used to describe the role of the elements in mediating the reality that they signify. The role of faith is central as it was for both Augustine and Cranmer, but the body of Christ is offered to faith; it is not created by our faith. There is a double eating in the eucharist. With our bodily mouths, we eat the bread and drink the wine, but spiritually and with the mouth of faith, we eat the body of Christ and drink his blood.

"... spiritually and with the mouth of our faith we eat the body of Christ and drink his blood. . . . the bread that we receive with our bodily mouths is an earthly thing, and therefore a figure; but the body of Christ that thereby is represented, and there is offered unto our faith, is the thing itself, and no figure. . . . we put a difference between the sign and the thing itself that is signified. . . ."[30]

The act of sacramental communion brings about a true union with Christ and a mutual indwelling of Christ and the believer:

"For Christ himself altogether is so offered and given us in these mysteries, that we may certainly know we be flesh of his flesh, and bone of his bones, and that Christ 'continueth in us, and we in him.' "[31]

Jewel stands close to the tap roots of the English Reformation and his theology reflects the outlook of the reformers both in language and style. Richard Hooker, on the other hand, is in the midst of establishing a tradition. In him, we find the beginning of a distinctively Anglican method in theology.[32] Hooker has a more metaphysical bent than Jewel. While Jewel's writings are saturated with scripture and laced with patristic quotations, Hooker's style reminds one more of Thomas Aquinas and the scholastics.

Hooker develops his sacramental theology within the framework of a theology of grace. "Grace," he says, "is . . . the very end for which [the sacraments] . . . were instituted."[33] The grace of the sacraments is mediated Christologically and involves a real communication of Christ's person along with his saving grace. Following in the tradition of Paul and Augustine, Hooker understands this participation in Christ in an ecclesial sense:

". . . this sacrament is a true and a real participation of Christ, who thereby imparteth himself even his whole entire Person *as a mystical Head* unto every soul that receiveth him, and . . . every such receiver doth thereby incorporate or unite himself unto Christ as *a mystical member of* him, yea of them also whom he acknowledgeth to be his own. . . ."[34]

Like Cranmer, Hooker's doctrine can be described as a doctrine of the real partaking of the body and blood of Christ in the eucharist rather than a doctrine of the real presence of Christ in the eucharist although, as we shall see, he by no means denies the latter. The real participation in the body and blood of Christ in the eucharist, however, is at the center of his eucharistic theology. Hooker supports this perspective by an appeal to scripture. According to Hooker, the operative words in the institution narrative are "Take and eat" and "Drink ye all of this." These words qualify the meaning of the words "This is my body" and "This is my blood" and indicate that they refer primarily to the act of receiving Christ rather than to a presence related to the elements. Unlike Zwingli, who interpreted the words of institution in the light of John 6, Hooker interprets them in the light of 1 Corinthians 10:16:

"If we doubt what those admirable words import, let him be our teacher for the meaning of Christ to whom Christ himself was a schoolmaster, let our Lord's Apostle be his interpreter, content we ourselves with his explication, My body, *the communion of my body*, My blood, *the communion of my blood*."[35]

In placing the emphasis in his theology on the real partaking of the body and blood of Christ in the eucharist rather than on the real presence, Hooker acknowledges, like Cranmer, that the primary purpose for which the eucharist was instituted is the nourishment of Christian believers. The eucharistic gifts are primarily spiritual food and drink. This early Anglican tradition sought to shift the axis of eucharistic theology away from its medieval center, where the primary question was the manner of the eucharistic presence in relation to the elements, and to reorient it around

176

the act of sacramental communion. In this way, it sought to relate the presence of Christ in the eucharist in a more integral
way to the sacramental acts of eating and drinking. In comment-
ing on the text "Except ye eat the flesh of the Son of man, and
drink his blood, ye have no life in you," Hooker recovers an
essential Johannine perspective:

"Life being therefore proposed unto all men as their end, they
which by baptism have laid the foundation and attained the first
beginning of a new life have here their nourishment and food
prescribed for *continuance of life* in them. Such as will live the life
of God must eat the flesh and drink the blood of the Son of
man, because this is a part of that diet which if we want we
cannot live . . . in the eucharist we so receive the gift of God,
that we know by grace what the grace is which God giveth
us . . . (and) understand . . . that his flesh is meat and his blood
drink, not by surmised imagination but truly, even so truly that
through faith we perceive in the body and blood sacramentally
presented the very taste of eternal life, the grace of the sacrament is here as food which we eat and drink."[36]

Where then does Hooker stand on the question of the eucharistic
presence? This is a question that has bewildered his interpreters.
Of the reality of the presence, Hooker is in no doubt. Without
the real presence, there would be no real partaking of the body
and blood of Christ in the eucharist. Hooker is quite explicit
about this:

". . . inasmuch as Christ's incarnation and passion can be available to no man's good which is not made partaker of Christ,
neither can we participate him without his presence. . . ."[37]

He relates the presence, however, primarily to the faithful communicant rather than to the elements of bread and wine:

"The real presence of Christ's most blessed body and blood is
not . . . to be sought for in the sacrament, but in the worthy
receiver of the sacrament."[38]

On the question of the relation of the presence to the elements
of bread and wine, he adopts a position of deliberate agnosticism:

"Let it therefore be sufficient for me presenting myself at the Lord's table to know what there I receive from him, without searching or inquiring of the manner how Christ performeth his promise; . . . what these elements are in themselves it skilleth not, it is enough that to me which take them they are the body and blood of Christ. . . ."[39]

Several factors account for Hooker's agnosticism. In the first place, he believes that the question of the manner of the real presence goes beyond the certain testimony of scripture. Secondly, he believes that it goes beyond the consensus of the early Church and the various Christian confessions. Thirdly, he thinks that the notion of a "substantial" presence, whether by way of transubstantiation or consubstantiation, is opposed to sound reason. Finally, disputes over the manner of the presence endanger piety by giving rise to fruitless speculation and dissension. The political situation also lies in the background here. Hooker is writing in defense of the state Church and is anxious to accommodate as wide a spectrum of belief as possible consistent with scripture and tradition.

All of these considerations reveal the emergence in Hooker of a distinctively Anglican approach to the issue of authority in matters of faith. It was a cardinal principle of the emerging Anglican tradition that nothing can be proposed as a necessary article of faith that goes beyond the certain testimony of scripture. Beyond this, agreement with the early Church, consent among the various Christian confessions, and the testimony of reason are further tests that serve either to confirm or deny the truth of a particular doctrine. This led to a distinction in Anglican theology between those doctrines that were regarded as necessary articles of faith and those matters that could be left in the realm of theological opinion. According to Hooker, the doctrine of the real partaking of the body and blood of Christ in the eucharist is clearly attested by scripture and has the universal consent of tradition. It is, therefore, a necessary article of faith. Particular theories, however, regarding the manner of the presence go beyond what is required by scripture, do not command universal acceptance, and are variously supported by reason. They ought, therefore, to be left in the realm of theological opinion. Hooker is drawing a distinction here between theology and faith. At the level of faith, all that is necessary is that we believe that the body and blood of Christ is really received in the eucharist by means of the sacramental signs. At the level of theology, it is legitimate to speculate about the manner of the presence as long as it does not endanger piety.

Hooker has his own theory about the manner of the eucharistic presence. He agrees with the Swiss reformers against Luther that to attribute ubiquity to the body of Christ is to confuse the two natures of Christ.[40] Christ's body is present in heaven; therefore, it cannot be present in the elements. However, because of the unity of Christ's person, the human nature participates in the universal presence of the divine nature by "conjunction." This gives it a "presence of force and efficacy" and an infinite "possibility of application."[41] The substance of the body of Christ is present only in heaven, but we on earth partake of its "force and efficacy" through "mystical participation."[42] His position, therefore, is very much like Calvin's. Like Calvin, he rejects a "substantial" presence of Christ in the eucharist because he equates a substantial presence with a local or physical presence of Christ in the elements.

What then, for Hooker, is the role of the elements in mediating the presence of Christ to the worthy receiver? In addressing this issue, Hooker attempts to steer a middle course between "Zwinglianism" on the one side and the doctrine of the medieval Church on the other. To explain the relationship between divine grace and the sacraments, Hooker, like Aquinas, employs the language of instrumental causality. The sacraments are not causes of grace in an absolute sense. God alone is the author of grace. The sacraments are causes only in a secondary or instrumental sense. God uses them as a means of imparting grace. As means of grace, however, the sacraments do not produce their effect automatically, but only conditionally. The sacraments are *moral instruments*, not mechanical or physical instruments.[43] Hooker is employing here what we would call a "personalist" rather than a naturalistic or mechanical model of sacramental causality. The operation of the sacraments is analogous to the offering and acceptance of a gift between free moral agents. It is conditional both on God's free offer of grace and upon the faithful response of the recipient. The offer of grace is unconditional in the sense that the sacraments depend upon the divine promise that is annexed to their institution:

" 'This is my body,' and 'this is my blood,' being words of promise, sith we all agree that by the sacrament Christ doth really and truly in us perform his promise. . . ."[44]

The acceptance of the gift, however, is conditional upon the free and faithful response of the recipient. The sacraments "really exhibit," but "they are not really nor do really contain in themselves that grace which with them or by them it pleaseth God to bestow."[45] Hooker draws a strict analogy between the offer of grace in baptism and the offer of grace in the eucharist:

"If on all sides it be confessed that the grace of Baptism is poured into the soul of man, that by water we receive it although it be neither seated in the water nor the water changed into it, what should induce men to think that the grace of the Eucharist must need be in the Eucharist before it can be in us that receive it?"[46]

"The bread and cup are his body and blood," therefore, "because they are causes instrumental upon the receipt whereof the *participation* of his body and blood ensueth."[47]

THE PURITAN TRADITION
The Puritans were the group within the Church of England that desired a "pure" reformation according to the Word of God. They regarded the established Church, and the Book of Common Prayer in particular, as imperfectly reformed, and they desired to see a reformation of the Church in England that was more in line with the model provided by Calvin's reform in Geneva. Both Anglicans and Puritans held a similar doctrine of the eucharist. What separated them was not theology,[48] but liturgical practice.

The fundamental disagreement between Anglicans and Puritans had to do with the way in which the worship of the Church is ordered. The Puritans insisted that the sole criterion for ordering the public worship of the Church was the Word of God in scripture. They wanted to see a form of worship that was modeled entirely on the Bible. This meant that forms of prayer, customs, and ceremonies not explicitly enjoined by scripture ought not to be retained. This was the basis for the long list of Puritan objections to the Book of Common Prayer. From the Puritan point of view, the Prayer Book contained a number of customs and ceremonies that they regarded as human traditions added to the Word of God, and that they regarded as nothing but relics of popery. Anglicans, on the other hand, argued that forms of prayer, customs, and ceremonies may be retained by the Church as long as they are not contrary to scripture. What was at stake were two fundamentally different understandings of the role of scripture and tradition in ordering the worship of the Church, and therefore, two fundamentally different conceptions of what constituted a Church that is fully reformed according to the Word of God.[49]

The Puritan movement was not at first a separatist movement.[50] It was a movement within the Church of England. Only a tiny minority of the Puritans were separatists. The vast majority of the Puritans remained within the Church of England, but hoped to achieve their aims within the established Church through a policy of sustained pressure on the monarchy, the bishops, and parliament. This policy, however, ultimately proved to be a failure. In 1640, when the Puritans gained the ascendancy in parliament, in a series of extreme moves, including the beheading of Charles I and Archbishop Laud, they established a Puritan Commonwealth under Oliver Cromwell. Parliament then moved swiftly to establish the Puritan reforms. An assembly of Puritan divines was held in Westminster in 1644, and in 1645, the Westminster Directory of Worship replaced the Book of Common Prayer. The Puritan Commonwealth came to an end with the restoration of the monarchy in 1661, and in 1662, the Book of Common Prayer was restored almost unchanged.[51] This final failure of the Puritan cause led to the separation of the Puritans from the Church of England. Many of them sailed to North America. Those that remained formed the first English Presbyterian and Congregationalist Churches.[52]

The differences between Anglican and Puritan traditions of eucharistic worship have their origins in a conflict that developed within the small community of English exiles in Frankfurt that had fled to the continent during the reign of Queen Mary and had been given permission by the city council to hold services in English in the Church of the White Ladies. A split developed within this congregation between those who favored a form of worship modeled on the liturgy used by Calvin in Geneva, and those who favored the adoption of the 1552 Book of Common Prayer.[53] In 1554, John Knox was invited to become a minister of this congregation. Knox disliked the Prayer Book, and he and a committee drew up an order of service modeled on Calvin's liturgy. This was unfavorably received by the supporters of the Prayer Book, and a "Liturgy of Compromise" was adopted in its place.

Soon afterwards, a further group of English exiles arrived in Frankfurt. This group was led by Richard Cox, who was a staunch supporter of the Prayer Book, and within two weeks, the Prayer Book supporters succeeded in deposing Knox, who left for Geneva, where he was later joined by a group of Calvinist supporters from the Frankfurt congregation. The "Coxians" who remained used a revised form of the 1552 Prayer Book.[54] Knox and his supporters formed a new English congregation in Geneva and adopted, with slight alterations, the order of worship originally intended by Knox for use in the Frankfurt congregation. This order of worship, commonly referred to as Knox's liturgy, provided the basic model for later forms of Puritan worship.[55]

Knox's liturgy was based on Calvin's Genevan liturgy of 1542. It has its origin, therefore, in the liturgical tradition of Strasbourg and Geneva, which, as we have already seen, has a common origin in the German mass of Diebold Schwarz, the first revision of the mass carried out in Strasbourg after the reformation. While Bucer and Calvin considerably modified Schwarz's mass, it is important to note that all the reformed liturgical rites of Strasbourg and Geneva owe their origin and structure to the eucharistic liturgy. Knox's liturgy is no exception. Knox, like Bucer and Calvin, intended the normal Sunday service to be a service of the Word culminating in the celebration of the Lord's Supper.

For pastoral and political reasons, however, the reformers were unable to achieve this ideal, so that only the first part of the eucharistic liturgy, the service of the Word, became the normal service on most Sundays. The practice in Knox's English congregation in Geneva was to celebrate the Lord's Supper once a month. On Sundays when the Lord's Supper was not celebrated, the service of the Word was followed up to the beginning of the order for the Lord's Supper.

In his order for the Lord's Supper, Knox followed the practice of Strasbourg and Geneva in separating the words of institution from the Eucharistic Prayer. The words of institution no longer function, as they did in the medieval mass, as words of consecration, but they are addressed to the congregation as the Word of God that provides the warrant for the celebration of the supper. The remarkable feature about Knox's liturgy, however, is its Eucharistic Prayer. Following Bucer and Calvin rather than Luther, Knox retained a reformed version of the canon, but the Eucharistic Prayer in Knox's liturgy is an entirely new composition that has no evident source either in the Strasbourg and Geneva liturgies, or in any of the historic liturgies of the Church. Nevertheless, while is departs drastically from all the historic models, it is remarkably resonant of the tradition of the Eucharistic Prayer in both its spirit and structure. It is a true *berakah* that renders thanks and praise to God for creation and redemption, while expressing thanks for the mystery of redemption in a way that reflects the distinctive theology and spirit of the Reformed tradition. While it does not contain an anamnesis or epiclesis in any recognizably historical form, the thanksgiving for redemption is explicitly rendered "in remembrance of his death until his coming again" and the doxology makes it clear that the whole action of thanksgiving is understood as a movement directed by the Holy Spirit:

"we thy congregation moved by thy Holy Spirit render thee all thanks, praise, and glory for ever and ever."

A fixed text is provided for the Eucharistic Prayer, but the rubric permits the minister to give thanks "either in these words following, or like in effect."[56]

This provision of a liturgical model with the freedom to adapt it became the hallmark of early Puritanism. The early Puritans did not object to liturgical forms, provided they did not exclude free prayer.[57] When the Genevan exiles returned to England after the accession of Elizabeth I, the model of worship that they favored was Knox's liturgy, with which they had become familiar on the continent. The early Puritans continued to print editions of Knox's liturgy into the second half of Elizabeth's reign. The Puritan printer Robert Waldegrave published an edition of Knox's liturgy in London in 1584.[58] This was reprinted with minor adaptations in the English trading community of Middleburg in Holland in 1586.[59] Attempts were made both in 1584–1585 and in 1587 to introduce this liturgy in Parliament to replace the Prayer Book, but both efforts failed. The publication of Knox's Genevan Service Book by the English Puritans and the efforts to have it authorized by Parliament make it clear that at this stage, the Puritans favored a form of liturgical worship on the Genevan model.

Originally, it was only the English Separatists (the Barrowists, Brownists, and Baptists) who opposed "free prayer" to liturgical forms. They insisted that this was the only form of prayer agreeable with the Word of God.[60] They believed that true spiritual worship is "from the heart" and ought to be guided by the free operation of the Spirit, which cannot be contained in any set forms. They were opposed, therefore, in principle to liturgical forms. Apparently through Separatist influence, one wing within the Puritan movement gradually came to espouse this ideal of free prayer in opposition to liturgical forms. This group, known as the Independents, are the original Congregationalists.[61] The Presbyterian wing of the Puritan movement continued to favor a form of worship modeled on the Genevan Service Book.

It is only with the establishment of the Puritan Commonwealth that the differing liturgical ideals of the Presbyterians and the Independents come fully into the light. When the Westminster Assembly was convened on July 1, 1643, it sought to reform the Church of England in a manner "most agreeable to God's holy Word." The Presbyterians were in the majority in the assembly, but the Independents constituted a vocal minority. The preparation of a service book was assigned to a subcommittee consisting of four Scottish representatives, four English Presbyterians, and one articulate Independent named Thomas Goodwin. After a long and fractious debate over the issue of freedom versus liturgical forms, the committee found itself unable to produce a liturgical rite, and instead produced a manual of directions to guide ministers in framing their own extemporaneous prayers. The order for the Sunday service retained the structure of the Genevan Service Book, but in place of the liturgical forms provided there, the Directory gave a detailed summary of what each prayer ought to contain. These outlines sufficiently resembled the liturgical forms provided in Knox's liturgy that they could be readily adapted to become "set forms" if the minister were inclined to use them in that way. The Directory, therefore, represents a compromise between the ideals of the Presbyterians and the Independents. The Presbyterians managed to retain a service book in the tradition of Geneva, but the Independents won the day on the issue of extemporaneous prayer.[62]

Following on the service of the Word, the order for the Lord's Supper in the Directory begins with an Exhortation. The Directory then continues:

"After this exhortation, warning, and invitation, the Table being before decently covered, and so conveniently placed, that the communicants may orderly sit about it, or at it, the minister is to begin the action with sanctifying and blessing the elements of bread and wine set before him (the bread in comely and convenient vessels, so prepared that, being broken by him, and given, it may be distributed among the communicants; the wine also in large cups), having first, in a few words, showed that those elements, otherwise common, are now set apart and sanctified to this holy use, by the Word of Institution and Prayer.

"Let the Words of Institution be read out of the Evangelists, or out of the first Epistle of the Apostle Paul to the Corinthians, chapter 11:23. I have received of the Lord, etc., *to the 27th verse, which the minister may, when he seeth requisite, explain and apply.*

"Let the prayer, thanksgiving, or blessing of the bread and wine, be to this effect:

"With humble and hearty acknowledgment of the greatness of our misery, for which neither man nor angel was able to deliver us, and of our great unworthiness of the least of all God's mercies: to give thanks to God for all his benefits, and especially for that benefit of our redemption, the love of God the Father, the sufferings and merits of the Lord Jesus Christ the Son of God, by which we are delivered; and for all the means of grace, the Word and sacraments; and for this sacrament in particular, by which Christ, and all his benefits, are applied and sealed up unto us, which, notwithstanding the denial of them unto others, are in great mercy continued unto us, after so much and long abuse of them all.

"To profess that there is no other name under heaven by which we can be saved, but the name of Jesus Christ, by whom alone we receive liberty and life, have access to the throne of grace, are admitted to eat and drink at his own table, and are sealed by his Spirit to an assurance of happiness and everlasting life.

"Earnestly to pray to God, the Father of all mercies, and God of all consolation, to vouchsafe his gracious presence, and the effectual working of his Spirit in us; and so to sanctify these elements, both of bread and wine, and to bless his own ordinance, that we may receive by faith the body and blood of Jesus Christ, crucified for us, and so to feed upon him, that he may be one with us, and we with him; that he may live in us, and we in him, and to him who hath loved us, and given himself for us.

"All which he is to endeavor to perform with suitable affections, answerable to such an holy action, and to stir up the like in the people. The elements being now sanctified by the Word and prayer, the minister, being at the table, is to take the bread in his hand and say, in these expressions (or other the like, used by Christ or his apostle upon this occasion):

"According to the holy institution, command, and example of our blessed Savior Jesus Christ, I take this bread, and having given thanks, I break it, and give it unto you.

"There the minister, who is also himself to communicate, is to break the bread, and give it to the communicants.

"Take ye, eat ye; this is the body of Christ, which is broken for you: do this in remembrance of him.

"In like manner the minister is to take the cup, and say, in these expressions (or other the like, used by Christ or the apostle upon the same occasion):

"According to the institution, command, and example of our Lord Jesus Christ, I take this cup, and give it unto you.

"Here he giveth it to the communicants.

"This cup is the New Testament in the blood of Christ, which is shed for the remission of the sins of many: drink ye all of it.

"After all have communicated, the minister may, in a few words, put them in mind

"Of the grace of God, in Jesus Christ held forth in this sacrament; and exhort them to walk worthy of it.

"The minister is to give solemn thanks to God.

"For his rich mercy, and invaluable goodness, vouchsafed to them in that sacrament; and to entreat for pardon for the defects of the whole service, and for the gracious assistance of his good Spirit, whereby they may be enabled to walk in the strength of that grace, as becometh those who have received so great pledges of salvation.

"The Collection for the Poor is to be ordered that no part of the public worship is thereby hindered."[63]

The structure of this order follows Knox's liturgy very closely, except that the Words of Institution now follow the Exhortation and immediately precede the Eucharistic Prayer. The most striking changes, however, are found in the rubric that precedes the Institution Narrative and in the contents of the Eucharistic Prayer itself. The rubric says that ". . . the minister is to begin the action with sanctifying and blessing the elements of bread and wine set before him . . . having first, in a few words showed, that those elements, otherwise common, are now set apart and sanctified to this holy use, by the Word of Institution and prayer." In the Eucharistic Prayer itself, the most striking change is the inclusion of an explicit "epiclesis" over both the community and the elements, which expresses very clearly Calvin's teaching regarding the eucharistic presence, the role of the Holy Spirit in the operation of the sacraments, and the union with Christ that is brought about in the act of communion.

What accounts for these changes, since they reflect a definite shift in emphasis between the Calvinist liturgies of the sixteenth century and the Puritan liturgies of the seventeeth? W. D. Maxwell has pointed out that the absence of an explicit invocation or "epiclesis" in Knox's liturgy was soon felt to be a distinct lack both by the Puritans in England and by the Presbyterians in Scotland. Both the Scottish Book of Common Order and the English Puritan liturgies have a common origin in Knox's Genevan Service Book, and there is evidence from early seventeenth-century Scottish sources that Knox's liturgy was supplemented quite early in Scotland by the addition of an explicit invocation or blessing over the elements. It seems likely, therefore, that the inclusion of an invocation in the Directory is the result both of Scottish influence and of the English Puritan eucharistic theology of the period.[64]

In his book *Eucharist and Institution Narrative*, R. Buxton has shown that the predominant theory of consecration held by both Anglicans and Puritans in the seventeenth century is that the elements are consecrated by "the Word of Institution and Prayer." By "Word of Institution" here is meant the Institution Narrative, and by "Prayer" is meant the Eucharistic Prayer, but more specifically an explicit invocation, blessing, or epiclesis over the elements. The Words of Institution in the Westminster Directory still function as they did in Knox's liturgy as the scriptural authority or "warrant" for the action of the Supper, but in their position immediately before the Eucharistic Prayer, they are linked more closely with the act of consecration than was the case in Knox's liturgy. Consecration is here understood as the "sanctification" or "blessing" of the elements, i.e., their being "set apart" from a "common" to a "holy use" in communion. This view of consecration parallels exactly the view held by Anglican theologians in the same period.[65] It is one of the ironies of Church history that it was the Puritans rather than the Anglicans who were able to give it explicit liturgical expression. Despite the efforts of the best seventeenth-century Anglican liturgists to restore an epiclesis in the Anglican liturgy, the Prayer of Consecration in the Book of Common Prayer of 1662 remained unchanged from that of 1552.

The final rubric in the Directory's order for the Lord's Supper is also worthy of note:

"The Collection for the Poor is to be ordered that no part of the public worship is thereby hindered."

Here the link between worship and the service of the poor is explicitly enjoined. The offerings of the people are a sign that the community's obligation to serve the poor is the direct implication of its participation in a common act of worship. Perhaps there is an echo here of Paul's perspective in 1 Corinthians 11. A community that celebrates the Lord's Supper and neglects the service of the poor lives in self-contradiction.

SEVENTEENTH-CENTURY ANGLICANISM
Hooker set the direction for Anglican eucharistic theology in the following century, although he never functioned as a magisterial figure in the way that Luther and Calvin did for their respective traditions. Anglican writers could vary considerably in theological style, in language, and in emphasis. Already a theological pluralism is evident when we compare the eucharistic theologies of Cranmer and Hooker. While both relate the eucharistic presence primarily to the faithful communicant rather than to the elements, Hooker's language is realist rather than spiritualistic and symbolical and there is no hint of "Zwinglianism" in his thought. Cranmer developed his eucharistic theology within the framework of a theology of faith, whereas Hooker developed his within the framework of a theology of grace, although these are by no means opposed to each other. Cranmer employed primarily Augustinian categories, whereas Hooker employs the categories of medieval scholasticism. These differences do not signal a difference in doctrine so much as differences in the thought worlds by means of which the doctrine was interpreted. In the sixteenth century, the worlds of the Bible, the patristic age, medi-

eval scholasticism, and Renaissance humanism clashed with each other and reverberated in different ways often within the same person and within the same Church tradition. While the sixteenth-century reformation was primarily a religious struggle, this struggle was being acted out in the midst of vast cultural changes, the implications of which are only slowly unfolded during the following centuries.

It was characteristic of seventeenth-century Anglican writers to insist on the real presence of Christ in the eucharist but to profess agnosticism concerning the manner of the presence in the tradition of Hooker. "Receptionism," as it is often called, remained the dominant theological position within the Church of England until the Oxford Movement in the early nineteenth century, with varying differences in emphasis. It is important to remember, however, that "receptionism" is a doctrine of the real presence, but a doctrine of the real presence that relates the presence primarily to the worthy receiver rather than to the elements of bread and wine.

During the seventeenth century, an early High Church tradition emerged within Anglicanism.[66] What distinguished this early High Church tradition from moderate Anglicanism was not so much its theology of the eucharist as its spirit and its liturgical ideals. The spirit of early High Church Anglicanism is expressed primarily in a heightened sacramental spirituality. The most obvious external evidence of this is in the arrangement of the churches, where the altar takes precedence over the pulpit and there is a heightened emphasis on the use of ceremonial and vestments.[67] For Cranmer and Jewel and the continental reformers generally, word and sacrament are essentially equivalent. Preaching and the sacraments are simply different ways in which the Word of God is proclaimed and faith nourished. Their piety is essentially a piety of the Word even when this is nourished sacramentally. While there is no disparagement of preaching among the seventeenth-century High Churchmen, and some of them rank among the best preachers the Anglican tradition has produced, the spirituality nourished by their preaching is sacramentally oriented.

While the High Churchmen represented a minority within the broader spectrum of Anglicanism, they included some of the most distinguished theologians of the period and gained considerable influence through the appointment of William Laud as Archbishop of Canterbury under Charles I. Laud emphasized all those features of the Prayer Book and its ceremonial to which the Puritans objected. While the ceremonial of Laud and the other seventeenth-century High Churchmen was modest compared with that introduced in the later stages of the Oxford Movement in the nineteenth century, it was enough to inflame the Puritans, and when Laud sought to force his will by autocratic means, both King and Archbishop lost their heads in the struggle.

The other feature that distinguished the early High Church tradition was its liturgical ideals, which are only partly indicated by the emphasis on ceremonial. From the very beginning, Anglicanism had established itself as a liturgical tradition. The seventeenth century saw a new flowering of research in the early liturgies. This brought with it a desire on the part of the High Churchmen to reform the Prayer Book liturgy in order to bring it more into line with the early models, particularly in the case of the Eucharistic Prayer. It also produced a spate of liturgy writing during the seventeenth and eighteenth centuries.[68] These ideals, however, were almost entirely unrealized in their own day and have only come to fruition with modern liturgical revision.

The eucharistic thought of seventeenth-century Anglicanism has often been treated in isolation from reformed thought on the continent. The leading seventeenth-century High Churchmen, however, read the writings of the continental reformers and their own eucharistic thought can only be understood within this wider historical context. Unlike their Oxford Movement successors, who set Anglican Catholicism over against the teaching of the Protestant reformers, the seventeenth-century High Churchmen were conscious of sharing a common confession of eucharistic faith in the real presence of Christ in the eucharist with the Reformation Churches on the continent, which they regarded as the true Catholic doctrine of the eucharist, agreeable with scripture and the early Church, as over against the later doctrine of transubstantiation:

". . . none of the Protestant Churches doubt of the real (that is, true and not imaginary,) presence of Christ's Body and Blood in the Sacrament; and there appears no reason why any man should suspect their common confession, of either fraud or error, as though in this particular they had in the least departed from the Catholic faith."[69]

In all of this, the seventeenth-century High Churchmen were in continuity rather than discontinuity with Cranmer, Jewel, and Hooker. In the matter of authority, Hooker's doctrine of authority continued to serve as the basis of Anglican eucharistic teaching. Scripture provided the touchstone, but the truth of scripture is confirmed by agreement with the early Church, the other Christian confessions, and sound reason.

The progenitor of the High Church tradition and its guiding spirit was Lancelot Andrewes. William Laud, as Archbishop of Canterbury, became its ecclesiastical statesman. John Cosin, Jeremy Taylor, John Bramhall, and Herbert Thorndike, nurtured in the tradition of Andrewes and Laud, were all leading theologians during the period before and after the Puritan Commonwealth (1644–1661).

Cosin and Taylor are typical of the eucharistic thought of the period. Both are deeply immersed in the thought world of both the Greek fathers and Augustine. Taylor's sacramental thought, in particular, is steeped in a Christian Platonism, which is fused with biblical typology, giving it a range and depth that captures the full scope of the patristic understanding of the sacraments as symbols.[70] Both Taylor and Cosin teach a doctrine of the real presence of Christ in the eucharist, but relate the presence primarily to the faithful communicant rather than to the elements of bread and wine. The mode of the presence is "spiritual," i.e., it belongs to the order of grace rather than to the order of nature. As in Hooker, the real presence functions as the presupposition of their sacramental thought rather than as its focus. The focus is on the grace conveyed by means of the sacramental signs.

In true Augustinian fashion, seventeenth-century Anglican writers distinguish between the *res* of the sacrament, i.e., the reality or grace conveyed by it, and the *sacramentum* or outward sign by means of which the grace is communicated to the faithful recipient.

". . . a Sacrament . . . comprehendeth two things in it,—that which is outward and visible, which the Schools call properly *Sacramentum* . . . and that which is inward and invisible, which they term *rem sacramenti*. . . . Thus in the Lord's Supper the outward thing, which we see with our eyes, is bread and wine; the inward thing which we apprehend by faith is the Body and Blood of Christ."[71]

At the same time, they maintain a "sacramental union" between the elements and the reality signified by them.

". . . the words of Christ make the form of this Sacrament to consist in the union of the thing signified with the sign . . . and . . . because the thing signified is offered, and given to us, as truly as the sign itself . . . we own the union betwixt the Body and Blood of Christ, and the Elements . . . we [do not, therefore] deny a Sacramental Union of the Body and Blood of Christ with the Sacred Bread and Wine, so that both are really and substantially received together. . . ."[72]

The union, however, does not abolish the distinction between the *sacramentum* and the *res*, otherwise the sacrament would cease to be a sacrament, since the nature of a sacrament always consists of two parts, a visible and an invisible, and an earthly and a heavenly. While the *sacramentum* and the *res* are joined, therefore, so that the offer of grace is clearly made to all, only the faithful recipient receives the *res* of the sacrament along with the outward signs. The outward signs are received by the mouth and enter into the stomach. The *res* of the sacrament, however, is only eaten by faith.

The bread and wine become a sacrament by means of their consecration in the Eucharistic Prayer. However, since the purpose of the sacrament is only attained in the act of communion, the consecration is not separated from the "use" of the elements in communion:

"It is important to remember that by consecration all the Caroline divines seem to have meant a setting apart for the sacred use of communion; this is in sharp contrast to the contemporary Roman view which regarded it as meaning the effecting of an objective change in the substance of the elements."[73]

Hooker had already spoken of consecration as the "hallowing with solemn benediction to use."[74] This represents a recovery of the patristic notion that consecration is brought about by the Eucharistic Prayer in the tradition of the Jewish *berakah*, rather than the medieval view that consecration is effected by the recital of the words of institution.

Anglican writers can even speak of a "conversion" or "change" in the elements as a result of consecration, but this is also a change in their use, not a change in their nature or substance. Whereas before consecration the elements served a "common" use, after consecration, they serve a "sacramental" use:

"The doctrine of the Church of England, and generally of the Protestants . . . is . . . that after the minister of the holy mysteries hath rightly prayed, and blessed and consecrated the bread and the wine, the symbols become changed into the body and blood of Christ, after a sacramental . . . manner. . . ."[75]

". . . The Protestants . . . none of them denies altogether but that there is a conversion of the Bread into the Body, (and consequently the Wine into the Blood,) of Christ; for they know and acknowledge, that in the Sacrament, by virtue of the words and blessing of Christ, the condition, use, and office of the Bread is wholly changed, that is, of common and ordinary, it becomes our mystical and sacramental food; whereby, as they affirm and believe, the true Body of Christ is not only shadowed and figured, but also given indeed, and by worthy communicants truly received."[76]

". . . because this is a Sacrament, the change must be understood to be sacramental also, whereby common Bread and Wine become the Sacrament of the Body and Blood of Christ; which could not be, did not the substance of the Bread and Wine remain, for a Sacrament consisteth of two parts, an earthly and heavenly. And so because ordinary bread is changed by consecration into a bread which is no more of common use . . . it is therefore said by some of the Fathers to be changed. . . ."[77]

While the theme of the presence of Christ in relation to the faithful communicants predominates in seventeenth-century Anglican eucharistic thought, it is not the only eucharistic theme that appears there. With the partial receding of the sixteenth-century polemical context and the renewed study of the Church fathers, the sacrificial aspect of the eucharist also begins to appear again in Anglican writings. The eucharist is described as a "commemorative" or "representative" sacrifice, which in no sense adds anything to the saving significance of the cross, and the ecclesial dimension of the eucharistic sacrifice stressed by Augustine comes into view again. In a sermon preached by John Buckeridge at the funeral of Lancelot Andrewes, there is a beautiful text that perfectly expresses this Augustinian emphasis:

"As Christ's cross was His altar where He offered Himself for us, so the Church hath an altar also where it offereth itself . . . not Christ the Head properly but only by commemoration, but Christ the members. For Christ cannot be offered truly and properly no more but once upon the cross. . . . This then is the daily sacrifice of the Church in St. Augustine's resolute judgment, even the Church itself, the universal body of Christ, not the natural body, whereof the Sacrament is an exemplar and memorial only, as hath been shewed. . . . We deny not then the daily sacrifice of the Church, that is, the Church itself, warranted by Scriptures and fathers."[78]

Morever, for Anglican writers, the sacrificial aspect of the eucharist can no more be severed from the communion aspect than can the consecration be separated from the act of communion. In the following text, the eucharist is modeled on a communion sacrifice:

". . . the Eucharist was instituted by the Lord for a memorial of Himself, even of His Sacrifice, and, if it be lawful so to speak, to be a commemorative sacrifice, not only to be a Sacrament and for spiritual nourishment. . . . [N]either of these uses thus instituted by the Lord together can be divided from the other. . . . The Sacrifice which is there is Eucharistic, of which Sacrifice the law is that he who offers it is to partake of it, and that he partake by receiving and eating, as the Savior ordered."[79]

We have described the characteristic Anglican doctrine of the eucharist as a doctrine of the real partaking of the body and blood of Christ by means of the sacramental signs of bread and wine. This "receptionist" understanding of the eucharist is a doctrine of the real presence, but a doctrine of the real presence that relates the presence primarily to the faithful communicants rather than to the elements of bread and wine. What accounts for this distinctive emphasis in Anglican eucharistic doctrine?

In our study of the eucharist in the Middle Ages, we saw that there developed a gradual separation between the act of consecration and the act of communion, so that the goal of the eucharist became the production of the real presence rather than the communion of the people. This resulted in a eucharistic piety that focused on the adoration of the host rather than the reception of communion. In medieval theology, it led to a preoccupation with the question of the manner of Christ's presence in the elements. Anglican theologians from Cranmer onwards were engaged in a project of reorienting eucharistic theology away from its medieval center and reuniting the act of consecration and the act of communion. For these theologians, the goal of the eucharist is not the production of the real presence, but the nourishment of Christian believers. The real presence is the presupposition rather than the focus of their thought. The consecration of the elements is not regarded as an end in itself, but is oriented toward the act of communion. Christ is not present in the eucharist as an object on the altar, but as spiritual food and drink to nourish the life of faith. With regard to the manner of the presence, they saw the sacramental presence and communication of the body and blood of Christ as an event in the order of grace. It is this that accounts for their rejection of transubstantiation, which they interpreted as a naturalistic explanation of the eucharistic presence, implying a local or physical presence of Christ in the order of nature. For these Anglican theologians, on the other hand, the presence of Christ in the eucharist is not an event in the physical world but a presence-in-grace that is offered to all but which can only be received by those who receive it with a living faith. The elements play an instrumental role in communicating the presence of Christ to the faithful receiver, but this does not occur in a mechanical manner but only within the freedom of the grace-faith relationship.

In all of this, High Church Anglicans and moderate Anglicans shared a common body of teaching. While the early Anglican High Church tradition can be distinguished from moderate Anglicanism in its sacramental spirituality and its liturgical ideals, it is difficult, if not impossible, to establish a clear distinction in the sphere of eucharistic theology. We can agree with Richard Buxton that the difference between the two outlooks reflects "variations of the basic early seventeenth-century position,"[80] which have more to do with piety than with doctrine. Moreover, as we have seen, it is just as difficult to draw a clear distinction between Anglican and Puritan theologies of the eucharist. While Anglicans and Puritans were locked in battle throughout this period, the battle was drawn along different lines than those of eucharistic theology. Anglicans, Puritans, and the Reformed Churches on the continent, while each possessed a very different spirit, and while different emphases can be discerned among them, shared a common tradition of eucharistic theology during this period.

JOHN AND CHARLES WESLEY

The latter part of the seventeenth century and the eighteenth century represent a time of profound political, cultural, and religious change in the life of the English nation.[81] It was the period of the Enlightenment, which exalted reason as the final arbiter of truth in all spheres of life, and rocked Europe to its foundations with its challenge to all forms of political and religious authority. The rationalism of the Enlightenment had a profound effect upon English religious life. In 1695, John Locke published his *Reasonableness of Christianity*, in which he tried to show that Christianity finds its ultimate vindication in reason. In the following year, John Toland published his *Christianity not Mysterious*, in which he sought to remove all supernatural elements from Christianity and reduce it to what could be established on the basis of reason. The practical effect of the Enlightenment on English religious life was to reduce Christianity to what could be rationally demonstrated, and to remove the dimension of mystery from Christian experience. This had its effect on both eucharistic thought and eucharistic life. In eucharistic thought, the rationalism of the period is reflected in the writings of Bishop Benjamin Hoadly, who published his *A Plain Account of the Nature and End of the Lord's Supper* in 1735. Hoadly explicitly denied any real presence of Christ in the sacrament, and held it to be a simple remembrance of the death of Christ. While this set off a pamphlet war with the High Churchmen and drew an able reply from the moderate Anglican theologian Daniel Waterland in his book, *A Review of the Doctrine of the Eucharist*, there is no doubt that a position such as Hoadly's was widely held in the eighteenth century. It is not surprising, therefore, that eucharistic life in the Church of England reached its lowest ebb during this period. When the Oxford Movement began in the early nineteenth century, "Hoadlyism" was a watchword for all that was wrong with the sacramental life of the Church of England.

The High Church tradition continued on as a vigorous minority throughout this period.[82] This tradition gained considerable importance as time went on, since it was through these High Churchmen that the seventeenth-century Anglican eucharistic tradition was mediated to John and Charles Wesley and to the leaders of the Oxford Movement. Two influential High Churchmen of the period were Robert Nelson and John Johnson. Both gave the sacrificial aspect of the eucharist a much more prominent role in their writings than it had in the works of the older High Churchmen. This heightened emphasis on the sacrificial character of the eucharist is also found in Daniel Brevint's *The Christian Sacrament and Sacrifice*, published in 1673. When John and Charles Wesley published their collection of eucharistic hymns in 1745, an abridgement of Brevint's treatise served as the introduction, and the hymns were arranged according to the headings in Brevint's work.

In 1689, the Roman Catholic King James II fled the country owing to popular fear of the restoration of Roman Catholicism in England. Parliament declared the throne vacant and offered it to William and Mary. This created a crisis, particularly for the High churchmen, many of whom held a doctrine of the divine right of kings, and whose memories of the Puritan revolution were fresh. About 400 clergy and 6 bishops refused to take the oath of allegiance to William and Mary because they felt bound by their oath of allegiance to James II. As a result, they became known as Non-Jurors, and were subsequently deprived of their parishes and bishoprics. The Non-Jurors were almost all High Churchmen who espoused the liturgical and spiritual ideals of the early seventeenth century. Once outside the established church some of the Non-Jurors adopted the 1549 Prayer Book or revised the Prayer Book more freely to bring it more into line with the liturgies of the early Church.

It is against this background that we can understand the revivals of eucharistic life that took place in the latter half of the eighteenth and the early nineteenth centuries. The first of these was the evangelical revival of John and Charles Wesley. The second was the Oxford Movement. It is not commonly known today either by Anglicans or by Methodists that the Wesleyan revival was as much a eucharistic revival as it was an evangelical revival.[83] The genius of the Wesleys, however, lies precisely in the unity that they saw between a sacramental and an evangelical vision of Christianity.

John and Charles Wesley grew up in Epworth, where their father, Samuel, was vicar of the parish church.[84] Samuel Wesley was a High Churchman. Though not a Non-Juror himself, he shared the religious sympathies of the Non-Jurors, and Robert Nelson was included in the circle of his friends. John and Charles, therefore, were introduced to High Church principles during their early years of growing up in the rectory in Epworth. Susanna, their mother, was also deeply formed in seventeenth-century eucharistic spirituality and, along with their father, implanted in her sons a high regard for the sacrament, which never left them.

John Wesley went to Oxford in 1720. During his time there, he was introduced to the spirituality of Jeremy Taylor and the Non-Juror William Law as well as to the writings of Thomas à Kempis. All of this contributed to his understanding of the Christian life as a life of growth in holiness. His brother Charles came up to Oxford in 1726 and gathered a small group that practiced a disciplined spirituality and frequent communion. The group was given various nicknames by the undergraduates, including "Holy Club," "Methodists," and "Sacramentarians." Because of his natural talents, John soon became the leader of the group. The group developed a keen interest in the early liturgies through the influence of the Non-Jurors. John also read widely in the Church fathers at this time and felt particularly attracted to the spirituality of the eastern fathers, and their understanding of the goal of the Christian life as perfection.

John was ordained a deacon by the Bishop of Oxford in 1725, and in the following year, was elected a fellow of Lincoln College. He was ordained priest in 1728. In 1733, he published a famous sermon entitled *The Duty of Constant Communion*, in which he urged the practice of regular and frequent communion. It is interesting to note that Wesley reprinted this sermon fifty-five years later, only four years before his death, and in a preface, he notes that he had not seen cause to alter any of the sentiments expressed in the sermon in the intervening years.[85] This is a clear indication that Wesley's thought and practice concerning the eucharist were consistent throughout his life.

On October 14, 1735, John and Charles, with a small contingent from the Holy Club, set sail on a missionary enterprise to Georgia. For the journey and for the support of his evangelical and pastoral work in Georgia, John took with him a library, the contents of which are highly instructive. Significantly, it included 500 copies of a treatise on the eucharist, which it is not now possible to identify with certainty. These were clearly intended for Christians and converts in Georgia. His personal library included some sixty books, mostly devotional classics and liturgical works by seventeenth- and eighteenth-century Anglican High Churchmen. Among these were William Beveridge's *Pendectae*, an impressive collection of early eastern liturgical texts, Daniel

Brevint's *Missale Romanum,* and John Johnson's *The Unbloody Sacrifice,* a treatise on the eucharistic sacrifice.

The next major influence on Wesley's life began to take shape while he was on board ship. Here he met for the first time a group of Moravians, whose joyful faith made a deep impression on him. After the failure of the mission in Georgia, Wesley returned to London, where he made contact with the Moravians again, and it was on May 24, 1738, in their meeting house at Aldersgate that he had his famous conversion experience. A preacher was expounding the doctrine of justification by faith, and Wesley began to feel things happen to him, which he describes in his Journal:

"In the evening, I went very unwillingly to a society in Aldersgate Street, where one was reading Luther's Preface to the Epistle to the Romans. About a quarter before nine, while he was describing the change which God works in the heart through faith in Christ, I felt my heart strangely warmed. I felt I did trust in Christ, Christ alone for salvation; and an assurance was given me that he had taken away my sins, even mine, and saved me from the law of sin and death."[86]

While Wesley went through a series of spiritual crises over the next year, all the elements that went into his unique vision of the Christian life are now present: justification by faith as the foundation of the Christian life; the inward appropriation of God's justifying grace in the experience of "new birth," "conversion," or the "assurance of faith"; the unfolding of the Christian life as a life of growth in holiness, a deep sacramental spirituality, and a vision of the goal of the Christian life as Christian perfection.

The doctrine of the eucharist that Wesley held throughout the course of his life was the doctrine of seventeenth-century Anglicanism that he had learned in the rectory at Epworth and that was reinforced by his Oxford experience. What is distinctive about Wesley's approach to the eucharist is that this doctrine is expressed within the framework of the unique theological vision of the Christian life that we have seen emerge from the variety of experiences and influences that had come to bear on Wesley's life. This was translated into the language of popular devotion in a collection of 166 eucharistic hymns, composed by Charles and John, which combine a rich sacramentalism with their joyful evangelical experience, giving to the Methodist people a treasury of devotion unique in the history of the Christian Church.

Wesley's theological vision is a unique synthesis of the Reformation doctrine of justification by faith, the Catholic doctrine of sanctification, and the evangelical experience of "new birth," "conversion," or the inward "assurance of faith." Albert Outler has shown that this is not a hodge-podge, but a genuine theological alternative to the classical Protestant and Catholic doctrines of grace.[87] The classical western doctrine of grace, which has its roots in Augustine, speaks of three aspects of divine grace: "preventing" or "prevenient" grace, "justifying" grace, and "sanctifying" grace. Prevenient grace is Augustine's term for the grace that precedes justification. It is the grace by which God leads us toward and prepares us for the gift of salvation. Justifying grace is the grace by which God freely accepts us in Jesus Christ, giving to us the gift of salvation through no merit of our own. It is the grace about which Paul speaks especially in Romans 5. Justification is for Wesley, as it was for Paul and the reformers, the foundation of the Christian life. Wesley insists, however, that God's justifying action must be inwardly and personally appropriated. This is the evangelical side of Wesley's theological vision. The "new birth," or "conversion" or the inward "assurance of faith" is the inward and personal appropriation by faith of God's justifying grace. At the level of personal experience, it is the moment when I know that I am a forgiven sinner, that God has accepted me. This forgiveness and acceptance, however, is entirely due to the initiative of grace. It is not the result of any merit on my part.

Wesley, however, does not stop there. The grace of justification is the foundation and the beginning of the Christian life, the basis of our acceptance before God. There is another aspect to God's graceful action toward us, however, which Wesley calls by its traditional name "sanctifying grace." Sanctifying grace is the action of God within us subsequent to justification by which we are transformed into the likeness of Jesus Christ. Wesley characteristically speaks of this process of sanctification as a growth in holiness, in line with the tradition of Catholic spirituality. The fullness of this transformation or growth in holiness he calls "Christian perfection" in the tradition of the eastern fathers.

For Wesley, both justification and sanctification are the work of grace and together constitute what he means by "salvation." Faith, however, is the means by which the grace of justification and sanctification are personally appropriated. Wesley insists, therefore, that faith is the necessary condition for both justification and sanctification. Moreover, when Wesley speaks of faith, he means active faith. It is, to use one of his favorite texts, "the faith that works by love" (Gal 5:6). Faith bears fruit in the love of God and neighbor. This is not, for Wesley, a new form of works righteousness; it is the work of faith, which is itself God's gift. The whole of the Christian life, therefore, in its foundation, its growth, and its fulfillment is the work of grace, acting by means of faith, and bearing its fruit in love.

". . . salvation . . . consists of two general parts: justification and sanctification."[88]

"Justification is another word for pardon. It is the forgiveness of all our sins and, what is necessarily implied therein, our acceptance with God."[89]

"And at the same time that we are justified—yea, in that very moment—sanctification begins. In that instant we are 'born again, born from above, born of the spirit.' . . ."[90]

"From the time of our being 'born again,' the gradual work of sanctification takes place. We are enabled 'by the Spirit' to 'mortify the deeds of the body' [Rom 8:11, 13], of our evil nature, and as we are more and more dead to sin, we are more and more alive to God. We go on from grace to grace. . . ."[91]

"It is thus that we wait for entire sanctification, for a full salvation from all our sins—from pride, self-will, anger, unbelief—or, as the apostle expresses it, 'go on unto perfection' [Heb 6:1]. But what is perfection? The word has various senses: here it means perfect love."[92]

"Faith is the condition, and the only condition of sanctification, exactly as it is of justification . . . (nevertheless, we cannot) perform one good action, but through . . . (God's) free, almighty grace, first preventing us and then accompanying us every moment."[93]

This is the theological framework within which Wesley discusses the sacraments.[94] For Wesley, the sacraments are the privileged means by which God's preventing, justifying, and sanctifying grace is conveyed. The sacraments are above all, for Wesley, "means of grace." By "means of grace," Wesley says,

"I understand outward signs, words, or actions ordained of God, and appointed for this end—to be the *ordinary* channels whereby he might convey to men preventing, justifying, or sanctifying grace."[95]

Wesley is very clear, however, that the sacraments are means of grace and not ends. If means and ends are confused, a confusion results between "outward" religion and the "inward" religion of the heart. True religion does not consist in outward observances, but "in a heart renewed after the image of God."[96] The sacraments are not the cause of our salvation: "the use of all means whatever will never atone for one sin. . . ."[97] The "whole value of the means," says Wesley, "depends on their . . . subservience to the end of religion,"[98] which is a renewed heart and the love of God and neighbor that flows from it. Outward reception of the sacraments is no substitute for this inward transformation of the heart:

". . . all outward means whatever, if separate from the Spirit of God cannot profit at all, cannot conduce in any degree, either to the knowledge or love of God."[99]

When the sacraments are separated from their end, therefore, they have no value. Used rightly, however, as a means, the sacraments have great value in the Christian life: ". . . the outward ordinances of God . . . profit much when they advance inward holiness, but when they advance it not are unprofitable and void. . . ."[100]

We can trust that God will convey grace through the means, for "whatever God hath promised, he is faithful also to perform,"[101] but we dare not trust in the means themselves, but only in God, who is alone the author of grace:

"It is he alone who, by his own almighty power, worketh in us what is pleasing in his sight. And all outward things, unless he work in them and by them, are mere weak and beggarly elements. Whosoever therefore imagines there is any intrinsic *power* in any means whatsoever does greatly err, not knowing the Scriptures, neither the power of God. We know that there is no inherent power in . . . the bread and wine received in the Lord's supper; but that it is God alone who is the giver of every good gift, the author of all grace; that the whole power is of him, whereby through any of these there is any blessing conveyed to our souls."[102]

It is significant that Wesley defines the sacraments as means that convey "preventing, justifying, or sanctifying grace." Wesley held that the sacraments are means of grace both before and after conversion. This is expressed in his conviction that the Lord's Supper is both a "converting" and "confirming" ordinance.[103] The Lord's Supper can be a means of bringing some to conversion; it can be the actual occasion on which some are converted, and it can be the means by which those who are already converted are sustained in the life of holiness that leads to perfection. This view of the sacraments was confirmed by Wesley's experience of many being converted at the large communion services that he held during the early days of the Methodist movement. Wesley's policy, therefore, was to admit to the Lord's table all who were conscious of their own sin and desired to receive whatever grace God wished to give in the sacrament. Wesley interpreted the dominical command to "Do this" as an invitation "to all those who either already are filled with peace and joy in believing, or who can truly say, 'The remembrance of our sins is grievous unto us; the burden of them is intolerable.' "[104] He says, "Let all, therefore, who truly desire the grace of God, eat of that bread and drink of that cup."[105]

Wesley acknowledges, both on the basis of scripture and pastoral experience that there is no one order in which God's grace works in the lives of men and women. God likewise employs the means of grace in a variety of ways to bring people to salvation:

". . . the means into which different men are led, and in which they find the blessing of God, are varied, transposed, and combined together a thousand different ways."[106]

It is false, therefore, to insist that God must act in people's lives according to a predetermined pattern. The measure of pastoral wisdom is to observe how the Spirit of God is at work in the lives of people and to lead them

". . . step by step through all the means which God has ordained; not according to our own will, but just as the providence and the Spirit of God go before and open the way."[107]

". . . the sure and general rule for all who groan for the salvation of God is this—whenever opportunity serves, use all the means which God has ordained. For who knows in which God will meet thee with the grace that bringeth salvation?"[108]

It is in their hymns above all that the Wesleys' doctrine of the Lord's Supper is most fully transmitted. Here we find the seventeenth-century Anglican doctrine of the eucharist refracted through the evangelical experience of the Wesleyan revival. We have already seen that the Wesleys published their collection of eucharistic hymns with an extract of Daniel Brevint's treatise *The Christian Sacrament and Sacrifice* as the preface. It will help us understand the theology of the hymns, therefore, if we first look at the theology of Brevint's treatise. There is nothing there that cannot be paralleled in earlier seventeenth-century Anglican writers. What is remarkable about the treatise is its scope and balance, and its recovery of eucharistic themes that had become marginalized or repressed in the tradition. This is particularly true of the eschatological perspective to which Brevint devotes a whole section. The sacrificial theme, which had appeared only hesitantly in the writings of early seventeenth-century Anglican writers because of their proximity to the polemical situation of the sixteenth century with its attack on the sacrifice of the mass, now receives a much more prominent place in Brevint's treatise. By taking this treatise as their starting point, therefore, the Wesleys were able to transmit to the Methodist people the full breadth of New Testament and patristic eucharistic themes in a way that had not been possible for centuries, and to do so in the language of popular devotion that enabled them to become part of the inner convictions and daily experience of hundreds of ordinary Christian people.

In his understanding of the operation of the sacraments, Brevint combines the language of sacramental signification and sacramental causality. As signs, the sacraments represent what they signify. The sacraments, however, are more than signs. They are means of grace, "moral instruments," which convey what they signify and represent. According to Brevint, there are three fundamental aspects to the eucharist: a past, a present, and a future aspect. The eucharist is, first of all, a memorial of the saving death of Christ. Secondly, it is present grace and nourishment for worthy receivers. Thirdly, it is a pledge that assures our participation in the life of the promised kingdom of God.

In his understanding of the eucharist as a memorial, Brevint recovers the authentic meaning of the eucharistic memorial as the effective representation in the present of the redemptive reality of events that took place once for all in the past:

"The main intention of Christ was not here to propose a bare image of his passion once suffered, in order to a bare remembrance; but, over and above, to enrich this memorial with such an effectual and real presence of continuing Atonement and strength, as may both evidently set forth Christ Himself crucified before our eyes, (Gal iii.1,) and invite us to his sacrifice, not as done and gone many years since, but, as to expiating grace and mercy, still lasting, still new, still the same that it was when it was first offered for us."[109]

In its eschatological aspect,

". . . the holy Communion has this third use, namely, of being a pledge and an assurance from the Lord, that in His good time he will crown us with everlasting happiness.

"Our Blessed Savior pointed at it when He said to his disciples, the holy cup being in his hand, that He would drink no more of that fruit till He should drink it new in the kingdom of his Father (Lk xxii.18). . . . Let them not whom He hath invited to eat and drink at Abraham's table trouble themselves about the room where our blessed Savior will feed them; . . . it is a sufficient assurance that in time He will also make them sit in that other palace where this holy man is now happy; and whosoever are admitted to the dinner of the Lamb slain (Mt xxii.4), unless they be wanting to themselves, must not doubt of being admitted to the wedding supper of the same Lamb, who once was dead, but now is living for ever (Lk xiv.16; Rv xix.9)."[110]

In treating of the sacrificial theme, Brevint is absolutely clear that the sacrifice of Christ on the cross took place once for all in the past and cannot be repeated, and that it atones completely for sin:

"As for the . . . expiation of sins, it is most certain, that the Sacrifice of Jesus Christ alone hath been sufficient for it; and that if all, both men and angels, were joined to it, it were not to add to, but to receive from its fullness."[111]

In what sense then can the eucharist be called a sacrifice? It can be called a sacrifice in at least three senses: in the first sense, the eucharist is a commemorative sacrifice:

". . . this Sacrifice, which, by a real oblation, was not to be offered more than once, is, by an eucharistical and devout commemoration, to be offered up every day . . . as . . . St. Augustin did explain when he said, that the holy flesh of Jesus Christ was offered up . . . in real deed upon the cross; and by a commemorative Sacrifice after he is ascended into heaven."[112]

Appealing again to Augustine, and also to Cyprian, Brevint also speaks of the eucharist as a sacrifice in a second ecclesial sense. The eucharist is not only a commemorative sacrifice of Christ's death, but it is the offering of the whole Church in union with Christ as its Head. The sacrifice of Christ and the sacrifice of Christians can no more be separated from each other "than parts are from the whole, or the body from its head":

"These two are so close coupled together, that St. Austin more than once, by the body of Christ in the holy Communion, understands Christ's mystical body, which is the Church. And St. Cyprian says expressly, that Christ and his people are contained and united together in the holy cup (that being represented by the wine, this represented by the water); so that Christ is not there without his people, nor the people without their Savior."[113]

Brevint also speaks of the eucharist as a sacrifice in a third sense. In line with the Epistle to the Hebrews, Brevint sees Christ as the eternal High Priest in heaven who continually presents before the Father his completed sacrifice on the cross as the basis of our acceptance before him. In making the memorial of Christ's death in the eucharist, therefore, the Church not only commemorates a past action, but Christians on earth now are united with Christ in the eternal pleading of his completed sacrifice in heaven.

". . . Jesus our eternal Priest, being, from the cross, where he suffered without the gate, gone up into the true sanctuary, which is heaven, there, above, doth continually present both his body in true reality, and us, as Aaron did the twelve tribes of Israel, in a memorial (Ex xxviii.29); and on the other side, we, beneath, in the Church, present to God his body and blood in a memorial; that under this shadow of his cross, and image of his Sacrifice, we may present ourselves before him in very deed and reality."[114]

The Wesleys' collection of eucharistic hymns follows the themes in Brevint's treatise very closely. These themes are reflected in the following verses from some representative hymns. A number of verses from the hymns bring out the character of the sacraments as signs and instruments, means of grace that effectually convey what they signify.[115]

"Author of our salvation, Thee
    With lowly thankful hearts we praise,
Author of this great mystery,
    Figure and means of saving grace.

"The sacred, true, effectual sign,
  Thy body and Thy blood it shows;
The glorious instrument Divine
  Thy mercy and Thy strength bestows."[116]

"Jesu, my Lord and God, bestow
All which Thy sacrament doth show,
  And make the real sign
A sure effectual means of grace,
Then sanctify my heart, and bless,
  And make it all like Thine.

"Great is Thy faithfulness and love,
Thine ordinance can never prove
  Of none effect, and vain;
Only do Thou my heart prepare
To find Thy real presence there,
  And all Thy fullness gain."[117]

"Draw near, ye blood-besprinkled race,
  And take what God vouchsafes to give;
The outward sign of inward grace,
  Ordain'd by Christ Himself, receive:
The sign transmits the signified,
The grace is by the means applied."[118]

The threefold character of the eucharist as a memorial of Christ's
death, as present grace, and as pledge of future glory is brought
out in Hymn 94:

"O what a soul-transporting feast
  Doth this communion yield!
Remembering here Thy passion past,
  We with Thy love are fill'd.

"Sure instrument of present grace
  Thy sacrament we find,
Yet higher blessings it displays,
  And raptures still behind.

"It bears us now on eagle's wings,
   If Thou the power impart,
And Thee our glorious earnest brings
   Into our faithful heart.

"O let us still the earnest feel,
   Th' unutterable peace,
This loving Spirit be the seal
   Of our eternal bliss!"

The hymns also put us in touch with the Passover and manna
traditions, which are placed in the context of Biblical typology
and linked with the Bread of Life discourse in John 6:

"Our Passover for us is slain,
The Tokens of His death remain,
   On these authentic signs imprest:
By Jesus out of Egypt led,
Still on the Paschal Lamb we feed,
   And keep the sacramental feast.

"That arm that smote the parting sea
Is still stretch'd out for us, for me;
   The Angel-God is still our Guide,
And, lest we in the desert faint,
We find our spirits' every want
   By constant miracle supplied.

"Thy flesh for our support is given,
Thou art the Bread sent down from heaven,
   That all mankind by Thee might live;
O that we evermore may prove
The manna of Thy quickening love,
   And all Thy life of grace receive!

"Nourish us to that awful day
When types and veils shall pass away,
   And perfect grace in glory end;
Us for the marriage feast prepare,
Unfurl Thy banner in the air,
   And bid Thy saints to heaven ascend."[119]

Hymn 72 is clearly epicletic in character and brings out the role of the Spirit in the realization of the sacrament.

"Come, Holy Ghost, Thine influence shed,
    And realize the sign;
Thy life infuse into the bread,
    Thy power into the wine.

"Effectual let the tokens prove,
    And made, by heavenly art,
Fit channels to convey Thy love
    To every faithful heart."

The hymns also set forth the sacrificial character of the eucharist in its various aspects as reflected in Brevint's treatise. The Wesleys, like Brevint, are absolutely clear that the cross is the all-sufficient act of expiation that atones for human sin. Nothing can add to the completeness of that sacrifice and it cannot be repeated. The eucharist can be called a sacrifice, however, in the three senses suggested by Brevint. The eucharist is a commemorative sacrifice. It is the sacrifice of the Church in which Christians are joined with Christ their head. It can also be called a sacrifice in the sense that in the eucharist, Christians are united with Christ in the continual offering of his completed sacrifice before the Father's throne as the foundation of their acceptance in him. These various aspects of the eucharistic sacrifice are evident in the following verses from the hymns.

"All hail, Redeemer of mankind!
Thy life on Calvary resign'd
    Did fully once for all atone;
Thy blood hath paid our utmost price,
Thine all-sufficient sacrifice
    Remains eternally alone:

"Angels and men might strive in vain,
They could not add the smallest grain
    T' augment Thy death's atoning power,
The sacrifice is all complete,
The death Thou never canst repeat,
    Once offer'd up to die no more."[120]

"The cross on Calvary He bore,
He suffer'd once to die no more,
   But left a sacred pledge behind:
See here!—It on Thy altar lies,
Memorial of the sacrifice
   He offer'd once for all mankind."[121]

"Memorial of Thy sacrifice,
   This eucharistic mystery
The full atoning grace supplies,
   And sanctifies our gifts in Thee:"[122]

"Would the Savior of mankind
   Without His people die?
No, to Him we all are join'd
   As more than standers by." [123]

"With Him, the Corner-stone,
   The living stones conjoin;
Christ and His church are one,
   One body and one vine;
For us he uses all his powers,
And all He has, or is, is ours."[124]

"For us He ever intercedes,
His heaven-deserving passion pleads,
   Presenting us before the throne;
We want no sacrifice beside,
By that great Offering sanctified,
   One with our Head, for ever one."[125]

Perhaps the most glorious of all the hymns is Hymn 93, which
brings out magnificently the eschatological perspective:

"Come, let us join with one accord
Who share the supper of the Lord,
   Our Lord and Master's praise to sing;
Nourish'd on earth with living bread,
We now are at His table fed,
   But wait to see our heavenly King;
To see the great Invisible

Without a sacramental veil,
  With all His robes of glory on,
In rapturous joy and love and praise
Him to behold with open face,
  High on His everlasting throne!

"The wine which doth His passion show,
We soon with Him shall drink it new
  In yonder dazzling courts above;
Admitted to the heavenly feast,
We shall His choicest blessings taste,
  And banquet on His richest love.
We soon the midnight cry shall hear,
Arise, and meet the Bridegroom near,
  The marriage of the Lamb is come;
Attended by His heavenly friends,
The glorious King of saints descends
  To take His bride in triumph home.

"Then let us still in hope rejoice,
And listen for th' archangel's voice
  Loud echoing to the trump of God,
Haste to the dreadful joyful day,
When heaven and earth shall flee away,
  By all-devouring flames destroy'd;
While we from out the burnings fly,
With eagle's wings mount up on high,
  Where Jesus is on Sion seen;
'Tis there He for our coming waits,
And lo, the everlasting gates
  Lift up their heads to take us in!

"By faith and hope already there,
Even now the marriage-feast we share,
  Even now we by the Lamb are fed;
Our Lord's celestial joy we prove,
Led by the Spirit of His love,
  To springs of living comfort led:
Suffering and curse and death are o'er,

And pain afflicts the soul no more
  While harbour'd in the Savior's breast;
He quiets all our plaints and cries,
And wipes the sorrow from our eyes,
  And lulls us in His arms to rest!"

These few verses give but an indication of the rich eucharistic theology that is to be found in the Wesleys' hymns. More than that, they only hint at the rich fare that the Wesleys believed was available to nourish Christian believers at the Lord's table, and that awaits them at the banquet table in the kingdom.

THE OXFORD MOVEMENT

In the early nineteenth century, the Wesleyan revival was followed by another renewal of eucharistic life in the Church of England called the Oxford Movement or the Anglo-Catholic revival. This new High Church movement is also known as the Tractarian movement, since the leaders of the movement sought to disseminate their views by means of a series of tracts known as the *Tracts for the Times*. The leaders of the movement were John Keble, Edward Bouverie Pusey, John Henry Newman, and Richard Froude. The systematic theologian of the movement was Robert Isaac Wilberforce. Its aim was the restoration of the Catholic heritage of the Church of England, and in particular a revival of its sacramental life.[126]

The most important contribution of the Oxford Movement was its sacramental interpretation of Christianity, expressed in what is called the "sacramental principle."[127] The sacramental principle is the belief that divine grace is primarily mediated to humanity by means of earthly, material, historical realities. In his *Apologia Pro Vita Sua*, Newman tells us that his adoption of the sacramental principle was confirmed by his reading of the Alexandrian theologians Clement and Origen.[128] Here Newman was in touch with the fountainhead of the Christian Platonism that we described in Chapter Two, with its understanding of symbols as earthly realities that participate in and mediate the divine reality.

In its widest application, the sacramental principle means that the whole created universe is a sacrament or symbol of the divine presence. In its more specific application, however, the central paradigm of the sacramental principle is the Incarnation. In the Incarnation, God mediated salvation in and through the earthly, created, human reality of Jesus of Nazareth. For the Tractarians, the Incarnation is the beginning of the redemptive transformation of creation. As the risen and ascended Lord, Jesus Christ is the beginning of a new creation, the head of a transformed humanity.

God continues to mediate the salvation, which was accomplished once for all through the incarnate life, death, and resurrection of Jesus by incorporating men and women into his risen humanity. The primary means by which this is brought about is by sacramental incorporation into the Church, the body of Christ, which is the earthly, visible, historical sign of the new creation. Through baptism, men and women are grafted sacramentally into Christ's humanity and become one body in him. In the eucharist, this participation in the body of Christ is continually renewed. Sacramental incorporation, therefore, has both a Christological and an ecclesiological dimension.

It is against the background of the centrality of the sacramental principle that we must understand the close connection that the Tractarians saw between the presence of Christ in the eucharist and the material elements of bread and wine. In their earlier writings, the Tractarians, like Hooker and the seventeenth-century Anglican theologians, acknowledged the real presence of Christ in the sacrament, but emphasized its mysterious character and avoided any philosophical explanation of the manner of the presence. In the course of defending their views, however, they were forced to give a more definite account of their position. It was R. I. Wilberforce who gave the Tractarian doctrine its fullest systematic exposition in his book *The Doctrine of the Holy Eucharist*.[129]

The Tractarians are agreed that there is a strict identity between the earthly body of Christ, his risen body, and his sacramental body. The only difference is in the manner or mode of the presence. While connecting the eucharistic presence of Christ more closely to the elements than did the earlier Anglican theologians, the Tractarians were entirely at one with them in insisting that the manner of the presence is spiritual and not physical or local. It is a presence in the order of grace and not a presence in the order of nature. Christ is present in the eucharist, however, in a specific way, namely, by means of sacramental signs.

There is nothing here that goes essentially beyond what can be found in the older seventeenth-century Anglican writers except by way of emphasis. The Tractarians, however, went decisively beyond the earlier Anglican theology in making a clear distinction between the presence of Christ in relation to the elements and the presence of Christ in relation to the worthy communicants. According to Tractarian teaching, the presence of Christ in relation to the elements is brought about by the act of consecration and is not dependent on their reception in communion. This position was given its clearest conceptual expression by Wilberforce, who distinguished not only between the *res* of the sacrament and its *sacramentum* as did the earlier Anglican writers, but also between the *res* and the *virtus* of the sacrament. The *res* of the sacrament is the reality signified by the outward signs, namely, Christ himself. The *virtus* of the sacrament is the blessing, effect, or grace that Christ gives to all who receive the sacrament in faith. The union between the *res* and the *sacramentum* is brought about by the consecration. After the consecration, Christ is objectively present in relation to the elements. This union between the *res* and the *sacramentum*, however, is a sacramental union, not the presence of an object in the physical world. Christ is not present in the elements in a physical or natural mode, but in a sacramental mode, that is, in the manner of a real symbol that participates in and mediates the reality that it symbolizes. The reality or *res* of the sacrament is offered to the communicants by means of the sacramental signs irrespective of their faith, but only those who receive the sacrament by faith receive the *virtus*, or grace of the sacrament. The purpose of distinguishing between the *res* and the *virtus* of the sacrament is to make it clear that Christ is objectively present in relation to the elements by means of their consecration, but present in grace only to those who receive him by faith.

The Oxford Movement, however, was not only a theological movement. It was also a parish movement, and the theological principles that were being worked out by the leaders of the movement were soon translated into practice in parish life. One of the forgotten aspects of the Oxford Movement is the close connection that the Tractarians saw between the revival of eucharistic worship and the social mission of the Church. Because of their belief in the sacramental principle, they saw an intimate relationship between sacramental worship and the transformation of the social and economic conditions of life. If Christ has taken our flesh in the incarnation, then the redemptive purpose of God includes the transformation of the whole material world. If grace is primarily mediated by earthly, material, created realities, then there must be a connection between the consecration and reception of the material elements of bread and wine in the eucharist and the transformation of society. Sacramental participation in Christ's body implies the transformation of the social and economic order.

In a recent article, R. W. Franklin has documented the relationship of the Oxford Movement to English industrial society in the early nineteenth century. The early leaders of the Oxford Movement were very much alive to the new social and economic conditions created by the Industrial Revolution of the eighteenth century and to the appalling slum conditions that had been created in the industrial centers of England. E. B. Pusey led a campaign to revive the sacramental life in these areas and to build parish churches in the new industrial towns. In these parishes, eucharistic worship and social concern were intimately linked:

"For adherents of Pusey, soon known as Puseyites, the eucharist gave new significance to earth as well as to eternity, to matter as well as to spirit. In their parishes justice began to flow from the eucharist: funds for workers' compensation, funds for worthy burial, and distribution centers for clothing, food and other necessities. From 1840 to 1900 the bond between worship and social justice was dramatized in Puseyite parishes in commercial districts."[130]

From 1835 to 1853, Pusey himself spent considerable time in the milltown of Leeds. The deplorable misery and poverty of this town was made famous by Friedrich Engels in his *The Condition of the Working Class in England.* The social thrust of the Oxford Movement was especially evident in the East End of London, where the Anglo-Catholic parishes united a revival of eucharistic worship and Catholic ceremonial with care for the poor.

By the end of the nineteenth century, the Anglo-Catholic movement tended to turn inwards upon itself, but the unity between liturgical life and social justice was maintained into the twentieth century, especially by the new Anglican religious orders and by a few daring spirits. One of the greatest of these was Frank Weston, Bishop of Zanzibar, who in a stirring address to the Anglo-Catholic Congress in 1923 recalled his hearers to the roots of the movement:

". . . if you are prepared to fight for the right of adoring Jesus in his Blessed Sacrament, then you have got to come out from before your Tabernacle and walk, with Christ mystically present in you, out into the streets of this country, and find the same Jesus in the people of your cities and your villages. You cannot claim to worship Jesus in the Tabernacle, if you do not pity Jesus in the slum. . . . And it is folly—it is madness—to suppose that you can worship Jesus in the Sacraments and Jesus on the Throne of glory, when you are sweating him in the souls and bodies of his children. It cannot be done. . . . You have got your Mass, you have got your Altar, you have begun to get your Tabernacle. Now go out into the highways and hedges. . . . Go out and look for Jesus in the ragged, in the naked, in the oppressed and sweated, in those who have lost hope, in those who are struggling to make good. Look for Jesus. And when you see him, gird yourselves with his towel and try to wash their feet."[131]

NOTES

1. For the progress of the reformation in England, see A. G. Dickens, *The English Reformation,* rev. ed. (London: Collins, Fontana Library, 1967).

2. Text in Charles Hardwick, *A History of the Articles of Religion* (London: George Bell & Sons, 1895), 289–353.

3. See G. J. Cuming, *A History of Anglican Liturgy*, 2d ed. (London: Macmillan, 1982), 45–47.

4. See C. W. Dugmore, *The Mass and the English Reformers* (London: Macmillan, 1958), 112ff.

5. Text in Colin Buchanan (ed.), *Background Documents to Liturgical Revision 1547–1549*, Grove Liturgical Studies, no. 35 (Bramcote, Notts.: Grove Books, 1983), 15–33.

6. Text of the 1549 eucharistic rite in Colin Buchanan, *Eucharistic Liturgies of Edward VI*, Grove Liturgical Studies, no. 34 (Bramcote, Notts.: Grove Books, 1983), 7–20 (Outline and canon in *PEER*, 234–243). For commentary, see Cuming, *Anglican Liturgy*, 51–59; idem, *The Godly Order: Texts and Studies Relating to the Book of Common Prayer*, Alcuin Club Collections, no. 65 (London: SPCK, 1983), Chap. 5.

7. Dix, *The Shape of the Liturgy*, 640–674; Gregory Dix, "Dixit Cranmer et non Timuit—I," *Church Quarterly Review*, 145 (1948): 145–176; Gregory Dix, "Dixit Cranmer et non Timuit—II," *Church Quarterly Review*, 146 (1948): 44–60.

8. G. B. Timms, *Dixit Cranmer* (London: A. R. Mowbray, 1946).

9. Dugmore, 182–201.

10. Peter Brooks, *Thomas Cranmer's Doctrine of the Eucharist: An Essay in Historical Development* (New York: Seabury Press, 1965).

11. Cyril C. Richardson, "Cranmer and the Analysis of Eucharistic Doctrine," *Journal of Theological Studies*, n.s., 16 (1965): 421–437. See also his earlier work, *Zwingli and Cranmer on the Eucharist* (Evanston, IL: Seabury-Western Theological Seminary, 1949).

12. Cranmer, *Works* PS 2.218. (PS refers to the Parker Society edition. Citations are by volume and page.)

13. Ridley, *Works* PS 274–275.

14. Text in Calvin, *Tracts and Treatises*, 2:212–20.

15. Cranmer, *Works* PS 1.79.

16. Cranmer, *Works* PS 1.395–396. This text illustrates the problem of Cranmer interpretation. Cranmer cannot mean that the substance of the body of Christ is in the elements, but that we are substantially united with Christ in communion. Richardson is clearly puzzled by this text (Richardson, *Zwingli and Cranmer*, 25, n. 67).

17. Cranmer, *Works* PS 1.70.

18. The phrase is found in Article 26 of Cranmer's *Forty-Five Articles* (1552). Text in Hardwick, 284.

19. Cranmer, *Works* PS 1.148. Cf. Richardson, *Zwingli and Cranmer*, 34–35.

20. *Original Letters relative to the English Reformation written during the reigns of King Henry VIII, King Edward VI, and Queen Mary*, PS 1.13.

21. See Cuming, *Anglican Liturgy*, 70–76.

22. Text in Buchanan, *Eucharistic Liturgies of Edward VI*, 21–33; PEER, 246–249. Commentary in Cuming, *Anglican Liturgy*, 77–81.

23. See Colin Buchanan, *What did Cranmer think he was doing?* Grove Liturgical Studies, no. 7 (Bramcote, Notts.: Grove Books, 1976).

24. John E. Booty (ed.), *The Book of Common Prayer 1559* (Charlottesville: University Press of Virginia, 1976).

25. Text of the "Black Rubric" or "Declaration on Kneeling," in Buchanan, *Eucharistic Liturgies of Edward VI*, 33.

26. For Jewel's eucharistic doctrine, see John E. Booty, *John Jewel as Apologist of the Church of England* (London: SPCK, 1963), Chap. 7. For Peter Martyr, see Joseph C. McLelland, *The Visible Words of God* (Edinburgh: Oliver & Boyd, 1957).

27. Jewel, *Works*, PS 1.448.

28. *Ibid.*, 2.1099.

29. *Ibid.*

30. *Ibid.*, 1.448–449.

31. *Ibid.*, 3.64.

32. For Hooker's sources, see John E. Booty, "Hooker's Understanding of the Presence of Christ in the Eucharist," in John E. Booty (ed.), *The Divine Drama in History and Liturgy* (Allison Park, PA: Pickwick Publications, 1984), 131–148; for his method, see W. Speed Hill (ed.), *Studies in Richard Hooker* (Cleveland: Case Western Reserve University Press, 1972); for his eucharistic theology, see Olivier Loyer, *L'Anglicanisme de Richard Hooker*, 2 vols. (Paris: Librairie Honore Champion, 1979), 1:475–542. For eucharistic developments during this period, see Richard F. Buxton, *Eucharist and Institution Narrative: A Study in the The Roman and Anglican Traditions of the Consecration of the Eucharist from the Eighth to the Twentieth Centuries.* Alcuin Club Collections, no. 58 (Great Wakering: Mayhew-

McCrimmon, 1976), and C. W. Dugmore, *Eucharistic Doctrine in England from Hooker to Waterland* (London: SPCK, 1942).

33. Hooker, *Laws* 5.50.3. Citations from Hooker are from *Of the Laws of Ecclesiastical Polity*, in John Keble (ed.), *The Works of . . . Mr. Richard Hooker*, 7th rev. ed. (Oxford: Clarendon Press, 1888), by book, chapter, and section.

34. *Laws* 5.67.7.

35. *Laws* 5.67.5.

36. *Laws* 5.67.1.

37. *Laws* 5.55.1.

38. *Laws* 5.67.6.

39. *Laws* 5.67.12.

40. *Laws* 5.53.1–4, 54.9, 55.1–9, 67.10.

41. *Laws* 5.55.9.

42. *Laws* 5.67.9,11,12.

43. Cf. *Laws* 5.57.4,5.

44. *Laws* 5.67.6.

45. *Laws* 5.67.6.

46. *Laws* 5.67.6.

47. *Laws* 5.67.5.

48. For Puritan sacramental theology, see E. Brooks Holifield, *The Covenant Sealed: The Development of Puritan Sacramental Theology in Old and New England, 1570–1720* (New Haven: Yale University Press, 1974).

49. See Horton Davies, *The Worship of the English Puritans* (London: Dacre Press, 1948).

50. For Puritans and Separatists, see Bryan D. Spinks, *From the Lord and "The Best Reformed Churches:" A study of the Eucharistic Liturgy in the English Puritan and Separatist Traditions 1550–1633*, Bibliotheca "Ephemerides Liturgicae" Subsidia, no. 33 (Rome: C.L.V.–Edizioni Liturgiche, 1984), 7–16.

51. See Cuming, *Anglican Liturgy*, Chap. 7.

52. For the eucharist in Congregationalism, see Bryan D. Spinks, *Freedom or Order? The Eucharistic Liturgy in English Congregationalism 1645–*

1980, Pittsburgh Theological Monographs, n.s., no. 8 (Allison Park, PA: Pickwick Publications, 1984).

53. See Dickens, 394–400.

54. Text in Robin Leaver (ed.), *The Liturgy of the Frankfurt Exiles 1555*, Grove Liturgical Studies, no. 38 (Bramcote Notts.: Grove Books, 1984). The text printed here is normally regarded as the "Liturgy of Compromise" drawn up by John Knox and Thomas Lever to appease the Prayer Book party before Cox's arrival and Knox's departure (see Spinks, *From the Lord*, 70–76), but Leaver argues that it was drawn up and put into use *after* Knox's departure.

55. Text and commentary in William D. Maxwell, *The Liturgical Portions of the Genevan Service Book* (London: Faith Press, 1965); Bard Thompson, *Liturgies of the Western Church* (Cleveland: Collins, 1961), 287–307. Commentary in Spinks, *From the Lord*, 76–84.

56. *PEER*, 252–257.

57. See Spinks, *From the Lord*, 22–28.

58. *Ibid.*, 114–119.

59. Text and commentary in Thompson, 311–341. Commentary in Spinks, *From the Lord*, 119–121.

60. See Davies, Chap. 7; Spinks, *From the Lord*, 28–32.

61. See Spinks, *From the Lord*, 32–34 and *Freedom or Order?*, Chap. 1.

62. Text and commentary in Ian Breward, *The Westminster Directory*, Grove Liturgical Studies, no. 21 (Bramcote, Notts.: Grove Books, 1980); Thompson, 345–371; eucharistic prayer in *PEER*, 267–269. Commentary in E. C. Ratcliff, "Puritan Alternatives to the Prayer Book," in *The English Prayer Book 1549–1662* (London: SPCK, 1963), 56–81; Spinks, *Freedom or Order?* Chap. 2.

63. *PEER*, 267–269 (concluding section added).

64. Maxwell, *Genevan Service Book*, 134–135; Ratcliff, 69–70; Spinks, *Freedom or Order?* 44–46.

65. Buxton, 142–144.

66. See G. W. O. Addleshaw, *The High Church Tradition* (London: Faber & Faber, 1941).

67. See G. W. O. Addleshaw and F. Etchells, *The Architectural Setting of Anglican Worship* (London: Faber & Faber, 1948), Chap. 4.

68. See W. Jardine Grisbrooke, *Anglican Liturgies of the Seventeenth and*

Eighteenth Centuries, Alcuin Club Collections, no. 40 (London: SPCK, 1958).

69. John Cosin, *Historia Transubstantiationis Papalis . . .,* translated in *Tracts for the Times,* vol. 1 (London: Rivington, 1840): 27.3 (citations from Cosin are by tract and page no. in this volume).

70. For Taylor's eucharistic teaching, see Harry Boone Porter, *Jeremy Taylor Liturgist,* Alcuin Club Collections, no. 61 (London: SPCK, 1979), Chap. 4.

71. James Ussher, cited in Paul Elmer More and Frank Leslie Cross, *Anglicanism: The Thought and Practice of the Church of England, Illustrated from the Religious Literature of the Seventeenth Century* (London: SPCK, 1962), 488.

72. Cosin, 27.13–15.

73. Buxton, 131.

74. *Ibid.* Cf. Hooker, *Laws* 5.67.12.

75. Taylor, *Real Presence,* cited in Darwell Stone, *A History of the Doctrine of the Holy Eucharist,* 2 vols. (London: Longmans, Green, & Co., 1909), 2:332.

76. Cosin, 27.12.

77. Cosin, 28.14.

78. Cited in Stone, 2:266–267.

79. Lancelot Andrewes, cited in More & Cross, 465.

80. Buxton, 131.

81. For the history of the period, see John R. H. Moorman, *A History of the Church in England,* 3d ed. (London: Adam & Charles Black, 1973), Chaps. 15 and 16.

82. See George Every, *The High Church Party 1688–1718* (London: SPCK, 1956).

83. See John C. Bowmer, *The Sacrament of the Lord's Supper in Early Methodism* (London: Dacre Press, 1951).

84. For Wesley's life and theology, the history of the revival, and bibliography, see Albert C. Outler, *John Wesley* (New York: Oxford University Press, 1964) (hereafter cited as Outler, *Wesley*); and Rupert Davies and Gordon Rupp, *A History of the Methodist Church in Great Britain,* 3 vols. (London: Epworth Press, 1965), vol. 1.

85. Text in Outler, *Wesley*, 332–344.

86. *Ibid.*, 66.

87. See Albert C. Outler, "John Wesley as Theologian—Then and Now," *Methodist History*, 12 (1974): 63–82.

88. Outler, *Wesley*, 273.

89. *Ibid.*

90. *Ibid.*, 274.

91. *Ibid.*, 275.

92. *Ibid.*

93. *Ibid.*, 278–279.

94. For Wesley's sacramental theology, see Ole E. Borgen, *John Welsey on the Sacraments: A Theological Study* (Nashville, TN: Abingdon Press, 1972).

95. Sermon 16, "The Means of Grace," in Albert C. Outler (ed.), *The Works of John Wesley*, vol. 1 (Nashville, TN: Abingdon Press, 1984), 381.

96. *Ibid.*, 378.

97. *Ibid.*, 382.

98. *Ibid.*, 381.

99. *Ibid.*, 382.

100. *Ibid.*, 379.

101. *Ibid.*, 391.

102. *Ibid.*, 382.

103. See Bowmer, 106–107.

104. Sermon 16, 389.

105. *Ibid.*, 390.

106. *Ibid.*, 395.

107. *Ibid.*

108. *Ibid.*

109. Daniel Brevint, *The Christian Sacrament and Sacrifice*, new ed. (Oxford and London: Hatchard & Son, 1847), 11.

110. *Ibid.*, 44–45.

111. *Ibid.*, 55.

112. *Ibid.*, 56.

113. *Ibid.*, 79–80.

114. *Ibid.*, 59.

115. The text of the hymns can be found in J. Ernest Rattenbury, *The Eucharistic Hymns of John and Charles Wesley* (London: Epworth Press, 1948).

116. Hymn 28, vv. 1–2.

117. Hymn 66.

118. Hymn 71, v. 1.

119. Hymn 44.

120. Hymn 124, v. 1.

121. Hymn 121, v. 2.

122. Hymn 123, v. 4.

123. Hymn 131, v. 1.

124. Hymn 129, v. 2.

125. Hymn 117, v. 2.

126. For an overview of the Oxford Movement on sacraments and liturgy, see Louis Weil, *Sacraments and Liturgy: The Outward Signs* (Oxford: Basil Blackwell, 1983). For the eucharistic theology of the Tractarians, see Alf Härdelin, *The Tractarian Understanding of the Eucharist* (Uppsala: Almquist & Wiksells, 1965). Bibliography in both.

127. See Härdelin, 60ff.

128. Martin J. Svaglic (ed.), (Oxford: Clarendon Press, 1967), 36.

129. (London, 1853).

130. R. W. Franklin, "Pusey and Worship in Industrial Society," *Worship*, 57 (1983): 388–389. See also Donald Gray, *Earth and Altar: The Evolution of the Parish Communion in the Church of England to 1945*. Alcuin Club Collections, no. 68 (Norwich: Canterbury Press, 1986).

131. "Our Present Duty," in *Report of the Anglo-Catholic Congress* (London, 1923), 185–186.

CHAPTER SEVEN

Contemporary Perspectives

FROM REFORMATION TO ECUMENISM

Very shortly after the initial period of the Reformation, and in sharp contrast to the sacramentalism of the major reformers, there developed a rapid decline of eucharistic life throughout the Churches of the reformation, a situation that has very largely persisted to the present day. This has expressed itself in a variety of ways in the different Church traditions. Much historical research remains to be done to discover the precise causes and stages by which this situation came about, but the general causes seem fairly clear.

In their reform of the mass, the reformers desired that it become a communal celebration in which all who participated also received the sacrament. Both Luther and Calvin desired a weekly celebration of the Lord's Supper. They wanted the norm for Sunday worship to be a celebration of both Word and sacrament. Pastorally, however, this proved to be an impossibility. Accustomed to attending mass every Sunday, but receiving communion on the average only once a year, the laity were not ready to receive it frequently. As a result, the reformers had to compromise, and the normal pattern throughout the reformation Churches became that of a quarterly celebration, with the normal Sunday service becoming a service of the Word. What this meant in practice was that despite the reformers' high regard for the sacrament, Protestants came to experience the Word rather than the sacrament as the normal means by which Christian faith and life are nourished, and the Lord's Supper became a periodic event rather than a part of the weekly rhythm of Christian life and worship.[1]

This pastoral situation received a certain theological justification from the teaching of the reformers themselves. For all of the importance that Luther attached to the sacrament, he said explicitly that the Word was of first importance and that one could do without the sacrament, but not without the Word.[2] Moreover, the very heart of Luther's reformation was a recovery of the Word of the gospel as the center of the Church's life. In order to achieve this end, he launched a fundamental attack on the sacramental system, which was the heart of medieval Catholicism. As a result, Protestantism tended to become a Word-oriented rather than a sacramentally-oriented form of Christianity. The reformers never intended to replace the sacrament by the Word, only to ground the sacrament in the Word, but in practice, the Word came to replace the sacrament as the center of Protestant experience.

The reformers' attack on the canon of the mass and the lack of historical knowledge in the sixteenth century concerning the history of the liturgy and the origin, development, and character of the Eucharistic Prayer led to a reform of the eucharistic liturgy that departed in fundamental ways from the historic shape of the early liturgies. In their reform of the liturgy, the reformers were concerned to instruct a laity that was woefully ignorant of even the most fundamental teachings of the gospel; hence, the Reformation liturgies placed a strong emphasis on teaching and exhortation. Also, the Reformation liturgies tend to have a strongly penitential character. Unwittingly at this point, the reformers were perpetuating the strong penitential element in the medieval mass that had come to overlay the thanksgiving character of the early liturgies. This resulted in a didactic, penitential, and even somber rite rather than a joyful celebration by the people of God in praise and thanksgiving for the mystery of redemption.[3]

In the English-speaking world, the long quarrel between Anglicans and Puritans with its unhappy result led to a polarization between the use of liturgical forms and extempore prayer in the English and North American Churches. This led to a liturgical rigidity on the one side and to a loss of liturgical tradition on the other. Furthermore, Methodists and Evangelicals who find their roots in the Wesleyan revival became cut off from their own roots when in contrast to Wesley himself, they came to express Wesley's evangelicalism in isolation from his sacramentalism.[4] Wesley never intended the preaching services of the Methodist societies to replace the eucharistic liturgy, but because these became the primary experience of worship for many of the Methodist people and had a quality of liveliness that was lacking in the way the liturgy was celebrated in many of the English parish churches, the preaching services eventually tended to become a substitute for the eucharist in Methodist experience and the balance in Wesley's own teaching was lost. By the same token, Wesley never intended his emphasis on the importance of the inward and personal appropriation of the gospel to develop into an individualistic form of Christianity lived out in isolation from the corporate life of the Christian community and its sacramental life.

In the eighteenth century, this general decline of sacramental life within Protestantism received powerful support from developments within the wider culture. The Enlightenment of the eighteenth century with its rationalistic outlook resulted in a further loss of symbolic consciousness and a loss of the sense of mystery in religious life, which left little room for sacraments. In the nineteenth century, the antisacramental currents that were already present in both the Reformation Churches and in the culture were reinforced by the conclusions of German Protestant historical scholarship, which tended to regard the development of Christian sacramentalism as the result of later Hellenistic influence on the soil of the gospel. It is only in our own century that liturgical scholarship has again recovered the Jewish origins of the Christian sacraments.

In the present century, a number of significant developments have taken place that have led to a remarkable renewal of eucharistic life in all the Churches and to a theological convergence on the eucharist that would have seemed impossible only a short time ago. The soil was prepared for this by both Roman Catholic and Protestant liturgical movements that have their beginnings in the nineteenth century, but that have achieved a new flowering in the period since the Second Vatican Council.[5] Paralleling the liturgical renewal movement itself, a number of developments in various fields of scholarship have stimulated the liturgical renewal and paved the way for a theological convergence on the eucharist, which has borne fruit in a series of ecumenical agreements.

Twentieth-century biblical and liturgical scholarship has confirmed the Jewish origins of the Christian eucharist and has severely challenged the nineteenth-century theory that the Christian sacraments owe their origins, or at least their principal development, to the Hellenistic mystery cults. As we saw in Chapter One, the Christian eucharist has its roots in Jewish meal tradition and Jewish eschatological expectation. While there is an overlap between the Jewish and the Hellenistic backgrounds with regard to the understanding of the eucharist as a memorial meal, it now seems clear that Paul's understanding of the eucharist as *anamnesis* has its primary background in Jewish tradition.

Liturgical research in the present century has given us a clearer picture of the shape and development of the early liturgy and of the origin and development of the Eucharistic Prayer. This has led to a new appreciation of the thanksgiving character of the meal as a whole and to the recovery by the western Churches of the tradition of the epiclesis. These results of liturgical research together with the movement of liturgical renewal have led to several major projects of liturgical revision on the part of a number of western Churches. The Roman Catholic Church led the way after the Second Vatican Council with a major revision of the eucharistic liturgy that introduced three new Eucharistic Prayers, all of which include an epiclesis. Other traditions in the West have also undertaken major revisions of their liturgies. Liturgical revision is being undertaken throughout the Anglican Communion and has borne fruit, for example, in the American *Book of Common Prayer* (1979), the English *Alternative Services Book* (1980), and the Canadian *Book of Alternative Services* (1985). With the appearance of the *Lutheran Book of Worship* (1978), the Eucharistic Prayer has been restored to Lutheran worship after 400 years. The United Methodist church in the United States in its publication *At the Lord's Table* (1981) has produced twenty-five new Eucharistic Prayers for the use of the Methodist people. In *A Sun-*

day Liturgy (1984), the United Church of Canada provides seven Eucharistic Prayers. These are examples of the kind of liturgical reform that is going on in all the Churches. All of these revisions are marked by a return to the basic shape of the early eucharistic liturgy and by a recovery of the tradition of the Eucharistic Prayer.[6]

Developments in historical and theological scholarship have paralleled these developments in biblical and liturgical research. The work of Max Thurian of the Community of Taizé has been seminal from the Protestant side. In his book *The Eucharistic Memorial*,[7] Thurian recovers the centrality of the *anamnesis*, which he interprets in the biblical and patristic sense, and recovers for Protestants the sacrificial aspect of the eucharist, which he interprets in the light of the eucharistic memorial. A similar development is reflected on the Roman Catholic side in the work of J. M. R. Tillard.[8]

The eucharistic sacrifice has been the thorniest theological issue dividing Roman Catholics and Protestants, so that a breakthrough on this issue is of fundamental importance. To the reformers, the sacrifice of the mass threatened the uniqueness and all-sufficiency of the sacrifice of the cross, the primacy of grace in the whole work of salvation, and the doctrine of justification by faith. The recovery by both Protestant and Catholic theologians of the biblical and patristic understanding of the eucharistic memorial, therefore, has been a key element in the overcoming of this centuries-old controversy. The eucharist is neither a repetition of the sacrifice of the cross, nor simply a mental recollection of an event that took place 2,000 years ago. Through the eucharistic memorial, the sacrifice of the cross is made sacramentally present in order that we may participate in its redemptive reality in the present. In the same way, when Jews celebrate the passover memorial, they participate in the redemptive reality of the exodus as a contemporary experience of liberation.

The Lutheran theologian Regin Prenter has developed an understanding of the sacrificial aspect of the eucharist out of that which is most distinctive in the Lutheran tradition, and has produced an interpretation of the eucharistic sacrifice that sees it as a safeguard and expression of the doctrine of justification by faith itself.[9] Prenter distinguishes between the death of a hero and the death of a martyr. The death of a hero is an act of self-assertion. The death of a martyr is an act of love witnessing to God's love. Jesus' death was a sacrifice because it was an act of love on our behalf. Our life and death can only become a true offering of love when they are taken up into his sacrifice offered on the cross. The eucharist can be called a sacrifice because it is "the constant presence in the Church of the sacrifice of Calvary."[10] In the eucharist, the sacrificial death of Christ is sacramentally present as the basis of our self-offering. Only as we are united to him in his sacrifice can our life and death become a true offering of love rather than an act of self-assertion. The eucharist, therefore, understood as a sacrifice, is the very opposite of a human work. It is the sacramental presence of God's own act of grace on the cross, through which alone our lives can become an acceptable offering to God. This is nothing else but justification by faith.

Along with the issue of the eucharistic sacrifice, the issue of the eucharistic presence of Christ has been a storm center of controversy, not only between the Roman Catholic Church and the Churches of the Reformation, but also between the Churches of the Reformation themselves. It is an odd feature of Church history that the community that gathers in the name of Jesus and is itself the body of Christ should have become embroiled in controversy about whether Christ is present in the eucharist or not and in what way. As a result of historical research, the sources of this strange phenomenon are no longer so difficult to discover. The roots of the controversies concerning the real presence of Christ in the eucharist and the relationship of the presence to the sacramental signs of bread and wine are to be found primarily in two parallel historical developments that took place between the patristic period and the Middle Ages. These two developments were the loss of the community's consciousness of itself as the body of Christ and the loss of a symbolic consciousness.

We have seen from our study of St. Augustine that in Augustine's time, the Christian community perceived the most intimate relationship between the presence of Christ in the community and the presence of Christ in the gifts of bread and wine on the altar, so much so that Augustine can say that it is your own mystery that you receive, because "you are the body and the members of Christ."[11] In the course of the Middle Ages, however, there developed a separation between the community and the gifts. The community gradually lost the earlier consciousness of itself as the body of Christ, and increasingly became a group of spectators who viewed the presence of Christ as an object on the altar. Parallel to this development went a gradual loss of symbolic consciousness, which is already signaled in the eucharistic controversies of the ninth and eleventh centuries. Because it was no longer understood that a symbol participates in and mediates the reality that it symbolizes, a polarization developed between a "symbolic" and a "realist" interpretation of the eucharistic presence. From the perspective of the realists, the symbolists had evacuated the reality of Christ from the eucharist and turned the bread and wine into mere symbols of a Christ who is absent. From the perspective of the symbolists, the defenders of a "real" and "substantial" presence were guilty of localizing Christ in the bread and wine. Since both sides in this long and weary controversy had lost an adequate understanding of the nature of symbols, no mediation was possible between the two positions.

The controversy about whether Christ is present in the elements or present in the believers is a spinoff from the same historical developments. It would never have occurred to an Augustine to separate the presence of Christ in the believers, who are the body of Christ, from the presence of Christ in the symbolic signs that the community offers and receives as the symbols of its renewed incorporation into Christ, the head of the body. When the community gathers to celebrate the eucharist, the living Lord is already present in his community, but through the proclamation of the Word and the the offering and sharing of the symbolic signs of bread and wine, he continues to nourish his community and to build it up in obedience and love.

Since the Middle Ages, eucharistic theology has tended to oscillate between an objective and a subjective interpretation of the eucharistic presence. Medieval and post-Reformation Catholicism, on the one hand, represents a tendency toward an extreme objectivization of the eucharistic presence as an objective presence of Christ in the elements on the altar. Modern Protestantism, on the other hand, has tended toward an extreme subjectivization of the eucharistic presence, seeing it primarily as an interior presence of Christ in the believer. As we are now able to see, both these tendencies represent a loss both of community and of symbolic consciousness. Christ is present in the eucharist neither in a physical mode like an object in nature, nor in a purely inward spiritual mode in the hearts of believers, but in a symbolic mode in the midst of a community celebration.

A renewal of sacramental theology has been going on for some time in Roman Catholic theology and various attempts have been made to reinterpret the doctrine of transubstantiation. Two of the theologians who have made a major contribution to this renewal are E. Schillebeeckx and P. Schoonenberg. Schillebeeckx's *Christ the Sacrament of the Encounter with God* was a pioneering work in sacramental theology.[12] Schillebeeckx adopted a personalistic model and interpreted the sacraments as the symbolic activity of the community of faith. The sacraments are communal symbols that mediate a personal encounter between Christ and the Church. Schoonenberg, in a similar manner, interpreted the real presence in personalistic categories.[13] The presence of Christ in the eucharist is not the presence of an object, but the personal presence of Christ in his community.

Both Schillebeeckx[14] and Schoonenberg stress that the presence of Christ in relation to the elements must not be isolated from his presence in the proclamation of the Word and in the community. The real presence is not an end in itself. It is Christ's self-gift to his community in the form of nourishing food and drink. The mode of Christ's presence in relation to the elements is sacramental. It takes place at the level of symbolic activity. Transubstantiation is interpreted as the Church's affirmation that the reality present and offered by means of the sacramental signs is Christ himself. It does not imply a local presence of Christ in the elements or any physical change in the elements. Both Schillebeeckx and Schoonenberg agree that while the doctrine of transubstantiation achieved its classical expression in Aristotelian categories, theologians today are free to explore the use of alternative philosophical categories provided that they do justice to the reality (= substance) that is present and offered by means of the sacramental signs.[15]

All of these developments have helped prepare the way for a series of ecumenical agreements on the eucharist that have taken place during the present century. Various interconfessional and bilateral discussions among the Churches have led to agreed statements on the eucharist.[16] Among these are the Leuenberg Agreement between Lutherans and Reformed[17] and the Anglican–Roman Catholic agreed statement on the eucharist.[18] In the United States, the Lutheran–Catholic dialogue has broken important new ground in the areas of the eucharistic sacrifice, the eucharistic presence, and eucharist and ministry.[19] All of these agreements have helped to prepare the way for the document *Baptism, Eucharist, and Ministry*[20] formulated by the Faith and Order Commission of the World Council of Churches at its meeting held in Lima, Peru, in 1982 as an expression of theological convergence on baptism, eucharist, and ministry. Particularly noteworthy is the fact that the Faith and Order Commission includes among its full members theologians of the Roman Catholic and other Churches that do not belong to the World Council of Churches. The Faith and Order Commission has invited all the Churches to prepare an official response to the document at the highest level of authority.

In the light of the historical background presented in this book, it is hardly necessary to write a lengthy commentary on the statement on the eucharist in the *BEM* document.[21] The meaning of the eucharist is presented under five headings:

A. The Eucharist as Thanksgiving to the Father
B. The Eucharist as Anamnesis or Memorial of Christ
C. The Eucharist as Invocation of the Spirit
D. The Eucharist as Communion of the Faithful
E. The Eucharist as Meal of the Kingdom

These sections set out the principal themes that we have discussed in this book. The first section discusses the eucharist as a thanksgiving meal in the tradition of the Jewish *berakah*. The second section discusses the eucharist as an *anamnesis* of Christ's death and resurrection and interprets the sacrificial aspect of the eucharist in the light of the biblical conception of the memorial. The third section discusses the role of the Spirit in the eucharistic celebration and the significance of the epiclesis. The fourth section discusses the eucharist as an act of communion in both its Christological and ecclesial sense, and the last section sets out the eschatological perspective. While acknowledging agreement on the reality of the presence of Christ in the eucharist, the document recognizes that some Church traditions relate the eucharistic presence of Christ more closely to the elements than do others, and it asks the question whether this difference can be accommodated within the agreement expressed on the other aspects of eucharistic doctrine. It remains for the Churches to answer this question. The final part of the document sets out the elements that belong to the historic shape of the eucharistic liturgy and to the Eucharistic Prayer.

RECOVERY OF THE SYMBOLIC

Throughout this book, we have stressed the character of the eucharist as a particular kind of symbolic activity. In Chapter Two, we saw that in the ancient world, a symbol was understood as a vehicle that mediated to the community the meaning of life in society and indeed in the cosmos as a whole. A symbol was understood to participate in the reality that it represented and to mediate that reality to those who participated in the symbol. Life in the world was understood to have a transcendent dimension that gave meaning to the whole. This transendent meaning was mediated in the community through symbolic activity. When the community recounted its myths and engaged in ritual symbolic activity, it participated in that transcendent meaning and was renewed in its life.

Through the course of the Middle Ages and in the early modern period, the West has experienced a gradual loss of this ancient symbolic consciousness. The final step in this cultural transition was effected by the scientific revolution and the Enlightenment of the seventeenth and eighteenth centuries. From the perspective of the Enlightenment thinkers, symbols are a survival from a primitive, superstitious, and less rational age. They are essentially ideas and representations that lack precision. What is required is that they be replaced by clear and distinct ideas and a rational account of reality. The ideal of the period, therefore, was the creation of a rational-scientific culture.[22] Religion, if it was retained at all, was to be retained in a rational form. In the nineteenth and twentieth centuries, however, a number of writers from a variety of disciplines have rediscovered the dimension of the symbolic, and in this section, we want to explore the resources these thinkers have to offer for a contemporary theology of the eucharist.

In philosophy, Ernst Cassirer and Susanne Langer were pioneers in the rediscovery of the symbolic.[23] More influential in recent years in philosophy and the study of religion is the phenomenological tradition.[24] The work of Paul Ricoeur is of particular importance here for the interpretation of symbols.[25] Historians of religion, especially Mircea Eliade, have highlighted the importance of the symbolic for the understanding of both ancient and modern cultures.[26] The rediscovery of the symbolic, however, has not been confined to the humanities. It is also to be found in the social sciences. In the psychoanalytic tradition, Freud and Jung pioneered in the realm of the symbolic through their explorations into the unconscious, showing the profound importance of symbols in the shaping of human personality.[27] Social anthropologists such as Clifford Geertz and Victor Turner have also shown the fundamental importance of symbols for the understanding of human society.[28] In the sociological tradition, the great social thinkers Max Weber, Emile Durkheim, and Karl Marx, and more recent thinkers such as Robert Bellah, have illuminated the relationship between symbols and society.

In our approach to these thinkers, we want to propose an analysis that distinguishes and correlates two broad tendencies in the interpretation of symbols that represent distinctive but overlapping concerns. One tendency is primarily concerned with the *meaning* of symbols as a phenomenon in human culture. The other tendency is primarily concerned with the psychological or social *function* of symbols. This distinction between "meaning" and "function" is somewhat arbitrary, but points on the one hand to the broadly phenomenological tradition in philosophy that is primarily concerned with hermeneutics, or the interpretation of symbols, and on the other hand to the psychological and sociological traditions that are concerned primarily with the way symbols function in the development and transformation of persons and societies. We shall call these two traditions the "symbolic realist" and the "sociological" traditions while recognizing that both traditions cross disciplinary lines. By correlating these two approaches, we hope to present the eucharist as a pattern of symbolic activity that mediates not only transcendent meaning, but also personal and social transformation.

This has important implications for the relationship between the eucharist and issues of social justice. It also has wider theological implications, for it can provide a point of mediation between the hermeneutical theologies of Europe and North America, which are primarily concerned for the interpretation of Christian symbols in a modern or postmodern culture, and the liberation theologies of Third World and other oppressed communities that employ a Marxist analysis and are concerned primarily with the ideological function of Christian symbols. By bringing the sociological tradition into relation with the hermeneutical tradition, we can face directly the clash between Marxist and non-Marxist interpretations of symbols.

The Symbolic-Realist Tradition
The term "symbolic realism" is used by Robert Bellah as a broad category that covers philosophers, historians of religion, anthropologists, and sociologists.[29] Included would be such thinkers as Mircea Eliade (Historian of Religion), Michael Polanyi (Philosopher of Science), Victor Turner and Clifford Geertz (Anthropologists), Paul Ricoeur (Philosopher of Religion), and Robert Bellah (Sociologist).

The principal feature of this tradition is its opposition to all forms of reductionism in the interpretation of symbols. According to these thinkers, symbols have an integrity of their own that cannot be reduced to other categories. Symbols have many levels of meaning and function in a variety of ways. For example, they embrace religious, philosophical, aesthetic, psychological, and sociopolitical meanings, but they cannot be reduced to any of these meanings or functions. They cannot, in other words, be translated into categories other than the symbolic without loss or distortion.

We can take the symbol of the Exodus as an example. On the sociopolitical level, it expresses the liberation of an oppressed people. In the Old Testament, however, another theological level of meaning is discerned in this event. It is interpreted as a divine act of deliverance or redemption. Both these levels of meaning are true, but neither can be reduced to the other. The power of the symbol consists precisely in the fact that it can hold together these different levels of meaning. The symbol, therefore, can never be replaced or displaced by any of its interpretations.

This is a direct attack on the position of the Enlightenment that symbols represent a primitive stage in the development of the race that needs to be superceded by rational thought. It is critical also of what Bellah calls the "symbolic reductionism" of Freud, Marx, and Durkheim. All these thinkers recognized the importance of symbols in the construction of society or the development of human personality, but they saw the symbols as masks for a truth that needs to be expressed in the categories of science or philosophy.

The symbolic realists also attempt to interpret symbols, but their aim is entirely different from that of the Enlightenment thinkers and their successors. The task of the interpretation of symbols does not have as its aim the abolition of the symbol or its replacement by an alternative conceptual scheme. Rather, the task of interpretation is to lead us back to a new appreciation of the symbol by disclosing its meaning. Symbolic consciousness, on this view, is the distinctively human mode of consciousness. From this perspective, the ancients were right and the Enlightenment thinkers were wrong. Rational thought is a truly human mode of reflection, but it is only one level of a multileveled symbolic universe of meaning. By abolishing symbols and replacing them with concepts, modern post-Enlightenment culture has become radically impoverished. Whole worlds of meaning have been closed to human consciousness. The loss of the symbol, in short, has dehumanized us. The aim of the symbolic realists is nothing less than the recovery of a full symbolic consciousness.[30]

It is precisely at this point, however, that hermeneutics, or the interpretation of symbols, comes into the picture. Modern persons, unlike the ancients, have lost the first naïveté of an unbroken symbolic consciousness. Symbols, therefore, require interpretation if their meaning is to be disclosed to us. This is the hermeneutical task. But the disclosure of the meaning present in the symbol is not to lead us away from the symbol, but back to it, so that we can reclaim it with what Ricoeur calls a second naïveté. This is the task that we are engaged upon in this book. It is a hermeneutical task. We are attempting what Ricoeur calls a "project of interpretation." The eucharist is a rich symbolic reality. Something of that richness is disclosed in the history of eucharistic traditions. Our project of interpretation is not to lead us away from that symbolic reality or away from those traditions that mediated that reality for earlier generations, but to lead us back through those traditions by way of interpretation to the symbolic reality itself, so that we can participate in the eucharist again with a new naïveté.

The Sociological Tradition

In our view, the analysis of the meaning of symbols by thinkers in the symbolic-realist tradition must be complemented by an analysis of their social function. The reasons for this will emerge in the course of our discussion. In fact, the symbolic realists acknowledge this. What they protest against is not that symbols have a psychological or social role, but the reductionism that equates their meaning with that role. We agree with the symbolic-realist critique of reductionism. Symbols do have an integrity of their own that cannot be reduced to other categories. What we want to disclose in this section, however, is the powerful resources that the great social thinkers, particularly Freud, Marx, Durkheim, and Weber have to offer for the understanding of symbols when their insights are released from their reductionist assumptions.

Robert Bellah has pointed out the implicit contradiction in the work of these thinkers between their assumptions and the conclusions to which they were led on the basis of those assumptions. All these thinkers accepted the Enlightenment assumption that the task of scientific work is to disclose the scientific or philosophical truth hidden under the fantastic disguise of symbolic representations. Yet their research led them to precisely the opposite conclusion; namely, that rational representations arise as a secondary level of reflection on the primary material of symbols.[31] Gregory Baum has analyzed this tradition in a penetrating manner in his book *Religion and Alienation*[32] and we shall take him as our principal mentor in this section.

The importance of Freud for the recovery of the symbolic can hardly be exaggerated. Freud, as a scientist, made the startling discovery that the development of the human personality could not be accounted for without attending to the symbolic dimension. Freud was led to this discovery through his investigation of dreams. Freud's great discovery was that dreams express the hidden and unconscious depth of the human personality in symbolic language. Through the interpretation of the symbolic language of dreams, we can gain access to the unconscious depths of our lives, their deepest wishes and inclinations, and their hidden conflicts. The symbolism of dreams, however, not only discloses the springs of the personality, it also provides a means by which we can confront the hidden dimensions of our lives and by so doing experience change, healing, and personal transformation. Symbols not only have meaning, they also have transforming power.[33]

Despite Freud's importance, however, there is a limiting factor in his analysis that requires a corrective. Freud did not perceive that his account of the development of the human personality implicitly reflected the society of his time. The European society of Freud's time was a highly individualistic society shaped by the ideals of individual freedom stemming from the Enlightenment. Society, according to Enlightenment theory, is an aggregate of individuals who come together into society by forming a social contract.[34] This has been the dominant ideology of European and North American societies since the time of the French and American revolutions. In such a society, it is possible to understand the psychological history of the individual exclusively in relation to the personal life history of the individual without reference to the structures of society that have shaped the individual's identity. This is precisely what Freud does. He was unaware in doing so that his account of the human person was in fact the function of an individualistic ideology.

The complementary truth about human persons is that our very individuality is powerfully shaped by the social matrix in which our personality is formed. From this perspective, personality itself is the product of a process of socialization. The social structures and institutions, the production process and the economic system, all have a profound influence on the shaping of human consciousness. In this case, the symbolic structure of human consciousness is not the reflection of our individual life history, but the reflection of the society in which we live. From this perspective, personal transformation and social transformation are intimately related. This is the perspective of the other thinkers that we shall discuss in this section. These thinkers differ, however, in their understanding of the way in which society shapes consciousness. They also differ in their understanding of the mutual relationship between personal consciousness and social consciousness.

Karl Marx has certainly been the most influential of the social thinkers who have developed a theory of symbols from this perspective. The central insight of Marx is that the symbolic structures of society, i.e., its institutions and its spiritual products such as art, religion, morality, politics, philosophy, etc. are a reflection or mirror image of the material basis of society.[35] Marx defines the material basis of society as the processes of production or the economic relationships that pertain in any given society. From this point of view, ideas or symbols are not neutral conceptions. Because they are the products of society, they serve an essentially social function. Marx called this social function "ideology."[36] To say that the social function of ideas or symbols is ideological is to say that they function as a legitimation of the existing economic and social order.

To understand what Marx means here, we have to understand his ideas in the context of the specific society of Marx's day. That society was the product of the Industrial Revolution.[37] The chief social products of the Industrial Revolution as Marx experienced them in England were the factory system and the creation of slum conditions. The factory workers of Marx's day worked under appalling conditions, with a fourteen-hour day and child labor as common practice. The development of factories led in turn to the evacuation of the countryside and the swelling of the towns and cities, creating large-scale slum conditions of unbelievable squalor. These are the specific historical conditions that led to the development of Marx's theories. Marx saw the root of these social conditions in the capitalist system, where economic capital and the means of production are concentrated in the hands of a few individuals while the vast majority of industrial laborers are forced to live and work in a situation that could only be described as one of suffering and alienation.

It is in this context that we must understand Marx's critique of religion.[38] Religion, in line with Marx's general theory of the relationship between society and its spiritual products, is an inverted reflection of the material conditions of society. Marx was not interested in the truth or falsity of religious ideas or symbols. Neither theoretical religion nor theoretical atheism were of any concern to him. What he was concerned about was the way religion functions in society, and the way Marx saw religion functioning in the society of his day was as a means of legitimating the set of material and social conditions we have described. Religion, for Marx, is not a transcendental idea or a supernatural revelation. It is a product of human beings. It is a reflection of social conditions that are themselves the product of economic relationships. Religious symbols serve both as a moral sanction and spiritual legitimation of existing social conditions and as an anesthetic (opium) to make these conditions bearable. Marx, therefore, proposed the abolition of religion because of its ideological role in society:

"Man . . . in his search for a supernatural being in the fantastic reality of heaven found only a reflection of himself. . . . Man makes religion, religion does not make man. . . . This state, this society produce religion, which is an inverted world consciousness because they are an inverted world. Religion is the general theory of that world . . . its spiritual . . . (and) moral sanction . . . its general ground of consolation and justification. . . .

"Religious misery is in one way the expression of real misery, and in another a protest against real misery. Religion is the sign of the afflicted creature, the soul of a heartless world, as it is also the spirit of spiritless conditions. It is the *opium* of the people.

"The abolition of religion as the *illusory* happiness of the people is the demand for their *real* happiness. The demand to abandon the illusions about their condition is the *demand to give up a condition that requires illusions*. Hence criticism of religion is in embryo a *criticism of this vale of tears* whose halo is religion."[39]

There is a double edge to Marx's critique of religion. It is expressed in the statement "Religious misery is in one way the expression of real misery, and in another a protest against real misery." Marx never developed the second half of this statement. He saw only the first half, the role of religion as the expression of social conditions. Can religion ever exercise a critical role in society as a protest against existing social conditions? Marx did not think so. The other social thinkers we shall consider did think so, or at least saw a positive function for religion in society as well as an alienating one. The first of these we shall discuss is Emile Durkheim.

The discovery of the symbolic took place in a dramatic way in the sociological work of Durkheim.[40] As a result of his early research, Durkheim held that there is a fundamental difference between traditional societies and modern society. His research led him to the conclusion that the social bond that holds traditional societies together is their common symbol system, their sharing in the same rites, values, dreams, and myths. His study of modern society, however, led him to the conclusion that the social bond is created by the division of labor and does not require a symbol system. According to this hypothesis, however, Durkheim found that he was unable to account for the way in which the social order communicates itself to the individual members of society. In midcareer, therefore, he changed his mind, and came to hold that modern society as well as traditional society cannot be accounted for without a symbol system that creates the consciousness of the individual members of society. With this discovery of the symbolic, Durkheim acknowledged that it was impossible to account for society and the formation of consciousness purely in terms of the material factors that enter into it. This challenges a rigid historical materialism that tries to account for the development of consciousness purely on the basis of the economic factor and the means of production.

Durkheim carried this analysis into his conception of religion. Religion, for Durkheim, is the symbolic representation of the depths and heights of society. Through the symbolic representations of religion, a society discovers its creative depths, its hidden potentialities, and its most daring dreams. This account of religion, however, would appear to coincide with the Marxist view of the social function of religion as a legitimation of the social order, and would seem to confirm the view that from a sociological standpoint, religion always fulfills an ideological function in society. Durkheim acknowledged the ideological role of religion in society, but he also allowed for its contrary. Since religion is grounded in the highest aspirations of society, it is able to generate a critique of the existing social order from the standpoint of society's own highest ideals. These ideals generate strong impulses toward change in society and account for the rise of reform movements within it. According to this sociological theory, therefore, religion has the capacity to exercise a critical and reforming function as well as an ideological function in society.

Max Weber is another sociologist who came to the conclusion that religion and religious symbols can exercise a transformative as well as an ideological function in society.[41] According to Talcott Parsons, "Weber's primary interest is in religion as a source of the dynamics of social change, not religion as reinforcement of the stability of society."[42] Weber's study of religion indicated that while in most historical periods, the dominant religions offer an ideological defense of the existing social order, there are also periods when religious trends have been a source of social criticism, and by offering a new vision of human life and society have exercised a role that has affected the transformation of culture and society. Religion, Weber concluded, is never purely and simply the reflection of society. It also contains within its traditions critical and creative elements. In his book *The Sociology of Religion*, he showed that even in the same religion and in the same historical period religion has quite different social and political meanings, depending on the class structure. Different social classes and groups in society adapt the symbolic meaning of the common religion to their collective aspirations, so that it is impossible to generalize in the way Marx did about the social function of religion. In each case, careful research and analysis is required to determine the social function that religion plays in a particular society.

Weber made "charism" the starting point for his study of religion as well as the key concept for his theory of social change. For Weber the dynamic element in religious institutions is the charismatic person. The charismatic person is not an individual set over against the community, but the person who intuits at a deep level and gives voice to the alienation of the community. The charismatic person is able to express and articulate the deepest experience and pain of a people. The other role of the charismatic person, however, is to propose a new imagination, or a new vision, by which this alienation can be overcome. We think immediately of the prophets, the apocalyptic writers, or of a figure like Martin Luther King in this connection. This breakthrough of imagination in the life of a people provides an alternative vision to that of the dominant society and nourishes hope for a new order of things. Imagination, therefore, exercises a significant role in social change.

Weber sees in society both a dominant trend that is imposed by the major institutions of society and countervailing trends sparked by personalities with charismatic gifts. The countervailing trends, however, do not arise out of the blue in the heads of charismatic persons. They are themselves in some sense determined by the dominant trend, but by way of protest rather than by way of legitimation. Weber, therefore, has picked up the other side of Marx's account of religion in which he acknowledges that in some sense religion is a protest against real misery as well as its expression.

Baum also points to another trend in the sociology of religion that is reflected in different ways in the thought of Karl Mannheim and Ernst Bloch.[43] These thinkers point toward the utopian role of religious symbols in the creation of society as well as their ideological role. This insight can extend the insight found in Weber that imagination plays a role in social change. Both Mannheim and Bloch in different ways point to the utopian mind-set of historical movements such as apocalyptic movements in Christianity and early forms of utopian socialism as a significant factor in the social and political dynamic of these movements. Utopian consciousness can play a role in social change. Ideological religion legitimates the existing social order. Utopian religion is critical of the existing order and proposes an alternative vision. Bloch belongs to the "warm current" of Marxism that stresses the role of the utopian imagination as opposed to the "cold current" of Marxism that stresses the scientific and largely deterministic character of the relationship between the economic base of society, analyzed in terms of the control of the means of production, and the spiritual products of society that Marx calls the ideological "superstructure." From Bloch's perspective, the symbols of the future have power in the production of society. They disclose the latent potentialities in the present and their unfulfilled possibilities for realization. Bloch has had a considerable influence on Christian theologians, particularly Jürgen Moltmann. In his book *Theology of Hope*,[44] Moltmann employed Bloch's insights and interpreted the biblical promise of the kingdom of God on the model of a utopian symbol that has power in the transformation of society and the creation of a new future.

In the work of the various thinkers we have discussed, we can see a number of possibilities for the social role of religious symbols. On the one hand, we can see the powerful ideological role that religion has played and continues to play in the life of society. On the other hand, we have also seen the possibility of other roles related to the religious imagination, which can propose an "alternative vision" for society. Alternative vision can take both utopian and other forms. In its utopian form, it can extrapolate from the eschatological and apocalyptic symbols in the Bible the vision of a new future. It can also propose new and unthought of possibilities for the present. In both these ways, the religious imagination can play a creative role in the transformation of society.

The Marxist critique of religion, however, is a powerful reminder of the ideological trend present in religion. Indeed, most sociological analysis of the function of religion in North American society only serves to confirm Marx's insight. Nevertheless, both Judaism and Christianity have produced countervailing prophetic and reform movements both within the mainstream and on the edges of the life of the religious community. From a strictly sociological perspective, therefore, religious symbols can play a transformative as well as an ideological role.

Theological Reflection on Symbols

So far, we have been describing a variety of approaches to the meaning and function of symbols from the point of view of the human sciences. We must now turn our attention to theological reflection on symbols.[45] From a theological perspective, the role of the symbol is to disclose the transcendent or the sacred. We would maintain, however, that religious symbols do not disclose a world different from this world, but the transcendent dimension that is present in all ordinary human experience. This point is of vital importance. What it means is that Christian symbolic activity, and, for our purposes, the symbolic activity that we call eucharist is not an escape into another sacral world, but the celebration of the divine presence in the whole of life with a view to its redemptive transformation.

In order to cast light on this conception of Christian symbols as disclosive of the transcendent in the world of our ordinary human experience, I turn to an article by Langdon Gilkey, in which he develops what he calls a "sacramental theory of religious symbolism," i.e., "one in which the divine is mediated to us through its presence within the finite."[46] Gilkey holds that there are three fundamental meanings of symbol in Christian theology, or three levels of symbolic mediation. At the first level of symbolic mediation, every finite being is a symbol of transcendence precisely as a finite creature. What it means to be a finite creature is to point to a transcendent ground or source and as such to be a symbol of the presence of the divine. This assumes that the world is not a closed system, but a reality open to mystery and to the possibility of ultimate meaning. As such, it can become symbolic of transcendent mystery and meaning.

At this level of symbolic mediation, finite beings are symbolic of the divine only in an obscure and ambiguous fashion. There arises, therefore,

". . . a second sense of the word 'symbol,' namely, those special and unique finite media through which a particular revelation of the ultimate and the sacred, universally present but universally obscured as well, is now manifested in a particular form to a historical community, and so through which a group becomes newly aware of its own status as symbol (in the first sense), as existing in and through the power of the divine. . . . In . . . (the Christian) tradition the originating symbols in this second sense, symbols of special revelation, or of redemptive grace, are the history of the community of Israel and the person of Jesus."[47]

Gilkey then goes on to describe the third level of symbolic mediation.

"In each tradition this presence of the Divine in and through special revelatory events and persons is over time communicated to the continuing community founded upon that special presence. This communication over time is in turn achieved through 'symbols' in a third sense. Again, finite entities have become media which point to, recall, and reintroduce by representation the originating presence of the holy in the revelatory symbols creative of that tradition."[48]

In the Christian tradition, this third level of symbolic mediation takes place primarily through word and sacrament.

"All Christian worship points to and finds its center in the revelatory events or symbols originative of that tradition, to the word in prophecy and Word made flesh. Correspondingly, the role of the tertiary symbols is to accomplish that pointing and centering, the sacraments of baptism and Eucharist with all of their manifold of symbolic power representing to us and in us these originating events, and the kerygma or proclamation opening up to us the transcendent meaning of these events and so calling us to decision and commitment in relation to them."[49]

Gilkey's reference here to the commitment called forth by the sacramental events is of fundamental importance.[50] In keeping with the analysis of symbols that we developed from the perspective of the human sciences, we want to show that religious symbols, and the eucharist in particular, not only disclose a world of transcendent meaning, but also serve as vehicles for social transformation. We have already indicated such a possible role for religious symbols from a strictly sociological standpoint. We now want to confirm this from a theological standpoint.

E. J. Kilmartin has shown that the root meaning of *sacramentum* in the western theological tradition includes the commitment to a new way of life.[51] The word *sacramentum* in Roman law meant an oath or pledge, which also implied a contractual obligation. The two essential ideas here are that one is bound to the party or parties to which the oath or pledge is given, and that one is committed to fulfilling the obligations of the contract. When the word *sacramentum* was taken over into Latin Christianity by Tertullian to refer to the Christian rites of baptism and eucharist, the implication is that participation in baptism and the eucharist means being bound to Christ in a covenant relationship and thereby committed to fulfill the obligations implied in that relationship by living a life in conformity with the demands of the gospel. A sacrament, therefore, is something more than a symbol of transcendence. It implies an obligation to live in accordance with that which is symbolized. The commitment to Christian action, therefore, is an integral part of the very meaning of the sacrament itself. "Baptism places the believer on the way of the life of Christ."[52] This obligation is renewed in the celebration of the Lord's Supper. "Whoever truly receives Jesus' saving service in the Eucharist knows he must serve in turn."[53] To participate in the eucharist, therefore, is to renew the covenant obligation to live out our lives in conformity with the gospel.

As a symbolic action, a sacrament functions in a manner analogous to a metaphor or a parable. The eucharist is an acted parable.[54] As such, it is inexhaustible in meaning. It is meant to fire our imagination, open up new possibilities for our living, and challenge our action in the world. Like the parables in the gospels, its many meanings put us in touch with the mystery of the kingdom and call us to bring the totality of our life in the world under God's rule.[55] The community that gathers for a common meal cannot hear the Word of God and share the bread and the cup without reflecting upon what that means for Christian obedience in a world without sufficient bread, and a world in which injustice, poverty, and oppression are ever present realities. When we reflect on the relationship between this meal that we celebrate and Jesus' meals with outcasts and sinners, we cannot fail to hear the call to extend our care and love to the outcast and the marginalized in our own society. To celebrate the Lord's death until he comes means to accept living under the sign of the cross in the present. To celebrate this meal as the anticipation of the meal in the kingdom is to acquire a new social and political vision. To observe our Lord taking the role of a servant and serving us at table shakes us out of our usual identities and roles and shows us a different way of relating to one another in humble service. To receive Christ's own life poured out for us is to learn what it means to give of ourselves. The eucharist as a symbolic action, therefore, provides a model not only for our meaning, but also for our doing. It is a vehicle both of disclosure and commitment.

EUCHARIST AND JUSTICE

In this final section, we want to explore the social implications of the eucharist, assuming, in the light of the preceding section, that the eucharist is a form of symbolic activity that has transformative possibilities for the life of society. This is a theme that has remained undeveloped through much of the history of the Church and needs to move to the center of our eucharistic reflection today, for the community that gathers to celebrate the eucharist cannot hear the Word of God and share the eucharistic bread and cup without reflecting on what that means for Christian obedience in a world of economic disparity, where many go hungry every day.[56] Reflection on the eucharistic bread causes us to reflect on an economic order in which the gap between the rich and the poor widens all the time. The connection between the eucharistic bread and the structures of society that permit bread to be shared or not shared must be made explicit if the eucharistic community is to be faithful in its living of the eucharist today. The celebration of the eucharist drives us toward a new social, economic, and political vision. The Canadian Catholic Conference of Bishops put the matter squarely in their Labor Day Message of 1974, *Sharing Daily Bread:*

"Man does not live by bread alone, but without bread he cannot live. . . . The food problem in Canada and in the world challenges especially those of us who pray, 'Give us this day our daily bread,' and who commune with the Servant Lord in consecrated bread. . . . the world food crisis puts to the test the Judeo-Christian vision of one human family under God. Whatever else may be said about the social thrust of the Scriptures, the fraternal responsibility to feed brothers and sisters who are hungry is a central imperative. This imperative theme is a dominant thread in the biblical tapestry—from the story of Joseph's plans to store food in famine-stricken Egypt to the narratives of the sharing of the loaves and fishes by Jesus; from the bold vision of the ancient prophets to the description of the first Christians, who together celebrated the Eucharist, 'the breaking of the bread,' and 'who shared their food gladly and generously.' . . . In the Scriptures, bread is a fundamental symbol of all God's gifts and mankind's task. Bread is the 'test' of both worship and brotherhood. For Christians, Jesus Christ is the Living Bread who kneads together the relationships between God and man, between people and daily bread, between the human spirit and eternal life, between justice and love."[57]

There are hints in the eucharistic tradition that can help us to make these links between eucharist and justice, but this task requires fresh theological work if we are to understand the full implications of our eucharistic participation for justice in our society and world today.

The link between worship and justice is already explicit in the Old Testament in the witness of the prophets.

"I hate, I despise your feasts, and I take no delight in your solemn assemblies. Even though you offer me your burnt offerings and cereal offerings, I will not accept them, and the peace offerings of your fatted beasts I will not look upon. Take away from me the noise of your songs; to the melody of your harps I will not listen. But let justice roll down like waters, and righteousness like an ever-flowing stream."[58]

In the New Testament, there is an intimate relationship between the worshiping assembly, the proclamation of the gospel, the building up of the Christian community, and the service of the poor and needy. This relationship is expressed in a variety of ways. The gospel is profoundly social in its meaning and implications. At the heart of Jesus' message was the proclamation of the coming reign of God. Against the Jewish background, this promised reign of God is not an otherworldly reality, but a kingdom in which the whole created earth is transformed. Jesus proclaimed the breaking in of this kingdom in his preaching. He also embodied it in his activity. In our discussion of the background of the New Testament eucharistic traditions in Chapter One, we saw that one of the primary images of the coming reign of God in the Old Testament is a great banquet or feast. Jesus' eating with outcasts and sinners was a sign of God's invitation to the outcast to share in the banquet table of the kingdom. Jesus' proclamation and activity breaks down social barriers and is a sign of the offer of participation in the coming reign of God to those who have been marginalized by society.

Both Luke and John connect tablesharing with service. In the context of his account of the institution of the Last Supper, Luke has the following text:

"A dispute also arose among them, which of them was to be regarded as the greatest. And he said to them, 'The kings of the Gentiles exercise lordship over them; and those in authority over them are called benefactors. But not so with you; rather let the greatest among you become as the youngest, and the leader as one who serves. For which is the greater, one who sits at table, or one who serves? Is it not the one who sits at table? But I am among you as one who serves.' "[59]

John has the account of Jesus' washing the disciples' feet in the context of the Last Supper.[60] Acts, likewise, connects the breaking of bread, the care of the needy, and the sharing of goods.[61] The connection between table-community and justice is made explicit by Paul in 1 Corinthians 10 and 11. By sharing in the one loaf and in the eucharistic cup, Christians are constituted as a *koinonia*, a community. Because there is one loaf, all who share in that loaf become one body, one community in Christ. Furthermore, Paul makes it clear that this eucharistic tablesharing, because it establishes the participants as one body in Christ, applies not only to the life of the community gathered for worship, but to the community in all of its social relationships within the life of the body of Christ. Worship and justice cannot be separated from each other. A contradiction takes place when the assembly meets for the eucharist and the poorer members of the community are deprived of food. We find a similar perspective in James:

". . . if a man with gold rings and in fine clothing comes into your assembly, and a poor man in shabby clothing also comes in, and you pay attention to the one who wears the fine clothing and say, 'Have a seat here, please,' while you say to the poor man, 'Stand there,' or 'Sit at my feet,' have you not made distinctions among yourselves, and become judges with evil thoughts? Listen, my beloved sisters and brothers. Has not God chosen those who are poor in the world to be rich in faith and heirs of the kingdom which he has promised to those who love him? But you have dishonored the poor man. Is it not the rich who oppress you, is it not they who drag you into court? Is it not they who blaspheme the honorable name which was invoked over you?"[62]

The close link that is found in the New Testament between worship and service is also reflected in the early liturgies and the patristic writings. There was a close relationship in the early liturgies between the offering of gifts and the care of the needy.[63] In his account of the liturgy in Rome in the middle of the second century, Justin Martyr tells us that those who have the resources "come to the aid of all who are in need, and we are always assisting one another."[64] During the Sunday liturgy, the contributions of the wealthy are deposited with the one who presides, and "he helps orphans and widows, and those who through sickness or any other cause are in need, and those in prison, and strangers sojourning among us; in a word, he takes care of all those who are in need."[65]

Similarly, Hippolytus says,

"If anyone has received anything to take to a widow, a sick person, or a church worker, he shall take it that day; and if he has not taken it, he shall take it the next day, adding to what there was something of his own, because the bread of the poor has remained in his possession."[66]

In the *Didascalia*, we find a passage similar to the one we saw in James:

"If a poor man or woman should arrive, whether from your own congregation or from another, especially if they are elderly, and there is no place for them, then you, the bishop, with all your heart provide a place for them, even if you have to sit on the ground. You must not make any distinction between persons, if you wish your ministry to be pleasing to God."[67]

There is a particularly striking text in John Chrysostom, where he tells us that love of the poor is a liturgy whose altar is more admirable than the one on which the eucharist is celebrated, "the latter being holy because it receives the body of Christ, the former because it is the body of Christ."[68]

We have noted similar links between worship and justice in Zwingli, Luther, the Westminster Directory, and the Oxford Movement. The pioneers of the liturgical movement in the United States showed a keen awareness of the relationship between sharing bread in the eucharist and the establishment of peace and justice,[69] and the examples could be multiplied. Taking these links in the tradition as clues, what we want to do in the last part of this section is to suggest a few lines of reflection that relate the principal eucharistic themes that are found in the *BEM* document and that we have discussed in this book to a justice perspective.

Memory and Hope

In Chapter One, we saw that the earliest eucharistic perspective in the New Testament is the eschatological perspective, the perspective that views the eucharist as an anticipation of the meal in the kingdom of God. This theme became marginalized in the eucharistic tradition and the themes of real presence and sacrifice assumed the center of the stage. In Christian theology generally today, the eschatological character of the Christian message has been recovered. This took place first of all in biblical studies, and was pioneered in systematic theology by Jürgen Moltmann in his *Theology of Hope.* It is a central theme in contemporary liberation theologies. The heart of the gospel is Jesus' proclamation of the coming reign of God. This message is rooted in God's promise in the Old Testament, which was the ground of Israel's hope in a new future, the promised reign of God. For Christian faith, the eucharist is a meal celebrated in anticipation of the promised kingdom. The centrality of this perspective needs to be recovered today both in eucharistic theology and in our celebration of the liturgy.[70]

This perspective is clearly linked to the theme of justice. A meal celebrated in prospect of the coming reign of God must give rise to a new social vision grounded in the promise of the kingdom. Such a vision challenges the status quo in society and the prevailing set of economic and social relationships. Sharing in a community meal anticipates a just sharing of all the gifts of creation in justice and love. It must give rise to a new set of relationships in society that reflect that vision. The community that celebrates the eucharist in prospect of the kingdom must ask itself whether its tablesharing in the eucharist is reflected in a just sharing of the gifts of the earth or whether some are deprived of the means of life because others hoard the world's goods for their own advantage. Eucharistic participation must lead first of all to a new social vision, then to a critique of our existing society in the light of that vision, and finally to advocacy for the poor and disadvantaged members of society and to social change. The community gathered around the table of the Lord must be prepared to have its entire common life in the world placed under both judgment and grace.

"The eucharist opens up the vision of the divine rule which has been promised as the final renewal of creation, and is a foretaste of it. Signs of this renewal are present in the world wherever the grace of God is manifest and human beings work for justice, love and peace. The eucharist is the feast at which the Church gives thanks to God for these signs and joyfully celebrates and anticipates the coming of the Kingdom in Christ (1 Cor 11:26; Mt 26:29)."[71]

If we connect this eschatological perspective with the eschatological judgment scene in Matthew 25:31–46, we see that to serve the least of our neighbors is to serve Christ himself:

"When the Son of man comes in his glory, and all the angels with him, then he will sit on his glorious throne. Before him will be gathered all the nations, and he will separate them one from another as a shepherd separates the sheep from the goats, and he will place the sheep at his right hand, but the goats at the left. Then the King will say to those at his right hand, 'Come, O blessed of my Father, inherit the kingdom prepared for you from the foundation of the world; for I was hungry and you gave me food, I was thirsty and you gave me drink, I was a stranger and you welcomed me, I was naked and you clothed me, I was sick and you visited me, I was in prison and you came to me.' Then the righteous will answer him, 'Lord, when did we see thee hungry and feed thee, or thirsty and give thee drink? And when did we see thee a stranger and welcome thee, or naked and clothe thee? And when did we see thee sick or in prison and visit thee?' And the King will answer them, 'Truly, I say to you, as you did it to one of the least of these my brothers and sisters, you did it to me.' "[72]

The service of the neighbor is the eschatological test of the authenticity of our eucharistic communities and of our commitments.

There is a justice dimension to the anamnesis also. In our study of the New Testament eucharistic traditions, we saw that the eucharist was not only interpreted from the eschatological perspective as a meal that anticipates the meal in the kingdom. It was also viewed as a "memorial" meal, a meal in which the Church "remembers" the death and resurrection of her Lord. We saw also that in Jewish and Greek traditions, the term *anamnesis* has a much richer meaning than the word "remember" normally conveys in English. To make the memorial of a past event is to "actualize" that event in the present. In Jewish understanding, this does not destroy the uniqueness of the event as an historical event that took place once for all in the past. To "actualize" a past event means to celebrate it in such a way that the contemporary community participates in its redemptive reality. When Jews celebrate the passover memorial, they celebrate the Exodus as a contemporary experience of liberation. This means that for a community to "remember" a past redemptive event liturgically is to experience that event as a liberative memory that opens up new possibilities in the present.

J. B. Metz calls the memory of the crucified Lord a "dangerous memory of freedom" in the midst of our modern society.[73] The eucharistic anamnesis functions as a subversive memory, because it calls in question the present order of things in the light of Jesus' passion and resurrection. It would appear that memory and hope are opposites, but Metz shows that it is through *anamnesis* that hope is rekindled. Memory not only opens up a vision of new possibilities for the present, it also nourishes a longing for a new future. Liberative memories create a horizon of expectation that refuses to allow us to be satisfied with present conditions, and, at the same time, prods us out of an attitude of resignation and despair.[74]

Metz also stresses the importance of the memory of suffering.[75] When we remember the suffering of Jesus on the cross, we include all of the victims of history. Understanding history from the point of view of the memory of suffering enables us to see history from the point of view of the underdog, the oppressed, the marginalized, and the outcasts in society. The memory of accumulated suffering can then become the source of socially emancipatory action. The memory of suffering creates a social and political conscience that is prepared to act on behalf of the suffering of others. It brings a new moral imagination into political life and a new partisanship on behalf of the weak and those who have no one to represent them.

Sacrifice

Does the language of eucharistic sacrifice have a justice aspect? Before we can answer this question, we have to ask first what the language of sacrifice means. The anthropologist J. Van Baal indicates that sacrifice has to do with communication, with the establishment of communion between the members of a community and between the community and God.[76] Sacrifice has to do with communication and communion in relationships, something that as contemporary persons, we can readily identify with. If this interpretation of sacrifice is correct, this would explain why the communion sacrifice played such an important role in Israel's early history. Augustine's description of sacrifice coincides with this: "a true sacrifice is any act which unites us in a holy communion with God."[77] Sacrificial language, however, is metaphorical language. It is rich in associations and cannot be given a single meaning.[78]

There is a risk and a cost involved in the establishment of communion. When a relationship is broken, it requires an act of costly love in order to reestablish communication and communion. There is no language more adequate than sacrifice to express this. The gift that creates the profoundest communion also involves the profoundest cost. For Christians, the paradigm of this self-giving love is God's action in the cross of Jesus. Rowan Williams explores this insight in his fascinating little booklet *Eucharistic Sacrifice—The Roots of a Metaphor*[79] and uses it to illuminate the sacrificial character of both the cross and the eucharist. God gives the gift of God's self in the event of the cross:

"God acts, offers, gives, in order to bring creation into fellowship with him; and, because that fellowship is so strange to fearful, self-enclosed, human beings, it requires a uniquely creative gift—a gift which involves God's manifesting himself without power or threat. He 'distances' himself from the stability of his divine life in order to share the vulnerability and darkness of mortal men and women. By the 'gift' of his presence—the presence in our world of an unreserved compassion and an unrestricted hope—he establishes communion; but this can be clearly shown only in conditions of final rejection and dereliction. The gift is consummated on the cross."[80]

The language of sacrifice attached itself in early Christianity not only to the cross, but also to the life of Christians and to the eucharist. The tenacity of this link between eucharist and sacrifice over the centuries reflects the instinct that Christians have had that somehow what is celebrated symbolically in the eucharist links Christians with God's act of self-giving in the cross of Jesus and points to the meaning of Christian discipleship as a way of self-giving love. To speak of the eucharist as sacrificial, therefore, is to say that through the offering and receiving of the eucharistic gifts Christians are drawn more deeply into the self-giving action of God that is here celebrated sacramentally.

To participate in the eucharist understood as a sacrifice is to participate in a liturgical action that draws us into the whole sacrificial action of Christ. To interpret Jesus' life and death as "sacrificial" is to say that it is a life and death that was lived out in such complete self-giving that it opens up for us the way of communion with God and our neighbor in the midst of the brokenness of our lives and of our world. To speak of the eucharist as a sacrifice is to say that in it is present sacramentally that mystery of sacrificial love that lies at the heart of God and that was poured out in the cross of Jesus.

All that old language about the eucharist as a "commemorative" sacrifice or a "communion" sacrifice only begins to make sense from that perspective. As we make the memorial of the death and resurrection of the Lord in the eucharist, we are drawn into Jesus' life and death as a living sacrifice. Jesus' sacrificial death on the cross can never be repeated. It is an historical action that took place once for all in the past. When we celebrate the eucharist, however, by making the memorial of Jesus' sacrifice, we are drawn into his action of suffering love. To celebrate the eucharist from this perspective, therefore, is to be drawn into a life of discipleship in which we are called to follow Jesus in his path of suffering love.

Sacrifice and justice, therefore, are intimately related. To celebrate the memorial of Christ's sacrifice in the eucharist is to be drawn into his action of suffering love on behalf of all our brothers and sisters. Community between God and humanity is only ultimately established by sacrificial love:

"The bond which unites God and man is celebrated—that is, effectively recalled and proclaimed—in the Eucharist. Without a real commitment against exploitation and alienation and for a society of solidarity and justice, the Eucharistic celebration is an empty action, lacking any genuine endorsement by those who participate in it. This is something that many Latin American Christians are feeling more and more deeply, and they are thus more demanding both with themselves and with the whole Church. 'To make remembrance' of Christ is more than the performance of an act of worship; it is to accept living under the sign of the cross and in the hope of the resurrection. It is to accept the meaning of a life that was given over to death—at the hands of the powerful—for the love of others."[81]

Presence and Epiclesis
Is there a justice perspective hidden even in the doctrine of the real presence? It is important today to insist on the sacramental mode of Christ's presence in the eucharist in order to avoid a false spiritualization. The danger today is the very opposite of the danger in the sixteenth century. The danger then was that people would believe in a physical miracle in the mass. The danger today is that people will fail to connect the acts of sacramental eating and drinking with their bodies and with the earth. We must eat and drink the elements with our bodies as a sign that the goal of the eucharist is the transformation of our entire bodily existence in the world. Otherwise we fall into a false spiritualization (dualism) that denies our bodily nature and undercuts our real relationships in the world at the social, economic, and political levels. The Christ who meets us in the eucharist meets us in and through the real structures of historical existence— matter, time, space, language, community, culture, and social, economic, and political relationships. Here both the ecclesial and the political dimensions of the eucharist come into view. The Christ who meets us in the eucharist unites us into community with himself and with one another and binds us to himself in the form of his servant presence in the world. The eucharist

binds us to Christ as a people called to engage in the transformation of history under the sign of the cross and in the light of the promise of the kingdom. The material signs of bread and wine, offered and shared by the community, are signs of the transformation of the entire material creation.

The Greek fathers, Ambrose, and the medieval theologians were not wrong, therefore, when they used transformationist language even of the elements. Where the medieval theologians went wrong was in divorcing transformationist language from symbolic language and in isolating the change in the elements from the context of the community meal. When transformationist language is united with symbolic language and placed in an eschatological perspective, the transformation of the elements becomes the sacramental sign of the transformation of the whole earth into the kingdom. This perspective is also related to the tradition of the epiclesis. In our study of the development of the epiclesis in the early liturgies, we saw that its roots lie in the eschatological perspective. In the New Testament, the Spirit is an eschatological gift. The epiclesis is a prayer for the transformation of both the gifts and the community in order that they may become signs of the transformation of the entire creation into the promised kingdom.

* * *

The eucharist is a community meal. This in itself has social implications, especially when the community that shares the meal comes together as the body of Christ. When the meal is celebrated in thanksgiving for the gifts of creation, the community that celebrates it cannot fail to seek justice for all God's creation. We know from scripture that the rule of God is a rule of righteousness and justice. We cannot celebrate the eucharist, therefore, without translating our worship into discipleship. To celebrate the memorial of the Lord's death until he comes means to accept living under the sign of the cross in this world, identifying with the victims of a fallen creation, and seeking to bring about a transformation of those conditions in society that victimize others. As Raimundo Panikkar has reminded us,

"The great challenge today is to convert the sacred bread into real bread, the liturgical peace into political peace, the worship of the Creator into reverence for the Creation, the Christian praying community into an authentic human fellowship. It is risky to celebrate the Eucharist. We may have to leave it unfinished, having gone first to give back to the poor what belongs to them."[82]

NOTES

1. See Jean-Jacques von Allmen, *The Lord's Supper* (London: Lutterworth Press, 1969), 17–18.

2. LW 32.15; 36.67.

3. See Maxwell, *Outline*, 72–73 and his discussion of the rites that follows.

4. See Paul S. Sanders, "The Sacraments in Early American Methodism," *Church History*, 26 (1957): 355–371.

5. For the history of the liturgical movement, see J. G. Davies (ed.), *A Dictionary of Liturgy and Worship*, s.v. "The Liturgical Movement."

6. See Geoffrey Wainwright, "Recent Eucharistic Revision," in Cheslyn Jones, Geoffrey Wainwright, and Edward Yarnold (eds.), *The Study of Liturgy* (New York: Oxford University Press, 1978), 280–288. See also Frank C. Senn (ed.), *New Eucharistic Prayers: An Ecumenical Study of their Development and Structure* (New York: Paulist Press, 1987). For the new Roman Catholic Eucharistic Prayers, see Enrico Mazza, *The Eucharistic Prayers of the Roman Rite* (New York: Pueblo Publishing Co., 1986).

7. Max Thurian, *The Eucharistic Memorial*, Part II—The New Testament (London: Lutterworth Press, 1961); *idem*, "The Eucharistic Memorial, Sacrifice of Praise and Supplication," in Max Thurian, (ed.), *Ecumenical Perspectives on Baptism, Eucharist and Ministry*, Faith and Order Paper 116 (Geneva: World Council of Churches, 1983), 90–103.

8. See J. M. R. Tillard, "The Eucharist, Gift of God," in *Ecumenical Perspectives on BEM*, 104–118. For a Roman Catholic reassessment of the teaching of the Council of Trent on the sacrifice of the mass, see the excellent recent study by David N. Power, *The Sacrifice We Offer: The Tridentine Dogma and Its Reinterpretation* (New York: Crossroad Publishing Co., 1987).

9. See Regin Prenter, *Creation and Redemption* (Philadelphia: Fortress Press, 1967), 487–514; *idem*, "Eucharistic Sacrifice According to the Lutheran Tradition," *Theology*, 68 (1964): 286–295. See also Gustaf Aulen,

Eucharist and Sacrifice (Philadelphia: Muhlenberg Press, 1958). For a Reformed perspective, see Alasdair I. C. Heron, *Table and Tradition: Toward an Ecumenical Understanding of the Eucharist* (Philadelphia: Westminster Press, 1983), 167–171.

10. Prenter, 491,

11. *Sermon* 272.

12. (New York: Sheed & Ward, 1963). For a summary, see Daniel H. Callahan, Heiko A. Oberman, and Daniel J. O'Hanlon (eds.), *Christianity Divided: Protestant and Roman Catholic Theological Issues* (New York: Sheed & Ward, 1961), 245–274. For the broader background of contemporary Roman Catholic thinking on the eucharist, see Kenan Osborne, "Eucharistic Theology Today," *Worship*, 61 (1987): 98–126. For the renewal of Protestant sacramental theology, see James F. White, *Sacraments as God's Self Giving* (Nashville, TN: Abingdon Press, 1983). For a recent ecumenical model, see Robert L. Browning and Roy A. Reed, *The Sacraments in Religious Education and Liturgy: An Ecumenical Model* (Birmingham, AL: Religious Education Press, 1985).

13. See Piet Schoonenberg, "Presence and the Eucharistic Presence," *Cross Currents*, 17 (1967): 39–54; *idem*, "The Real Presence in Contemporary Discussion," *Theology Digest*, 15 (1967): 3–11.

14. For Schillebeeckx on the real presence, see Edward Schillebeeckx, "Transubstantiation, Transfinalization, Transfiguration," *Worship*, 40 (1966): 324–338; *idem*, *The Eucharist* (New York: Sheed & Ward, 1968).

15. For a review of modern Roman Catholic thought on the real presence, see Joseph M. Powers, *Eucharistic Theology* (New York: Herder & Herder, 1967), Chap. 4.

16. See John Reumann, *The Supper of the Lord: The New Testament, Ecumenical Dialogues, and Faith and Order on Eucharist* (Philadelphia: Fortress Press, 1985), 78–137.

17. *Ibid.*, 99–100.

18. Anglican-Roman Catholic International Commission, *The Final Report* (London: SPCK, 1981).

19. Paul C. Empie and T. Austin Murphy (eds.), *Lutherans and Catholics in Dialogue*, vol. 3: *The Eucharist as Sacrifice*, vol. 4: *Eucharist and Ministry* (Washington, DC: United States Catholic Conference; New York: U.S.A. National Committee of the Lutheran World Federation, 1967, 1970).

20. Faith and Order paper, no. 111 (Geneva: World Council of Churches, 1982).

21. For background and commentary, see Reumann, 137–201. See also S. W. Sykes, "Story and Eucharist," *Interpretation,* 37 (1983): 365–376, who interprets the *BEM* themes from the perspective of a theology of story.

22. See Ernst Cassirer, *The Philosophy of the Enlightenment* (Boston: Beacon Press, 1955), Chap. 1.

23. See Ernst Cassirer, *An Essay on Man* (New Haven: Yale University Press, 1944); idem, *The Philosophy of Symbolic Forms,* 3 vols. (New Haven: Yale University Press, 1953–1957); Susanne K. Langer, *Philosophy in a New Key: A Study in the Symbolism of Reason, Rite, and Art,* 3d ed. (Cambridge, MA: Harvard University Press, 1957).

24. See Jacques Waardenburg, "Symbolic Aspects of Myth," in Alan M. Olson (ed.), *Myth, Symbol, and Reality* (Notre Dame: Notre Dame University Press, 1980), 41–68.

25. See Paul Ricoeur, "The Symbol . . . Food for Thought," *Philosophy Today,* 5 (1960): 196–207; idem, *The Symbolism of Evil* (New York: Harper & Row, 1967); idem, *Interpretation Theory: Discourse and the Surplus of Meaning* (Fort Worth, TX: Texas Christian University Press, 1976), Chap. 3. See also David M. Rasmussen, *Symbol and Interpretation* (The Hague: Martinus Nijhoff, 1974).

26. See his *Images and Symbols* and *Myth and Reality.*

27. See Sigmund Freud, *A General Introduction to Psychoanalysis* (New York: Washington Square Press, 1952), Chap. 10: "Symbolism in Dreams"; Carl G. Jung, *Man and his Symbols* (New York: Dell Publishing Co., 1968); Wallace B. Clift, *Jung and Christianity* (New York: Crossroad, 1983), Chaps. 7 and 8.

28. See Clifford Geertz, "Ethos, World-View and the Analysis of Sacred Symbols," *Antioch Review,* 17 (1957–1958): 421–437; idem, "Religion as a Cultural System," in M. Banton (ed.), *Anthropological Approaches to the Study of Religion* (London: Tavistock, 1966). For an introduction to Turner and primary bibliography, see Mary Collins, "Ritual Symbols and the Ritual Process: The Work of Victor W. Turner," *Worship,* 50 (1976): 336–346; Urban T. Holmes, "Ritual and the Social Drama," *Worship,* 51 (1977): 197–213.

29. See Robert N. Bellah, "Christianity and Symbolic Realism," *Journal for the Scientific Study of Religion,* 9 (1970): 89–96.

30. See Norman O. Brown, *Love's Body* (New York: Random House, 1966).

31. Bellah, 90–92.

32. (New York: Paulist Press, 1975).

33. *Ibid.*, 116–25.

34. See Jean Jacques Rousseau, *The Social Contract* (New York: Hafner Publishing Co., 1957).

35. See Arthur F. McGovern, *Marxism: An American Christian Perspective* (Maryknoll, NY: Orbis Books, 1980), 26–34.

36. See Baum, 34–37.

37. See McGovern, 12.

38. For Marx's writings on religion, see Karl Marx, *On Religion*, Saul K. Padover (ed.), (New York: McGraw-Hill, 1974).

39. *Ibid.*, 35–36.

40. See Baum, 125–133.

41. *Ibid.*, 163–178.

42. Max Weber, *The Sociology of Religion*, with an Introduction by Talcott Parsons (Boston: Beacon Press, 1964), xxx.

43. See Baum, 99–107, 274–83.

44. (London: SPCK, 1967).

45. For theological reflection on symbols and the relation between liturgy and symbol, see David N. Power, *Unsearchable Riches: The Symbolic Nature of Liturgy* (New York: Pueblo Publishing Co., 1984).

46. Langdon Gilkey, "Symbols, Meaning, and the Divine Presence," *Theological Studies*, 35 (1974): 255.

47. *Ibid.*, 258.

48. *Ibid.*, 259.

49. *Ibid.*, 260.

50. See Regis A. Duffy, *Real Presence: Worship, Sacraments, and Commitment* (San Francisco: Harper & Row, 1982).

51. Kilmartin, "Sacraments . . . Perspectives and Principles," 98–101.

52. *Ibid.*, 100.

53. *Ibid.*, 101.

54. See Jeremias, *Parables*, 227–229.

55. See John Dominic Crossan, *In Parables* (New York: Harper & Row, 1973).

56. There is a growing literature in this area. See especially, Monika H. Hellwig, *The Eucharist and the Hunger of the World* (New York: Paulist Press, 1976); Rafael Avila, *Worship and Politics* (Maryknoll, NY: Orbis Books, 1977); David Hollenbach, "A Prophetic Church and the Catholic Sacramental Imagination," in John C. Haughey (ed.), *The Faith that Does Justice* (New York: Paulist Press, 1977); Mark Searle (ed.), *Liturgy and Social Justice* (Collegeville, MN: The Liturgical Press, 1980); John H. McKenna, "Liturgy: Toward Liberation or Oppression?" *Worship*, 56 (1982): 291–308; Tissa Balasuriya, *The Eucharist and Human Liberation* (London: SCM Press, 1979); Joseph A. Grassi, *Broken Bread and Broken Bodies: The Lord's Supper and World Hunger* (Maryknoll, NY: Orbis Books, 1985).

57. *Sharing Daily Bread*, Labour Day Message: September 2, 1974 (Ottawa: Canadian Catholic Conference, 1974), 2–4.

58. Am 5:21–24. Cf. also Is 58:5–9; Is 1:10–17; Jer 7:2–12, 21–23.

59. Lk 22:24–27.

60. Jn 13:1–17.

61. Acts 2:42–46; 4:32–35. See Stanislas Lyonnet, "La Nature du Culte dans le Nouveau Testament," in J.-P. Jossua and Y. Congar (eds.), *La Liturgie après Vatican II* (Paris: Editions du Cerf, 1967).

62. Jas 2:2–7.

63. See Edward J. Kilmartin, "The Sacrifice of Thanksgiving and Social Justice," in Mark Searle (ed.), *Liturgy and Justice*, 57–58; also M. Francis Mannion, "Stipends and Eucharistic Praxis," *Worship*, 57 (1983): 194–199.

64. *1 Apology* 67.1.

65. *Ibid.*, 7.

66. Hippolytus, *Apostolic Tradition* 24.

67. *Didascalia* 12.

68. *Homilies on 2 Corinthians* 20. Cf. *Homilies on Matthew* 50.

69. See Paul B. Marx, *Virgil Michel and the Liturgical Movement* (Collegeville, MN: The Liturgical Press, 1957); Kenneth R. Himes, "Eucharist and Justice: Assessing the Legacy of Virgil Michel," *Worship*, 62 (1988): 201–224.

70. See Geoffrey Wainwright, *Eucharist and Eschatology* (London: Epworth Press, 1971).

71. *BEM*, 14.

72. Mt 25:31–40.

73. Johann B. Metz, *Faith in History and Society* (New York: Seabury Press, 1980), 88.

74. *Ibid.*, 90–91. See also 184–204.

75. *Ibid.*, Chap. 6.

76. See J. Van Baal, "Offering, Sacrifice and Gift," *Numen*, 23 (1976): 161–178.

77. *City of God* 10.6.

78. See David N. Power, "Words That Crack: The Uses of 'Sacrifice' in Eucharistic Discourse," *Worship*, 53 (1979): 386–404. See Also Sykes, "Story and Eucharist."

79. Grove Liturgical Studies, no. 31 (Bramcote, Notts.: Grove Books, 1982). For an evangelical reply and Williams' response, see Colin Buchanan (ed.), *Essays on Eucharistic Sacrifice in the Early Church*, Grove Liturgical Studies, no. 40 (Bramcote, Notts.: Grove Books, 1984).

80. Williams, 28.

81. Gustavo Gutierrez, *A Theology of Liberation* (Maryknoll, NY: Orbis Books, 1973), 265.

82. Raimundo Panikkar, "Man as a Ritual Being," *Chicago Studies*, 16 (1977): 27.

Bibliography

Allmen, Jean-Jacques von. *The Lord's Supper*. London: Lutterworth Press, 1969.

Amar, Joseph P. "Perspectives on the Eucharist in Ephrem the Syrian." *Worship*, 61 (1987): 441–454.

Aulen, Gustaf. *Eucharist and Sacrifice*. Philadelphia: Muhlenberg Press, 1958.

Balasuriya, Tissa. *The Eucharist and Human Liberation*. London: SCM Press, 1979.

Barclay, Alexander. *The Protestant Doctrine of the Lord's Supper*. Glasgow: Jackson, Wylie & Co., 1927.

Baptism, Eucharist and Ministry. Faith and Order paper, no. 111. Geneva: World Council of Churches, 1982.

Borgen, Ole E. *John Wesley on the Sacraments: A Theological Study*. Nashville, TN: Abingdon Press, 1972.

Bouley, Alan. *From Freedom to Formula: The Evolution of the Eucharistic Prayer from Oral Improvisation to Written Texts*. Washington, DC: Catholic University of America Press, 1981.

Bouyer, Louis. *Eucharist: Theology and Spirituality of the Eucharistic Prayer*. Notre Dame: University of Notre Dame Press, 1968.

Bowmer, John C. *The Sacrament of the Lord's Supper in Early Methodism*. London: Dacre Press, 1951.

Brevint, Daniel. *The Christian Sacrament and Sacrifice*, new ed. Oxford: Printed for J. Vincent. London: Hatchard & Son, 1847.

Brilioth, Yngve. *Eucharistic Faith & Practice Evangelical and Catholic*. London: SPCK, 1930.

Brooks, Peter. *Thomas Cranmer's Doctrine of the Eucharist: An Essay in Historical Development*. New York: Seabury Press, 1965.

Browning, Robert L., and Roy A. Reed. *The Sacraments in Religious Educa-*

tion and Liturgy: An Ecumenical Model. Birmingham, Alabama: Religious Education Press, 1985.

Buchanan, Colin. *What Did Cranmer Think He Was Doing?* Grove Liturgical Studies, no. 7. Bramcote, Notts.: Grove Books, 1976.

—— (ed.). *Essays on Eucharistic Sacrifice in the Early Church.* Grove Liturgical Studies, no. 40. Bramcote, Notts.: Grove Books, 1984.

Buxton, Richard F. *Eucharist and Institution Narrative: A Study in the The Roman and Anglican Traditions of the Consecration of the Eucharist from the Eighth to the Twentieth Centuries.* Alcuin Club Collections, no. 58. Great Wakering: Mayhew-McCrimmon, 1976.

Camelot, P. Th. "Réalisme et Symbolisme dans la doctrine eucharistique de S. Augustin." *Revue des Sciences Philosophiques et Théologiques,* 36 (1947): 394–410.

Chenderlin, Fritz. *"Do This as my Memorial": The Semantic and Conceptual Background and Value of Anamnesis in 1 Corinthians 11:24–25.* Analecta Biblica, no. 99. Rome: Biblical Institute Press, 1982.

Jasper, R. C. D., and G. J. Cuming. *Prayers of the Eucharist: Early and Reformed.* 3d ed., rev. and enl. New York: Pueblo Publishing Co., 1987.

Cuming, G. J. *A History of Anglican Liturgy.* 2d ed. London: Macmillan, 1982.

Dix, Gregory. *The Shape of the Liturgy.* Additional notes by Paul V. Marshall. New York: Seabury Press, 1982.

Dugmore, C. W. *Eucharistic Doctrine in England from Hooker to Waterland.* London: SPCK, 1942.

——. *The Mass and the English Reformers.* London: Macmillan, 1958.

Finkelstein, Louis. "The Birkat Ha-Mazon." *Jewish Quarterly Review,* n.s., 19 (1928–29): 211–262.

Gilkey, Langdon. "Symbols, Meaning, and the Divine Presence." *Theological Studies,* 35 (1974): 249–267.

Grassi, Joseph A. *Broken Bread and Broken Bodies: The Lord's Supper and World Hunger.* Maryknoll, NY: Orbis Books, 1985.

Gray, Donald. *Earth and Altar: The Evolution of the Parish Communism in the Church of England to 1945.* Alcuin Club Collections, no. 68. Norwich: Canterbury Press, 1986.

Hänggi, Anton, and Irmgard Pahl. *Prex Eucharistica.* Spicilegium Friburgense, vol. 12. Fribourg, Switzerland: Editions Universitaires, 1968.

Härdelin, Alf. *The Tractarian Understanding of the Eucharist*. Uppsala: Almquist & Wiksells, 1965.

Hellwig, Monika K. *The Eucharist and the Hunger of the World*. New York: Paulist Press, 1976.

Henning, E. M. "The Architectonics of Faith: Metalogic and Metaphor in Zwingli's Doctrine of the Eucharist." *Renaissance and Reformation*, n.s., 10 (1986): 315–365.

Heron, Alasdair I. C. *Table and Tradition: Toward an Ecumenical Understanding of the Eucharist*. Philadelphia: Westminster Press, 1983.

Himes, Kenneth R. "Eucharist and Justice: Assessing the Legacy of Virgil Michel." *Worship*, 62 (1988): 201–224.

Holifield, E. Brooks. *The Covenant Sealed: The Development of Puritan Sacramental Theology in Old and New England, 1570–1720*. New Haven: Yale University Press, 1974.

Hollenbach, David. "A Prophetic Church and the Catholic Sacramental Imagination." In John C. Haughey (ed.), *The Faith that Does Justice*, New York: Paulist Press, 1977.

Jeremias, Joachim. *The Eucharistic Words of Jesus*. London: SCM Press, 1966.

Jones, Cheslyn, Geoffrey Wainwright, and Edward Yarnold (eds.). *The Study of Liturgy*. New York: Oxford University Press, 1978.

Jorissen, Hans. *Die Entfaltung der Transubstantiationslehre bis zum Beginn der Hochscholastik*. Münster: Aschendorff, 1965.

Kavanagh, Aidan. "Thoughts on the Roman Anaphora." *Worship*, 39 (1965): 515–529; 40 (1966): 2–16.

Keifer, Ralph A. "The Unity of the Roman Canon: An Examination of its Unique Structure." *Studia Liturgica*, 11 (1976): 39–58.

Kilmartin, Edward J. "Sacrificium Laudis: Content and Function of Early Eucharistic Prayers." *Theological Studies*, 35 (1974): 268–287.

———. "A Modern Approach to the Word of God and Sacraments of Christ: Perspectives and Principles." In Francis A. Eigo (ed.), *The Sacraments: God's Love and Mercy Actualized*. Villanova, PA: Villanova University, 1979.

Köhler, Walther. *Zwingli und Luther. Ihr Streit über das Abendmahl nach seinen politischen und religiösen Beziehungen*. 2 vols. Leipzig, 1924; Gütersloh, 1953.

Ligier, Louis. "From the Last Supper to the Eucharist." In Lancelot Sheppard (ed.), *The New Liturgy*, 113–150. London: Darton, Longman & Todd, 1970.

————. "The Origins of the Eucharistic Prayer: From the Last Supper to the Eucharist." *Studia Liturgica*, 9 (1973): 161–185.

Lubac, Henri de. *Corpus Mysticum: L'Eucharistie et l'Eglise au Moyen Age.* 2d rev. ed. Paris: Aubier, 1949.

McCue, James F. "The Doctrine of Transubstantiation from Berengar through Trent: The Point at Issue." *Harvard Theological Review*, 61 (1968): 385–430.

McDonnell, Kilian. *John Calvin, the Church, and the Eucharist.* Princeton, NJ: Princeton University Press, 1967.

McKenna, John H. *Eucharist and Epiclesis: The Eucharistic Epiclesis in Twentieth Century Theology.* Alcuin Club Collections, no. 57. Great Wakering: Mayhew-McCrimmon, 1975.

————. "Liturgy: Toward Liberation or Oppression?" *Worship*, 56 (1982): 291–308.

McLelland, Joseph C. *The Visible Words of God.* Edinburgh: Oliver & Boyd, 1957.

Macy, Gary. *The Theologies of the Eucharist in the Early Scholastic Period.* Oxford: Clarendon Press, 1984.

Martelet, Gustave. *The Risen Christ and the Eucharistic World.* London: Collins, 1976.

Mayer, Cornelius P. *Die Zeichen in der geistigen Entwicklung und in der Theologie Augustinus.* 2 vols. Würzburg: Augustinus-Verlag, 1969–1974.

Mazza, Enrico. *The Eucharistic Prayers of the Roman Rite.* New York: Pueblo Publishing Co., 1986.

Mitchell, Nathan. *Cult and Controversy: The Worship of the Eucharist Outside Mass.* New York: Pueblo Publishing Co., 1982.

Osborne, Kenan. "Eucharistic Theology Today." *Worship*, 61 (1987): 98–126.

Power, David N. "Words That Crack: The Uses of 'Sacrifice' in Eucharistic Discourse." *Worship*, 53 (1979): 386–404.

————. *Unsearchable Riches: The Symbolic Nature of Liturgy.* New York: Pueblo Publishing Co., 1984.

————. *The Sacrifice We Offer: The Tridentine Dogma and Its Reinterpretation.* New York: Crossroad Publishing Co., 1987.

Powers, Joseph M. *Eucharistic Theology.* New York: Herder & Herder, 1967.

Prenter, Regin. "Eucharistic Sacrifice According to the Lutheran Tradition." *Theology,* 68 (1964): 286–295.

Pruett, Gordon E. "Cranmer's Progress in the Doctrine of the Eucharist, 1535–1548." *Historical Magazine of the Protestant Episcopal Church,* 45 (1976): 439–458.

Rattenbury, J. Ernest. *The Eucharistic Hymns of John and Charles Wesley.* London: Epworth Press, 1948.

Reumann, John. *The Supper of the Lord: The New Testament, Ecumenical Dialogues, and Faith and Order on Eucharist.* Philadelphia: Fortress Press, 1985.

Richardson, Cyril C. *Zwingli and Cranmer on the Eucharist.* Evanston, IL: Seabury-Western Theological Seminary, 1949.

———. "Cranmer and the Analysis of Eucharistic Doctrine." *Journal of Theological Studies,* n.s., 16 (1965): 421–437.

Rordorf, Willy, et al. *The Eucharist of the Early Christians.* New York: Pueblo Publishing Co., 1978.

Sasse, Hermann. *This Is My Body: Luther's Contention for the Real Presence in the Sacrament of the Altar,* rev. ed. Adelaide, South Australia: Lutheran Publishing House, 1977.

Schillebeeckx, Edward. "Transubstantiation, Transfinalization, Transfiguration." *Worship,* 40 (1966): 324–338.

———. *The Eucharist.* New York: Sheed & Ward, 1968.

Schoonenberg, Piet. "Presence and the Eucharistic Presence." *Cross Currents,* 17 (1967): 39–54.

———. "The Real Presence in Contemporary Discussion." *Theology Digest,* 15 (1967): 3–11.

Schweizer, Eduard. *The Lord's Supper According to the New Testament.* Philadelphia: Fortress Press, 1967.

Searle, Mark, (ed.). *Liturgy and Social Justice.* Collegeville, MN: The Liturgical Press, 1980.

Seasoltz, R. Kevin. *Living Bread, Saving Cup: Readings on the Eucharist.* Collegeville, MN: The Liturgical Press, 1982.

———. "Justice and the Eucharist." *Worship,* 58 (1984): 507–525.

Senn, Frank C., (ed.). *New Eucharistic Prayers: An Ecumenical Study of their Development and Structure.* New York: Paulist Press, 1987.

Spinks, Bryan D. *Luther's Liturgical Criteria and His Reform of the Canon of the Mass.* Grove Liturgical Studies, no. 30. Bramcote, Notts.: Grove Books, 1982.

————. *From the Lord and "The Best Reformed Churches:" A Study of the Eucharistic Liturgy in the English Puritan and Separatist Traditions 1550–1633.* Bibliotheca "Ephemerides Liturgicae" Subsidia, no. 33. Rome: C.L.V.—Edizioni Liturgiche, 1984.

————. *Freedom or Order? The Eucharistic Liturgy in English Congregationalism 1645–1980.* Pittsburgh Theological Monographs, n.s., no. 8. Allison Park, PA: Pickwick Publications, 1984.

Stephens, W. Peter. *The Theology of Huldrych Zwingli.* Oxford: Clarendon Press, 1986.

Stevenson, Kenneth. *Eucharist and Offering.* New York: Pueblo Publishing Co., 1986.

Stone, Darwell. *A History of the Doctrine of the Holy Eucharist.* 2 vols. London: Longmans, Green, & Co., 1909.

Swidler, Leonard, (ed.). *The Eucharist in Ecumenical Dialogue.* New York: Paulist Press, 1976 [= *Journal of Ecumenical Studies*, 13 (1976)].

Sykes, Stephen W. "Eucharist and Story." *Interpretation*, 37 (1983): 365–376.

Talley, Thomas. "The Eucharistic Prayer of the Ancient Church According to Recent Research: Results and Reflections." *Studia Liturgica*, 11 (1976): 138–158.

————. "From *Berakah* to *Eucharistia*: A Reopening Question." *Worship*, 50 (1976): 115–137.

————. "The Eucharistic Prayer: Tradition and Development." In Kenneth Stevenson (ed.), *Liturgy Reshaped.* London: SPCK, 1982.

————. "The Literary Structure of the Eucharistic Prayer." *Worship*, 58 (1984): 404–420.

Thurian, Max. *The Eucharistic Memorial*, Part II—The New Testament. London: Lutterworth Press, 1961.

————, (ed.). *Ecumenical Perspectives on Baptism, Eucharist, and Ministry.* Faith and Order Paper 116. Geneva: World Council of Churches, 1983.

Tillard, J. M. R. "La triple dimension du signe sacramentel." *Nouvelle Revue Théologique*, 83 (1961): 225–254.

————. "Roman Catholics and Anglicans: The Eucharist." *Lumen Vitae*, 28 (1973): 117–175.

Wainwright, Geoffrey. *Eucharist and Eschatology*. London: Epworth Press, 1971.

White, James F. *Sacraments as God's Self Giving*. Nashville, TN: Abingdon Press, 1983.

Wilberforce, R. I. *The Doctrine of the Holy Eucharist*. London, 1853.

Williams, Rowan. *Eucharistic Sacrifice—The Roots of a Metaphor*. Grove Liturgical Studies, no. 31. Bramcote, Notts.: Grove Books, 1982.

Yarnold, Edward. *The Awe-Inspiring Rites of Initiation: Baptismal Homilies of the Fourth Century*. Slough, England: St. Paul Publications, 1972.

Young, Frances M. *The Use of Sacrificial Ideas in Greek Christian Writers from the New Testament to John Chrysostom*. Patristic Monograph Series, no. 5. Cambridge, MA: Philadelphia Patristic Foundation, 1979.

Index of Names

Subject Index

and Calvin, 158–159
early development, 57–63
and justice, 262–263
in Knox's liturgy, 183–184
in liturgical revision, 230
origin, 54–56
in Westminister Directory, 187–189

Eschatological perspective
in Aquinas, 113–114
in Brevint, 207–208
and justice, 256–258, 262
in the New Testament, 3–4, 5–8
in Wesleys, 210–211, 213–215

Eucharistic piety
in Anglicanism, 190–191, 196–197
in the Middle Ages, 107, 122–125
in Reformation churches, 227–230

Eucharistic Prayer
in the Book of Common Prayer, 166–167, 171–173
and continental reformers, 144–145, 160–161, 228
early development, 41–52
in Knox's liturgy, 183–184
in liturgical revision, 230–231
origin, 39–40
theology of, 52–54
in Westminster Directory, 184–188

Faith and the sacraments
in Augustine, 90–94
in Calvin, 150–152, 159
in early Anglicanism, 168–171, 174–175, 176–178, 192–194, 196–197
in Luther, 128–129, 130–132
in the Middle Ages, 108, 109, 110, 115–116
in Oxford Movement, 217–218

in Wesley, 201–204
in Zwingli, 135–139, 142–143

Frequency of communion
in the Middle Ages, 122–123
in Reformation churches, 144, 161, 183, 227–228
in Wesley, 200

Genevan Service Book. See Knox's liturgy

Grace and the sacraments
in Aquinas, 113–114
in Augustine, 92–94
in Brevint, 207
in Calvin, 149–152
in early Anglicanism, 174–177, 179–180, 193, 196–197
in Luther, 130–132, 143–144
in Oxford Movement, 215, 216, 217–218
in Wesleys, 201–206, 209–210
in Zwingli, 135–136

Holy Spirit, See Epiclesis

Institution narrative
in Anglicanism, 171–173, 176–177
in early liturgies, 39–42, 44–48
in Luther, 130–131, 133–135, 143–145
in the New Testament, 9–17, 29–31
in Reformed tradition, 136, 160–161, 183
in Westminster Directory, 185–188

Justice and the eucharist
in the Bible, 33, 34, 252–255
in contemporary theology, 250–252, 256–263
in the early Church, 254–255
in Luther, 129–130
in Oxford Movement, 217–219

284